Education in the United Kingdom

Edited by

Liam Gearon

David Fulton Publishers
London
Published in association with the
University of Surrey Roehampton

David Fulton Publishers Ltd
Ormond House, 26–27 Boswell Street, London WC1N 3JZ

First published in Great Britain by David Fulton Publishers in 2002

Copyright © David Fulton Publishers 2002

British Library Cataloguing in Publication Data
A catalogue record for this book is available from the British Library.

ISBN 1-85346-715-4

Typeset by Servis Filmsetting Ltd, Manchester
Printed and bound in Great Britain by The Cromwell Press, Trowbridge, Wilts.

Contents

Foreword

Those who read this book, either as newcomers to the field or as experienced practitioners within it, will do so at a time of transforming change. See the chapters which follow, therefore, as signposts guiding us in understanding this change, and pointing to the kinds of education service we are developing in the United Kingdom, both to effect it and to learn how to live with its consequences.

Will the change be a united one, coherent and uniform across the nation? Probably not: indeed, devolution already means that the four countries of the UK organise their education systems differently. One characteristic of United Kingdom education in the new century is that it is not united, and this may become even more pronounced should future governments devolve powers down to the English regions. We will find different emphases and styles. At the time this book is being written, for instance, those who determine the English system are powerfully centralist in their determination to raise educational standards (countable measures of performance), even when this might mean a loss of quality (leading to disaffected teachers, over-stretched administrations and – who knows? – over-tested pupils). It is not so – at least, it is not so apparent – in other parts of the UK and it will be interesting, as the century unfolds, to see whether strict central control (in the English fashion) is as effective in building a first-class education service as are less intrusive approaches. We should also expect to find other kinds of diversity: for instance, in parts of the curriculum (as in Wales, where schools are required to teach pupils Welsh), in statute and regulation, in assessment and inspection, and in the very offices of state that govern the education systems of each country.

Divergences of this kind, however, lie only at the surface. Beneath, we are likely to see the broad structures of British education shaped by the same underlying imperatives. These will be common both laterally, from north to south, from east to west, in town and country, and vertically, from the toddler attending preschool mornings, through to the retired couple finding, for no other reason than that it satisfies their minds and spirits, that at last they have the time to study. Education at the start of the century involves a greater proportion of the population than it ever has before, and this national engagement with the need to know more, and to become more skilful, will increase still further as the century gathers years. Our prosperity depends upon it, and so does the resilience and strength of our democracy. So structures and organisational patterns of educational provision, though they may differ in detail across the United Kingdom, will become increasingly dominated by the need to embrace its people ever more actively in the processes of education, wherever they are, and throughout their lives.

During this time of change, three themes are likely to be particularly significant:

- Our futures are digital ones. Though this book considers education in different parts of the United Kingdom, our children and young people will increasingly come to be educated in a virtual world, where geographical distance is immaterial. Look in this book, therefore, for signposts to an education system developing not only in a neighbourhood, regional and national context, but in a global one as well.
- We know education to be a powerful instrument in eliminating social exclusion, understanding that economic divisions between rich and poor damage national prosperity. That is why education occupies so central a position in the political agenda, and why people who work in education are agents of social change. How, in the future, will governments organise the balance between statutory controls and professional freedoms among these change agents? Can any government dare to allow its educators free rein? Can any population afford to allow its governments too much control over its educators?
- Look carefully and you may see another theme emerging, more quietly but no less influential for being so: the recognition that education does more than confer upon people the knowledge and skills they can later sell in the employment market place. In the 1980s and 1990s, the function of the nation's education service became ever more closely identified with jobs and the national economy: in England, this was marked by the fusion into one of two of the great Departments of State (Education and Employment), though in June 2001 it was reframed as the Department for Education and Skills. In the twenty-first century, will the assumptions which linked them still hold so strongly, or will we reassert other, equally important, values in our education service, ones which cannot easily be measured on an economic scale, involving the emotional, perhaps even the spiritual, lives of those who learn?

All societies must make decisions about how the population is to be educated. Look in this book to discover the mechanisms we have developed in the UK for carrying out this enormous undertaking. As you study them, ask: what values inform them? What do our structures and organisations – be they supple and responsive, brittle or stiff – tell us about the spirit which animates the machinery of our education system?

Professor Mike Newby
Dean of the Faculty of Arts and Education, University of Plymouth
Chair of the Universities Council for the Education of Teachers (1998–2001)

Contributors

James Arthur is Professor of Education and Head of Educational Research at Canterbury Christ Church University College. He has written widely on denominational education and recently completed *Education with Character: The Moral Economy of Schooling* (Routledge 2002). Professor Arthur has been a member of a number of Church education bodies and has lectured at international conferences on Catholic schools held in Australia, South Africa and the USA.

Alistair B. Cooke, OBE, has been General Secretary of the Independent Schools Council since 1997. He played a significant part in establishing the Independent Schools Inspectorate, through which ISC schools are accredited, and the ISC Teacher Induction Panel which oversees the new induction scheme in ISC schools.

Vaneeta-marie D'Andrea has had over 20 years' experience in higher eduction in the USA before moving to the UK.

Karen Evans is Professor and Head of the School of Lifelong Education and International Development at the University of London Institute of Education. She has directed international and comparative studies of learning and work in Europe, North America and the Commonwealth, and leads the Professional and Work-Related Learning Research Group at the Institute of Education.

Linda Gillard is a Senior Lecturer in Science Education at the University of Surrey Roehampton, She worked as a science teacher in Humberside, Ayrshire and Essex before working in primary and secondary initial teacher education. Currently, she is researching induction as part of professional development for primary and secondary teachers.

David Gosling has had experience teaching in Africa as well as the UK.

John Gray is Dean of Research at Cambridge University and before that was Director of Research at Homerton College, Cambridge from 1994 to 2001. He was previously Professor of Education at Sheffield University. He has been a Visiting Professor at the London Institute of Education and was elected as a Fellow of the British Academy in 2000. His main research interests lie in the areas of school effectiveness, school improvement and dynamics of change.

J. Mark Halstead is Professor of Moral Education at the University of Plymouth.

David W. Lankshear has been a head teacher of a Church of England Primary school, a diocesan adviser and a diocesan director of education. He is currently Deputy General Secretary of the National Society and Schools Officer of the Church of England Board of Education.

Liz Laycock has been involved in Primary education for several decades as a classroom teacher, an advisory teacher and in higher education and ITE. She was Programme Convenor for the Primary PGCE and Director of Programmes in the Faculty of Education at University of Surrey Roehampton.

Chris Lloyd is Head of the School of Education Studies at the University of Surrey Roehampton. She worked as a teacher in mainstream and special schools and as an advisory teacher for Special Educational Needs before moving into the University sector in 1991. Her teaching and research interests are in the areas of disability in education and inclusion.

Peter Long is Senior Lecturer in Early Childhood Education and Coordinator of the Early Childhood Centre, University of Surrey Roehampton. He is an Ofsted accredited inspector of primary schools and has also worked as a Registered Inspector of Nursery Education and as an Ofsted accredited trainer of Registered Inspectors of Nursery Education.

Laura Lundy is Senior Lecturer in Law at Queen's University Belfast. She is Chair of the Northern Ireland Human Rights Commission's Working Party on Education Rights for the proposed Bill of Rights.

Pat Mahony has been Professor of Education at the University of Surrey Roehampton since 1995. She has published widely in the areas of social justice and teacher education and is currently British editor of *Women's Studies International Forum*.

Paul Meredith is Reader in Education Law in the Faculty of Law at the University of Southampton. He is a member of the Executive Board of the European Association for Education Law and Policy and a member of the Editorial Board of the *European Journal for Education Law and Policy*.

Linda Merricks is Head of Adult and Community Learning at the University of Surrey.

Ian Morrison is Programme Director for Undergraduate Studies in the Faculty of Education at Cambridge University, having for many years held a similar appointment at Homerton College.

Mike Newby is Dean of the Faculty of Arts and Education in the University of Plymouth. He has been active at the national level over many years in the field of teacher education and training.

Jacqueline Nunn began her career as a teacher of English in secondary schools in London. She has extensive experience in teacher education and professional development and is currently Head of School of Initial Teacher Education at University of Surrey Roehampton.

Martin O'Callaghan is Principal of St Mary's University College, the main work of which is teacher education.

Lucy Palfreyman is Deputy Finance Officer at the Institute of Education, University of London. Her areas of responsibility include research finances.

Lindsay Paterson is Professor of Educational Policy in the Faculty of Education, Edinburgh University. He has written on many aspects of the sociology of education, in particular on the effects of social disadvantage and on the expansion of higher education, as well as on Scottish politics and culture.

Robert Phillips is Senior Lecturer in the Department of Education, University of Wales Swansea. He has written extensively on history education, education policy and schooling in Wales.

Sally Power is Professor of Education and Head of the School of Educational Foundations and Policy Studies at the Institute of Education, University of London. Her research interests include contemporary education policy, public and private education and the relationship between education and social class.

David Woodhead is National Director of the Independent Schools Council information service (ISCis) and Deputy General Secretary of ISC.

Introduction

Liam Gearon

Education in the United Kingdom is designed as an accessible and *outline* guide to the main features of an education system that by its very nature is always changing – and in a time of devolved governance this is even more the case.

There is no shortage of material about education. Specialist and technical academic texts about curriculum, assessment, government policy, educational research and so forth abound. Even the most dedicated professionals complain that there is too much to digest. Yet colleagues and I working in initial teacher training have been struck by the need for a text that provides a basic but critical guide to the complexities of education across age phases and in a time of devolved government within the United Kingdom.

The book was thus conceived to be of particular use to those entering the education profession for the first time, to newly qualified teachers and to those such as governors whose responsibilities mean that they need a ready grasp of the education system and the main features of its organisation. It is not, nor could it pretend to be, a comprehensive single-volume guide to education in the United Kingdom, but in each chapter you will find:

- a chapter summary;
- points for discussion;
- Internet sites;
- further reading and references.

Because of its general scope, the book will also be of use to the general reader in the UK, and internationally, who desires an understanding of the main trends in education within England, Northern Ireland, Scotland and Wales.

Education in the United Kingdom is divided into five parts:

- Part I: School Structures and Organisation.
- Part II: Curriculum, Assessment and Inspection.
- Part III: Denominational and Independent School Provision.
- Part IV: University Education and Initial Teacher Training.
- Part V: Continuing Professional Development and Educational Research.

Part I: School Structures and Organisation

This part has four chapters, one each for England, Northern Ireland, Scotland and Wales. Each author examines key structures and organisational features, including distinctive administration and legislation, and the effects of particular forms of local, national and devolved governance on teaching, learning and inspection. As well as legal perspectives for the different regions, these chapters provide important historical and political perspectives on education in the United Kingdom.

Part II: Curriculum, Assessment and Inspection

This section has five chapters. The aim is to provide a broad focus on the key features of education in terms of curriculum, assessment and inspection across the different age phases. The major focus is on England and Wales, though most authors refer to regional variations. There are chapters on the following: early years education; primary schools; secondary schools and sixth forms; and further education. There is a separate chapter on the main principles and trends in special educational needs.

Part III: Denominational and Independent School Provision

This part has four chapters, covering: Church of England schools; Roman Catholic schools; faith and diversity in religious school provision; and independent schools. Regional variations are identified where the authors deem this appropriate, but the intention here is to highlight aspects of education in the UK that, for religious or ideological reasons, seem to be marginalised or given scant attention in many educational texts, especially in initial teacher training.

Part IV: University Education and Initial Teacher Training

This part contains three chapters, covering: university education; models of teacher training; and induction for new teachers. The university sector, since 1992, has undergone a particularly rapid period of change with the creation of the new universities. At the same time, initial teacher training and the induction of new entrants to the profession have changed drastically. This part provides some insight into the transformation.

Part V: Continuing Professional Development and Educational Research

This part contains two chapters, covering: continuing professional education; and educational research. Both chapters demonstrate the opportunity that teachers and related professionals have for career development. These chapters also highlight critical reflection in education as an independent academic enquiry, as much as a career opportunity. The final chapter of the book thus focuses on education as a vibrant research discipline – one that extends education in the UK into an international dimension.

As editor, I would like to thank all contributors for their time, energy and commitment to this project, accepting that any flaws are my responsibility, and hoping that you, the reader, will find the book useful and engaging.

PART I:
School Structures and Organisation

CHAPTER 1

England

Paul Meredith

CHAPTER SUMMARY

- The governance of education in the past 20 years has been in a process of virtually continuous change and conflict. There has been a large outpouring of legislation, which has transformed the organisational structure. It has been – and remains – an area of acute political conflict.
- The Education Act 1944 originally envisaged a balanced partnership between the central department and local education authorities (LEAs), LEAs being very significant players with a strong strategic planning role.
- LEAs' strategic planning and other functions came under particular attack during the tenure of the Conservative government from 1979 to 1997. If the Conservative government had retained power in 1997, LEAs as we know them might have gone almost out of existence.
- Under the present government, and particularly by virtue of its first major education measure, the School Standards and Framework Act 1998, LEAs have obtained a crucial role in promoting and improving standards in schools. However, the secretary of state enjoys extensive powers of prescription, control and intervention. The organisational structure is highly centralised and authoritarian.
- The role of LEAs in the future is open to question, particularly by virtue of the advance of private sector involvement in the provision of educational services in the maintained sector – a development the government is embracing with some enthusiasm, but that raises critical questions relating to democratic control and accountability.

Introduction

The structure and organisation of the governance of schools in England throughout the past two decades has been in a process of almost continuous change and – arguably – conflict. The relative position of each of the key players in the governance of schools – the secretary of state and the central department with responsibility for education, local education authorities (LEAs), school governing bodies, headteachers,

teachers and parents – has changed significantly over this period of radical reform by virtue of a constant outpouring of education legislation. Most of this legislation has been enacted by successive governments in the name of raising standards and enhancing accountability on the part of the providers of education to their consumers (perceived, in general, as parents). Much of this legislation has, however, caused profound changes in the structure and organisation of school governance at every level, and has brought about shifting patterns in the distribution of power between the several partners involved. Indeed, the balance of power between the central department and LEAs as originally established under the Education Act 1944 – the foundation statute of the current schools system in England, though now entirely replaced by subsequent legislation – today bears hardly any resemblance to the reality of the distribution of power.

It is fair to say that the changes in structure and organisation since 1979 have been dramatic and in many cases deeply controversial. They have by no means been achieved through broad consensus. Indeed, in the past two decades education has been deeply politicised: this is not to say that education was not previously an area of political and social controversy – comprehensive reorganisation of secondary education in the 1960s and 1970s was quite evidently a movement of central political and social significance. But the political momentum underpinning educational reform in the past 20 years has grown enormously, to the point where education and educational reform are perceived to be a central element within the government's domestic policy agenda. This was seen most clearly in the May 1997 general election campaign, in which the Labour Party notoriously adopted the campaign slogan of 'education, education, education'; and in the June 2001 general election, the government's education policy was again clearly a central feature of political debate. Indeed, there is no indication that education in the foreseeable future will cease in any way to be at the centre of the political stage.

Key structures and organisational features

The original concept of a balanced partnership under the Education Act 1944

The framers of the Education Act 1944 envisaged a balanced partnership between the key elements within the organisational structure of schools provision – the central department, LEAs, governing bodies and headteachers. The central department – whose name has changed with some regularity over the years, but is currently the Department for Education and Skills – would be responsible, among many other matters, for overall policy direction, for securing resources from the Treasury for education expenditure and for approving, modifying or rejecting proposals submitted by LEAs (or school governors) for structural changes to the organisation of the provision of schools at local level. LEAs for their part would be responsible for the organisation of the provision of schools at local level, for distributing funds to schools, for the formulation of curricular policies, for many staffing matters and for the provision of many key services, including school transport and educational welfare services. At the level of the individual school, the headteacher played the pivotal role, with a substantial degree of direct day-to-day control over the delivery of the curriculum, discipline and the overall smooth running of the school, advised and supported by the governing body.

This represents only the broadest outline of the allocation of responsibilities as originally envisaged under the 1944 Act, but what is clear is that the Act enshrined a significant element of decentralisation of power from the central department downwards to the LEAs, which were seen as having a highly significant strategic planning role, as well as a vital role in determining curricular policy and in providing many important support services for individual schools. The role of LEAs as strategic planners of the provision of schools in their respective areas was especially important, and was a clear recognition of the constitutional position of LEAs as a critical element in the overall statutory structure of education, with a democratic legitimacy for the policies they adopted, and democratically accountable to their local electorate for the way in which they implemented those policies.

That balance of power between the central department and LEAs was directly reflected in the 1944 Act itself (see Harris 1993: 24–8). The minister (later known as secretary of state) had a very broad function under section 1(1) of the 1944 Act to:

> promote the education of the people of England and Wales and the progressive development of institutions devoted to that purpose, and to secure the effective execution by local authorities, under his control and direction, of the national policy for providing a varied and comprehensive educational service in every area.

While this symbolically important provision clearly envisaged the existence of a national policy for education and a degree of central control and direction, it none the less recognised the vital role of LEAs as the executors of that policy. Furthermore, the LEAs themselves were given specific responsibility under sections 7 and 8 of the Act for securing the provision of efficient education throughout the primary, secondary and further education stages to meet the needs of the population of their area (Education Act 1944: s. 7) and for the provision of sufficient schools within their area (*ibid.*: s. 8). These key statutory responsibilities of LEAs enshrined their crucial strategic planning role. Although with respect to strategic planning LEAs were not infrequently subject to considerable central government pressure – notably over the comprehensive reorganisation of secondary schools in the 1960s and 1970s, and subsequently over the removal of surplus places in the light of falling rolls – they none the less enjoyed wide discretion as to the nature, organisation and structure of schools in their respective areas. Although the final determination of structural proposals lay with the secretary of state, LEAs held the initiative power with respect to making proposals for matters of structural reorganisation, and this was fundamental to their strategic planning role (see Meredith 1995).

The relationship between the central department and LEAs as envisaged under the 1944 Act may therefore be characterised as one of genuine partnership: although it would be wrong to suggest that this was an equal partnership, the central department always having the ultimate control through formulation of national policy and the capacity to exert pressure on LEAs through control of resources, LEAs were none the less significant players. Furthermore, although the secretary of state held certain specific powers of intervention in the affairs of LEAs – for example, under section 68 of the 1944 Act she or he could issue directions to an LEA where satisfied that it was acting unreasonably – such powers of intervention were very difficult to invoke in practice. In one very well known instance in 1975–6, the then Labour secretary of state (Fred Mulley) issued a section 68 direction to the Conservative-controlled Tameside Metropolitan Borough Council requiring it fully to implement plans for comprehensive reorganisation of schools in the area which had been submitted by the council in the previous year, when it was under Labour control, and been approved by the secretary of state. When the secretary of state sought to enforce his direction in the courts, the LEA challenged its legality: it was held unanimously by the Court of Appeal and the House of Lords that the direction had been improperly issued, as the secretary of state had not been truly satisfied in law that the LEA was proposing to Act 'unreasonably'. The secretary of state may have wholeheartedly disagreed with the LEA's actions and thought them politically misguided and educationally unsound, but he could not properly categorise them as 'unreasonable' unless satisfied that the LEA was acting in a way in which no reasonable authority possibly could act (see *Secretary of State for Education and Science* v. *Tameside Metropolitan Borough Council* [1977] AC 1014). This case very significantly undermined the secretary of state's capacity to direct LEAs to take a particular course of action, and served to underpin the autonomy of LEAs and strengthen their capacity to resist central departmental pressure.

The erosion of the balanced partnership

While the partnership between the central department and LEAs had come under increasing strain during the 1960s and 1970s, particularly over comprehensive reorganisation, in which context many LEAs strongly resisted pressure by the Labour governments of 1964–70 and 1974–9 to reorganise their secondary schooling, it was arguably not until the Conservative government under Margaret Thatcher came to power in May 1979 that there was a genuinely sustained attack on the role, authority and relative autonomy hitherto enjoyed by LEAs. Since 1979 we have witnessed a huge outpouring of education legislation by both Conservative and Labour governments, profoundly affecting the structure and organisation of the governance of schools. It is possible in a brief chapter only to outline some of the key features of these structural changes, but the main recurring themes have been: the increasing centralisation of power in the hands of the central department and the secretary of state; the undermining of the functions of LEAs, particularly in the context of strategic planning, leading ultimately to the possibility that LEAs as we have known them may no longer exist; and an ever-increasing regime of prescription, inspection and control from above.

During the tenure of the Conservative government from 1979 to 1997, the role of LEAs was greatly diminished by virtue of the combined effect of vigorous centralisation of power in the hands of the central department and the secretary of state, and devolution of power to the governing bodies of individual schools. Centralisation took many forms, but perhaps the most obvious was the establishment of the National Curriculum under the Education Reform Act 1988 (ss 1–25; see also Education Act 1996: ss 350–374), which in a fundamental way undermined the considerable curricular policy-making functions enjoyed hitherto by LEAs. The National Curriculum is now well established and widely accepted, although it is noteworthy that the process of its formulation is remarkably centralised, the secretary of state being advised by the Qualifications and Curriculum Authority – a statutory body appointed by her and operating under her control and direction. In the other direction, many LEA functions were devolved to governing bodies: devolution took the form of the considerable enhancement of the functions of governing bodies in relation to crucial matters of expenditure and staffing through schemes of local management.[1]

Arguably of even greater significance to LEAs, however, was the erosion of their strategic planning role: this came about through a number of developments, including loss of their capacity to plan the intake of pupils into schools in order to ensure balanced numbers by virtue of the introduction of open enrolment,[2] and the government's encouragement of school governing bodies to seek grant-maintained status, thereby opting out of LEA control.[3] In the event, opting out never attained the momentum originally envisaged by the Conservative government. Little more than 1,000 schools were accorded grant-maintained status, and the pace of opting out had declined greatly by the time of the 1997 general election. Had the Conservative government been returned to power in 1997, it is highly likely that many more schools would have opted out of LEA control. The opting out process was, however, ended by the incoming Labour government, and grant-maintained schools have been returned to the LEA fold under the School Standards and Framework Act 1998, mainly as foundation schools. The School Standards and Framework Act also abolished the Funding Agency for Schools, which had been established by the Conservative government under the Education Act 1993 (ss 3–12 and 20), with responsibility for the distribution of central government grants to schools in the grant-maintained sector, and with important strategic planning functions. Indeed, in areas with a high proportion of pupils in attendance at grant-maintained schools, the Funding Agency took over (either wholly or in part) the relevant LEA's strategic planning role – in particular, the LEA's fundamental statutory responsibility for ensuring the provision of 'sufficient schools' within its area.[4]

Had the grant-maintained schools programme developed on a wider scale, the strategic planning role of LEAs would in all probability in due course have been lost, and it is arguable that the very *raison d'être* for the existence of LEAs would have disappeared. Indeed, in a White Paper issued in June 1996, *Self-government for Schools* (Cm 3315), the then Conservative government indicated its vision of a distinctly residual role for LEAs:

> Their role should be to provide those services and undertake those functions which schools cannot carry out for themselves and which no other agency is better placed to carry out. This role should be tightly specified to the minimum consistent with the efficient and effective operation of the education service. (*ibid.*: 49, para. 5)

The future of LEAs in the period leading up to the 1997 general election was thus in considerable jeopardy. What would have happened had the Conservative government retained power can only be conjecture. In the event, however, a Labour government under Tony Blair was elected in May 1997 and again in June 2001. The incoming Labour government in 1997 lost no time in bringing forward proposals for major legislation relating to schools in its White Paper of July 1997, *Excellence in Schools* (Cm 3681). The subsequent legislation, the School Standards and Framework Act 1998, introduced wide-ranging structural changes which profoundly affect the organisation and structure of the governance of schools today, from the secretary of state down through LEAs to the individual school. Many aspects of the Conservative government's education policies – not least the strong trend towards centralisation and the government's commitment to a rigorous programme of inspection of both schools and LEAs – have in fact been endorsed and consolidated by the Labour government. There have, however, been some important structural changes – especially to the organisational framework of maintained schools – and many significant new initiatives, some of which have imposed important new obligations upon LEAs. The organisation and structure of school governance is therefore clearly in a state of rapid and radical change. Furthermore, there is no end in sight to this radical reform programme: at the time of writing (July 2001), we are awaiting a new government White Paper and a new Education Bill which will make further important structural changes, notably by promoting the role of the private sector in the functioning of LEAs and public sector schools. We shall return to these latest developments in the concluding section of this chapter. In the meantime, however, we shall outline the organisation and structure of schooling under the currently applicable legislation.

Administration and legislation: the current structure and organisation of school governance

In this section it is proposed, first, to outline very briefly the key overall statutory responsibilities of the three essential tiers in the organisational structure – the secretary of state, LEAs and governing bodies. We shall then go on to examine how these three tiers interact in practice against the background of the government's core educational goal of raising standards.

Key statutory responsibilities

The secretary of state's overriding duty under the Education Act 1996 is to 'promote the education of the people of England and Wales' (s. 10), and to exercise her powers 'with a view to improving standards, encouraging diversity and increasing opportunities for choice' (s. 11(2)). Beyond this very general duty, however, the secretary of state has at her disposal a very considerable range of powers of prescription and control and of intervention in the affairs of LEAs and schools. Perhaps most importantly the secretary of state is ultimately responsible for the promulgation of the National Curriculum (Education Act 1996: s. 356). She also has wide powers of prescription, exercised through the promulgation of regulations on many aspects of educational provision and of very important codes of practice addressed in particular to LEAs and school governing bodies. These Codes of Practice are issued in the contexts of the assessment and identification of children with special educational needs (Education Act 1996: s.313), school admissions and school admissions appeals (School Standards and Framework Act 1998: s.84) and LEA–school relations (*ibid.*: s.127). The secretary of state also has extensive powers with respect to the rationalisation of school places (*ibid.*: s.34 and schedule 7), and very important powers with respect to approving, modifying or rejecting LEAs' education development plans (*ibid.*: s.7). Perhaps of greatest importance, however, from the point of view of the relationship between the secretary of state, LEAs and individual schools, are the secretary of state's powers of intervention and direction. Such powers were included in the Education Act 1944, notably section 68, the power to issue directions to LEAs or governing bodies where satisfied that the LEA or governors were acting unreasonably, and section 99, the power to issue directions where satisfied that the LEA or governors were acting in breach of a statutory duty. These powers still exist, in sections 496 and 497 of the Education Act 1996, but, as discussed above in the context of the *Tameside* case, have been extremely difficult to exercise in practice. Of far greater significance today is a new power conferred on the secretary of state under section 8 of the School Standards and Framework Act 1998 (inserting a new section 497A into the Education Act 1996) to intervene in the running of LEAs. This new provision is of immense importance and is an emphatic assertion of the secretary of state's power of intervention. This power is of such importance that it merits more detailed discussion below.

The key overriding statutory responsibilities of LEAs, now enshrined in sections 13 and 14 of the Education Act 1996, are to 'contribute towards the spiritual, moral, mental and physical development of the community by securing that efficient primary education, secondary education and further education are available to meet the needs of the population of their area' (Education Act 1996: s.13). They are required to secure the provision within their respective areas of sufficient primary and secondary schools (*ibid.*: s.14(1)), ensuring that they are sufficient in number, character and equipment to provide for all pupils an education that is 'appropriate' in the sense that it offers 'such variety of instruction and training as may be desirable' in view of the pupils' different ages, abilities and aptitudes (*ibid.*: s.14(2) and (3)). LEAs have a further very general but none the less symbolically important duty, imposed by section 5 of the School Standards and Framework Act 1998, to ensure that they carry out their functions with a view to promoting high standards in primary and secondary education.

The key statutory responsibilities of school governing bodies are now to be found in sections 36 to 44 of the School Standards and Framework Act 1998. Their general powers are set out in schedule 10. The obligation placed upon LEAs to promote high standards is paralleled by a similar duty placed on school governors to 'conduct the school with a view to promoting high standards of educational achievement at the school' (School Standards and Framework Act 1998: s.38(2)).

This very broad statement of the key overriding statutory responsibilities of the secretary of state, LEAs and school governors offers no more than a skeletal framework.

The reality of the relationships between the key elements within the organisational structure is inevitably much more complex and is best seen in context.

Practical interaction between the three tiers in context

An insight into the interaction between the three tiers can be obtained by examining their respective roles in the context of the government's key goal of raising standards in schools (see Meredith 1998), the centrepiece of its education policy. In the 1997 White Paper, *Excellence in Schools*, the government stressed that schools themselves should bear the primary responsibility for raising standards, but that they should do so in active partnership with the other key players in the educational field:

> The main responsibility for raising standards lies with schools themselves. But they will be more effective in doing so if they work in active partnership with LEAs, Ofsted and the DfEE. The LEA's role is to help schools set and meet their targets. Ofsted's role is to inspect performance by individual schools and LEAs, and provide an external assessment of the state of the school system as a whole. The DfEE's role is to set the policy framework, promote best practice, and to provide pressure and support in relation to LEAs as LEAs themselves do for their schools. (DfEE 1997: 27, para. 16)

This paragraph encapsulates the government's perception of the relationship, bringing about what it described as 'the right balance of pressure and support' for both schools and LEAs in order to optimise their chances of improving performance and raising standards.

At the level of the individual school, one of the keys to improvement in standards, as set out in the White Paper, would be the setting and subsequent monitoring of 'challenging targets for improvement' (*ibid.*: 26, para. 12).

In the setting of targets, both the central department and LEAs would play a significant proactive role: national performance and benchmark data would initially be set by the central department; each LEA would then be required to set benchmark data and guidance for all maintained schools in its area; each school would then issue a draft version of its own targets. Schools would enter into discussions with their LEA in relation to their draft targets. If agreed, these would then be established for a three-year period, though subject to annual review. In the absence of agreement, the LEA might invoke the new 'early warning' system under section 15 of the School Standards and Framework Act 1998, which is applicable to underperforming schools and requires an action plan setting out the governing body's proposals for improvement.

Target-setting would not be limited to the level of individual schools: each LEA would be required to draw up an Education Development Plan (EDP) setting out its proposals for developing the provision of education for children in its area by raising standards and improving performance.[5] Each LEA would be required to submit its EDP for approval by the secretary of state, who would have power of approval, modification or rejection. EDPs have become of great significance, giving the central department and the Office for Standards in Education (Ofsted) a considerably enhanced capacity for direct involvement at local level in the process of delivering improved standards. In the event of the secretary of state and an LEA being in irresolvable conflict over the content of an EDP, the secretary of state might direct Ofsted to conduct an inspection of the LEA. This possibility clearly manifests the secretary of state's determination to maintain rigorous control over the formulation of EDPs.

It is clear that school performance targets and EDPs are crucial elements in the government's drive to improve standards. Also of critical importance, however, are the mechanisms that have been developed for tackling underperforming schools. The key agency in this context is Ofsted, which conducts periodic inspections of individual schools under Part I of the School Inspections Act 1996, and whose reports are of immense significance in providing a direct mechanism of intervention from the top of the organisational structure – the secretary of state – down to the level of the individual school. A complex remedial regime exists for schools identified in inspection reports as having 'serious weaknesses' or, in more extreme cases, as requiring 'special measures'. LEAs are empowered in specified circumstances to issue schools with 'early warning' notices under the School Standards and Framework Act, setting out action they require the governing body to take in order to remedy specified defects, and the period within which such action should be taken (School Standards and Framework Act 1998: s.15). LEAs are empowered in specified circumstances to appoint additional governors to a school's governing body (*ibid.*: s.16) or to suspend the school's delegated budget (*ibid.*: s.17). The secretary of state is also empowered to appoint additional governors (*ibid.*: s.18) or, in a grave situation, to give a direction that a school shall be closed down (*ibid.*: s.19). Direction to close a school may be given as part of what is referred to in the White Paper as the 'fresh start' programme (DfEE 1997: 30, paras 29–30), under which a failing school may be: closed, its pupils being transferred to nearby successful schools; absorbed by another school by amalgamation; or discontinued and then reopened with a new name and under new management.

Taken together, the regime described above for target-setting for individual schools, the formulation of EDPs, inspection of schools and specific action to tackle failing schools amounts to a rigorous network of monitoring and control from the central department downwards through LEAs to the level of individual schools. What is clear is that the regime is markedly authoritarian in nature, the central department having firm control over the other elements in the structure, through setting benchmark standards, through the process of approving EDPs, through the Ofsted inspection process and ultimately through the secretary of state's power to intervene at individual school level in the event of serious and continuing failure. This catalogue of central powers of intervention is, however, incomplete: there remains one further extremely significant power of intervention – the power of the secretary of state to intervene directly in the running of LEAs by way of issuing specific directions.

Under the most radical provision for central departmental intervention in the affairs of LEAs yet seen, the secretary of state was given the power by virtue of section 8 of the School Standards and Framework Act 1998 (inserting new sections 497 A and B into the Education Act 1996) to issue directions to an officer of the LEA concerned (it is presumed that this would normally be the chief education officer) if satisfied that the LEA is 'failing in any respect' to perform any function relating to schools to 'an adequate standard' or at all. If the secretary of state is satisfied that such a state of affairs exists – whether by virtue of the findings of an Ofsted inspection of the LEA, or through complaints submitted by parents, adverse press publicity or by any other means – she may direct an officer of the LEA 'to secure that that function is performed in such a way as to achieve such objectives as are specified in the direction' (Education Act 1996: s. 497A(3)).

Furthermore, the secretary of state may direct that the functions themselves should be taken over by someone outside the LEA nominated by the secretary of state. It would be hard to envisage a more radically interventionist power than this. One might have thought that this would be an extreme measure of last resort, and only very rarely invoked in situations of catastrophic failure by an LEA to carry out its functions to a satisfactory standard. This has proved to be far from the case: following adverse Ofsted inspection reports on a significant number of LEAs, the secretary of state has not hesitated to invoke section 497A, leading in some of these cases to the LEA's functions being taken over by outside agencies – generally private educational entrepreneur companies which in the recent past have been entering the sphere of public sector education with a view to profit. This raises a major debate about the privatisation of public sector education services, to which we shall return in the following section, on initiatives and prospects.

This section has sought to place the organisational structures in the context of the government's central goal of raising standards. There is little doubt that LEAs under the School Standards and Framework Act have a significant role to play in driving up standards, especially in ensuring that schools set targets at an appropriate level, in monitoring the extent to which those standards are achieved and in taking action where schools are perceived to be underperforming. It is, however, clear that the real driving force within the three-tier structure is at the centre, the secretary of state today having powers of prescription, control and intervention never envisaged in the Education Act 1944.

Conclusion: initiatives and prospects

It should be evident from the discussion above that the relationship between the three tiers in the structural organisation have been subject to significant changes and tensions over the years. LEAs, in particular under the Conservative government in the 1980s and 1990s, lost a great deal of their strategic planning role, and it is possible that this critical function would have been almost entirely surrendered in time to the Funding Agency for Schools if the Conservative government had remained in office. Under the 1997 Labour government's first major education measure, the School Standards and Framework Act 1998, the erosion of the LEA strategic planning function was at least in part ended, particularly by the abolition of the Funding Agency and the return of grant-maintained schools to the LEA fold. However, a major new challenge faces LEAs today, raising fundamental questions as to their future. This arises from the increasing trend, strongly promoted by the government, towards the involvement of the private sector in the provision of public sector education, particularly through the provision of services hitherto provided by LEAs.

The involvement of the private sector in the provision of public sector education is by no means new: LEAs and school governors have bought in private sector services for many years; for instance, in relation to the provision of services such as meals, transport and cleaning. That is relatively uncontroversial. In the recent past, however, the nature and scale of private sector involvement has grown remarkably, with crucial educational services provided by LEAs being 'outsourced' to private sector companies. Examples include the school improvement service and the ethnic minority achievement service in the London Borough of Hackney being outsourced to Nord Anglia plc (see Education and Employment Select Committee, 2000, p. viii), and the whole school education service of the London Borough of Islington being outsourced to Cambridge Education Associates (*ibid.*). Other LEAs where private sector companies have been brought in to take over education services to date have included Liverpool, Leicester, Leeds and the London Borough of Haringey. In large part, outsourcing has arisen as a direct result of intervention by the secretary of state in the affairs of the LEAs concerned under section 497A of the Education Act 1996, discussed above. In such cases the secretary of state, generally following adverse Ofsted reports relating to the management of the LEA, has taken the decision to intervene. Following reports from private management consultants on the running of the LEA, tenders have been obtained from private sector educational entrepreneur companies for the running of particular education services within the LEA, and a contract with the successful company has subsequently been drawn up for the provision of those services.

This represents a hugely important and controversial development which, if continued and expanded on a wide scale, will raise serious questions as to the future of LEAs. It also raises serious constitutional questions about the accountability of the private sector companies for their provision of the services taken over. Traditional forms of democratic accountability by the LEA to its electorate do not apply in the same way to private sector companies: such companies may be accountable through being required, on pain of incurring financial penalties, to meet targets and deadlines incorporated specifically into their contracts. But it is very difficult to see how individual parents or children affected by the provision of educational services can realistically hold such companies to account. And, in the event of severe failure by a private sector company in the provision of educational services, and possible bankruptcy, it is possible to envisage huge disruption to the provision of education in the area and severe harm being done to the children affected.

Despite these concerns, the government has embraced private sector involvement in public sector educational provision with considerable enthusiasm. At the time of writing, this has mainly taken the form of companies taking over certain LEA services; the government has, however, strongly encouraged other forms of private sector involvement, notably by taking over the management of individual schools, a trend still in its infancy but which we can fully expect to develop considerably in the foreseeable future. Indeed, at the time of writing we are awaiting publication of a White Paper on education and a new Education Bill, which, it is anticipated, will make provision for expansion of private sector involvement in the running of maintained schools. If the trend towards private sector involvement continues as expected, there will be a new and very important player in the educational field, and we can fully expect that the nature and ethos of the three-tier organisational structure will undergo yet more radical transformation.

POINTS FOR DISCUSSION

1 In what ways were the powers of LEAs eroded under the Conservative government between 1979 and 1997? If the Conservative government had remained in office, what functions would LEAs have had today?
2 In what respects did the School Standards and Framework Act 1998 restore the strategic planning role of LEAs?
3 In what respects can it be argued that the School Standards and Framework Act 1998 was a centralising measure?
4 Section 8 of the School Standards and Framework Act 1998 (inserting section 497 A and B into the Education Act 1996) gives the secretary of state a very powerful measure of intervention in the affairs of LEAs: what is the extent of this power and why is it so controversial?
5 In what ways are private sector educational entrepreneur companies becoming involved today in the provision of public sector education? Do you regard this as a welcome development? What are the possible consequences in terms of accountability?

INTERNET SITES

Department for Education and Skills: www.dfes.gov.uk
House of Commons Select Committee for the Department for Education and Skills: www.parliament.uk/commons/selcom/edskillshome.htm
National Curriculum Online: www.nc.uk.net/home/html
Ofsted: www.ofsted.gov.uk

NOTES

1 Originally introduced under Education Reform Act 1988 (ss 33–51). See also Education Act 1996 (ss 101–26).
2 Introduced under Education Reform Act 1988 (ss 26–7). See also School Standards and Framework Act 1998 (s. 86(5)).
3 Opting out was introduced originally under Education Reform Act 1988 (ss 52–104).
4 Originally under s. 8, Education Act 1944. See also s. 14, Education Act 1996.
5 EDPs are now a statutory requirement under the School Standards and Framework Act 1998 (ss 6–7).

FURTHER READING

Ford, J., Hughes, M. and Ruebain, D. (1999) *Education Law and Practice*. London: Legal Action Group.

Hyams, O. (1998) *Law of Education*. London: Sweet & Maxwell.

Poole, K., Coleman, J. and Liell, P. (1997) *Butterworths Education Law*. London: Butterworths.

Education and the Law. London: Carfax Publishing, Taylor and Francis (quarterly journal).

Education Law Journal. London: Jordans (quarterly journal).

REFERENCES

DfEE (1996) *Self-government for Schools*, Cm 3315. London: DfEE.

DfEE (1997) *Excellence in Schools*, Cm 3681. London: DfEE.

Education and Employment Select Committee (2000) *The Role of Private Sector Organisations in Public Education*, Seventh Report, 1999–2000, HC 118. London: The Stationery Office.

Harris, N. (1993) *Law and Education: Regulation, Consumerism and the Education System*. London: Sweet & Maxwell.

Meredith, P. (1995) 'The future of local education authorities as strategic planners', *Public Law*, 234–43.

Meredith, P. (1998) 'The fall and rise of local education authorities', *Liverpool Law Review*, 20(1), 41–62.

CHAPTER 2

Northern Ireland

Martin O'Callaghan and Laura Lundy

CHAPTER SUMMARY

This chapter:

- Puts schools in Northern Ireland in a broad historical context that explains why schooling is more politicized than in England and Wales and outlines the shortcomings of 30 years of direct rule.
- Spells out the implications of devolved government and describes Northern Ireland's dual system of state and church schools and the system of their governance and funding.
- Looks at the way educational administration was dealt with in the period of direct rule and how it is dealt with under devolved government, and examines the work of the five Education and Library Boards and the Council for Catholic Maintained Schools.
- Gives an overview of the Northern Ireland Curriculum and the modes of assessment within schools and by public examinations, and describes how the Education and Training Inspectorate functions.
- Surveys current and planned developments in education, including the review of the curriculum, the review of selection at 11 and the Northern Ireland Bill of Rights.

Introduction

The brief historical overview that follows is divided into two parts: the period before the abolition of the Northern Ireland Parliament in 1972; and the period of direct rule from 1971 to 1999. The short period from the setting up of a devolved government in 1999 to the present day is referred to throughout the chapter.

The development of schooling in Northern Ireland is in many respects similar to that in England and Wales. Differences are due in part to cultural factors and in part to political factors. One of the main differences is that the administration of schools in Northern Ireland is politicized differently, the major factor being the political and religious division in society.

With the partition of Ireland in 1921, Northern Ireland was set up as a separate polit-ical entity, still part of the UK but with a devolved parliament and government. In the disturbed decades preceding partition, English reforms increasing public control over schools and lessening the influence of churches were not introduced in Ireland. Almost all the National (primary) Schools in Ireland, established from 1827 on and publicly funded, were *de facto* denominational schools, and this situation continued in both parts of Ireland after partition. Within about 20 years of partition, however, the Protestant churches in the North had mostly transferred their schools to state control, while the Catholic Church kept its schools. The state schools are known as 'controlled schools' and the Catholic schools as 'maintained schools'.

Both kinds of schools had their recurrent costs, including teachers' salaries, paid by the government. In the case of controlled schools, capital costs were met by the govern-ment, while maintained schools had to find 50 per cent of their capital costs. The state share of capital costs for maintained schools has increased over the years to the point where schools that agree to waive their right to a majority on the board of governors can receive 100 per cent of capital costs.

Following the Butler Act 1944, the Northern Ireland government introduced similar measures in 1947. This led to the possibility of secondary and university edu-cation for many people from less advantaged backgrounds. When comprehensive edu-cation was introduced to England in the 1960s it was not introduced in Northern Ireland, except in one small area. The system of selection of children for grammar school at age 11, perceived by many to be unjust to children, is the single most con-tentious issue.

Following the introduction of direct rule from Westminster in 1971, Northern Ireland experienced less change than elsewhere in the UK, and very often the wrong change or change for the wrong reasons, compounded by a lack of action from some Ministers of Education owing to the multiplicity of their responsibilities. The worst effect of this was the tendency to by-pass the time-honoured process of consulting edu-cational professionals in order to identify the needs of the educational system and find solutions. The latest solution was imported from England whether Northern Ireland had a problem for it or not.

Key structures and organisational features

Department of Education

Under the system of direct rule that was in place until 1999, the overall responsibility for the internal government of Northern Ireland rested with the Northern Ireland Office, under the Secretary of State for Northern Ireland. The Department of Education, Northern Ireland (DENI) was headed by a British minister. As a result of the Belfast Agreement in 1998, devolution was restored in December 1999 and the Department of Education (DE) is now headed by a locally elected Minister for Education (at the time of writing, Martin McGuinness of Sinn Fein). Before 1999 DENI had responsibility for the whole range of education, from nursery to further and

higher, as well as sport and recreation, the youth service, libraries and community relations. As a result of the reallocation of functions between departments under the new
devolved arrangements, the DE is now focused on schools and libraries, its other functions being divided between two new departments, the Department of Higher and
Further Education, Training and Employment (DHFETE) and the Department of
Culture, Arts and Leisure (DCAL).

Education and Library Boards

In Northern Ireland educational services are administered by regional education bodies
known as Education and Library Boards (ELBs). There are five of these: Belfast, South
Eastern, Southern, Western and North Eastern. ELBs are responsible for many of the
functions carried out by local education authorities (LEAs) in England and Wales,
including curriculum support, education welfare services, the assessment and statementing of children with special educational needs and the appointment of staff in controlled schools. The Council for Catholic Maintained Schools is responsible for
appointments in maintained Catholic schools. All appointments to ELBs are made by
the DE.

However, whereas LEAs are composed of directly elected local representatives, legislation in Northern Ireland provides that ELBs should not have more than two-fifths
of their members nominated by local district councils. This measure, which was
designed to ensure that no one political grouping could have overall control of an education authority, was introduced following a major review of local government in
Northern Ireland in 1970. The review had been planned as a tidying up exercise, but
was hastened by the commencement of civil unrest, and in particular allegations that
unionists were using their majorities on local authorities to discriminate against the
minority Catholic population. Education had not been one of the major areas of
concern. However, it was considered that educational administration would benefit
from the same changes that were taking place throughout local government. Each ELB,
therefore, has the following representation: members of the local district councils;
persons representing the interests of transferors; representatives of the trustees of
maintained schools; and persons deemed to be suitable by reason of their interest in
the services for which the ELB is responsible.

Categories of school

Until 1989 Northern Ireland had basically only two categories of school: controlled
schools (managed by the ELB for the area) and voluntary schools (owned and managed
by trustees, normally the local churches). There are two types of voluntary school:
maintained (including voluntary primary and secondary schools) and voluntary
grammar (which are permitted to select pupils on the basis of ability). The majority of
voluntary maintained schools are controlled by the Catholic Church. In order to facilitate the management of these schools the Education Reform (Northern Ireland) Order
1989 transferred responsibility for all Catholic maintained schools to a statutory body,

the Council for Catholic Maintained Schools (CCMS). The 1989 Order also introduced a new category of school, the grant-maintained integrated school, whose primary focus is to provide a religiously mixed environment that is capable of attracting reasonable numbers of both Catholic and Protestant pupils. Northern Ireland has 22 independent schools out of a total provision of 190 pre-school centres, 91 nurseries, 916 primary schools (including 79 with nursery classes and 24 preparatory departments in grammar schools), 165 secondary schools and 47 grammar schools. There are three special schools and 22 hospital schools.

Types of educational provision

Northern Ireland's school system is distinctive in a number of ways. More than half the children in Northern Ireland attend Catholic schools. Some Catholic children attend non-Catholic schools and very few non-Catholic children attend Catholic schools. Some people think this is one of the causes of 'the troubles', and urge religiously integrated schools as part of the solution to the problems of division in society. Others see the causes of the troubles as political in origin (colonisation and partition), producing profound social and economic division, and not solvable by integrated schooling. Both points of view are inclined to agree that as a just and equal society is gradually established the social division will decrease and children will be able to mix more easily than they can now.

Another of the most notable differences from its neighbouring systems is that it maintains a grammar–secondary school divide. At the age of 11, pupils undertake a centrally organised aptitude test, which is used to determine which children will attend grammar schools (35 per cent in 1994). However, the system of selection for post-primary schools is currently under review, and the prospects for reform are explored in the final section of this chapter.

A further significant difference is the school starting age, which in Northern Ireland is four, with nursery provision offered to three-year-olds.

Finally, there are two forms of educational provision that are peculiar to Northern Ireland: Irish-medium schools, where children are taught through Irish in more than half the compulsory subjects (excluding English); and integrated schools, where children are educated in a religiously mixed environment (both Catholic and Protestant pupils). The DE is under a statutory obligation to encourage and facilitate both of these distinctive types of education. It fulfils this obligation to a large extent by providing funding to two educational charities, Comhairle na Gaelscoiliochta (the Council for Irish Medium Education) and the Northern Ireland Council for Integrated Education.

School government and funding

Every grant-aided school in Northern Ireland is managed by a board of governors, which includes representatives of parents, teachers and the DE or local ELB, along with either trustee representatives (usually the Catholic Church in voluntary schools), transferors (the Protestant churches in controlled schools) or foundation governors (the parents who established the school) in grant-maintained integrated schools. The head-teacher is also a member, albeit a non-voting one. The precise composition of the board is determined to a large extent by the source and level of funding the school receives. Thus schools that receive their funding directly from the DE have DE representatives, while those that receive it from the ELB have ELB representatives. Although the DE has released proposals to move towards a common funding formula, in which all schools will receive their budget allocation from ELBs, there is no plan to alter the DE nominations in voluntary and grant-maintained schools. Moreover, in voluntary schools the precise balance of members between the state and trustee appointments is determined by the level of funding for capital costs. In voluntary schools that receive grant aid of 85 per cent of their capital costs, the trustee representatives are in the majority on the board. However, in 1993, following concerns about the levels of attainment in voluntary schools (the majority of which are Catholic), voluntary schools were allowed to opt for 100 per cent funding of capital costs (see Cormack *et al.* 1991). In such cases, the balance of membership changes, with the result that the trustees no longer constitute a single majority grouping on the board.

Since 1990, the management of all schools has been devolved to boards of governors and principals in key areas such as admissions, discipline and securing delivery of the Northern Ireland Curriculum. Moreover, schools that did not previously control their own budgets have had financial responsibility devolved to them under the local management of schools (LMS) scheme. As in England and Wales, the ability of governors to carry out the extensive range of duties allocated to them has been queried. In particular, one research study concluded that many governor tasks are simply left to the headteacher, with the result that the management structure is akin to 'one of a Chief Executive with a relatively weak Board of Directors' (McKeown 1997).

Administration and legislation: local, national and devolved governance

After 27 years of direct rule from Westminster, devolution was reintroduced to Northern Ireland in December 1999, restoring both executive and legislative responsibility to local politicians. As a result of the Northern Ireland Act 1998, executive powers are exercised by ministers and Northern Ireland departments on 'transferred' matters such as education. The division within Northern Ireland's political parties is such that it had been anticipated that there would be occasions when it would be difficult for a minister to command the trust of his or her opponents (either on certain contentious issues or, indeed, at all). In view of this legislation, the Northern Ireland Act 1998 contains a series of safeguards to ensure that the actions of ministers are not party political and that decisions on potentially contentious issues have the backing of both communities. First among these checks and balances is the system of cross-party statutory committees. These have the power to: consider and advise on departmental budgets; approve secondary legislation and take the committee stage of relevant primary legislation; call for persons and papers; initiate enquiries and make reports; and consider and advise on matters brought to the committee by the minister.

The Assembly also has legislative responsibility in relation to education. After the Northern Ireland Parliament was abolished in 1972, legislation for Northern Ireland on various matters, including those pertaining to education, was by way of Order in Council at Westminster (see Hadfield 1992). Debate on this legislation was limited and, possibly as a consequence of this, the general approach taken to law reform has been to reproduce the legislative proposals that had previously been adopted in Great Britain (see Lundy 1998). Since 1986 there have been four major Education (Northern Ireland) Orders, each mirroring (albeit with a one- to three-year delay) provisions at Westminster. For example, the Education Reform (Northern Ireland) Order 1989 replicates many of the major changes in the English and Welsh Education Act 1988, including open enrolment, the statutory curriculum, the reform of governing bodies and LMS. In many instances the law is identical (for example, special educational needs). In other areas, the legislation has been tailored to reflect the local political and cultural context (such as the inclusion of the theme of education for mutual understanding in the Northern Ireland Curriculum).

Given that there is now a realistic prospect that educational reform will be determined by locally based politicians for the first time in over 20 years, it will be interesting to see whether the law in Northern Ireland will continue to follow the pattern of England and Wales, or whether something wholly distinctive will emerge. Early indications are that the Assembly is willing to go its own way: for instance, one of the first things the Minister for Education did was to abolish the highly contentious school league tables. Changes might also occur at the organisational level. Despite the reorganisation of the departments after devolution, the DE is unaffected in its obligations to schools. However, the fate of the ELBs is less certain. In 1997 there was a legislative proposal to reduce the number from five to four. Although the amalgamation was contested when it was proposed via Westminster, economic pressures might force a rethink when the issue is considered locally: reorganisation was mentioned in a number of the manifestos for the 1998 election to the Assembly. The categories of school are unlikely to be affected: public opinion and the influence of the churches are likely to sustain the existing structures. However, it will be interesting to see how certain types of school, such as integrated and Irish-medium, fare, given that they have the specific support of political parties who for the first time have a direct say in the operation of the education system. However, there can be little doubt that the single biggest issue that faces the Assembly in the context of education is the question of selection at 11, an issue explored below.

Teaching and learning: inspection frameworks

The curriculum

The Northern Ireland Curriculum was phased in after 1990, following the introduction of the National Curriculum in England and Wales. It was drawn up by the Northern Ireland Curriculum Council, which later merged with the Council for Examinations and Assessment to form the Council for the Curriculum, Examinations and Assessment (CCEA).

The Education Reform (Northern Ireland) Order 1989 sets out the minimum educational entitlement for pupils aged from four to 16 years. The Order requires schools to provide a curriculum for all pupils that 'promotes the spiritual, moral, cultural, intellectual and physical development of pupils at the school and thereby of society; and prepares such pupils for the opportunities and experiences of adult life'. The curriculum is defined in terms of four Key Stages, which cover the 12 years of compulsory schooling. The only difference from the Key Stages in England and Wales is that Key Stage 1 spans four years, rather than three, and Key Stage 2 spans three.

In addition to the Northern Ireland Curriculum, schools can develop additional curriculum elements to express their particular ethos and meet pupils' individual needs. In the first review, begun in 1994 and implemented in 1996, schools were given more freedom in the amount of time they could devote to non-core activities. A second, more radical, review began in 1999 and is still ongoing. More details are given below.

Key Stages 1 and 2

The curriculum for Key Stages 1 and 2 includes: religious education, English, mathematics, science and technology, history and geography (known as the environment and society area of study); art and design, music and physical education (known as the creative and expressive area of study); Irish, in Irish-speaking schools only; and four educational cross-curricular themes (education for mutual understanding, cultural heritage, health education and information technology). The cross-curricular themes are not separate subjects but are woven through the main subjects of the curriculum.

Key Stages 3 and 4

Compulsory for Key Stage 3 are:

- religious education;
- English and mathematics;
- science, technology and design;
- history and geography;
- art and design, music and physical education;
- French, German, Italian, Spanish or Irish;
- six educational themes, four as in Key Stages 1 and 2, plus economic awareness and careers education.

Compulsory for Key Stage 4 are:

- religious education;
- English, mathematics, science;
- one of history, geography, business studies, home economics, economics, politics;
- physical education;
- a modern language;
- the six educational themes as in Key Stage 3.

The structure of the curriculum

Each subject in the Northern Ireland Curriculum has a Programme of Study, which sets out the opportunities that should be offered to all pupils, subject to their age and ability, in terms of the knowledge, skills and understanding at each Key Stage. Teachers use the Programmes of Study as a basis for planning schemes of work. Each Programme has Attainment Targets, which define the expected standards of pupil performance in terms of level descriptors. These provide the basis for judgements on pupils' attainment at the end of each Key Stage.

The Foreword to the new curriculum was like the English curriculum in that it promised the development of the whole child: moral, physical etc. In practice this did not really happen. The curriculum was overtly subject-based and, in the opinion of some, had too much content and was pitched at too high a level. This led to prescription of the amount of time to be spent on the subjects of the curriculum. Many teachers found that this regime not only reduced the time available for 'fringe areas' but also, by setting attainment levels in all subjects, reduced the flexibility available to the teacher.

Common curriculum in religious education

After the introduction of the Northern Ireland Curriculum the four main Christian churches in Northern Ireland established a working group to produce an agreed syllabus that could be used in all schools to fulfil the statutory obligation to teach religious education. This agreed syllabus does not cover all the issues any particular school would wish, but leaves scope for attention to be given to particular aspects of each denomination. This syllabus is being reviewed by an inter-church group as part of the overall review of the curriculum.

Educational themes

The six educational (cross-curricular) themes are strands of knowledge, skills, attitudes and values that cut across curricular boundaries. Their statutory nature indicates the importance attached to them. Their objectives are meant to be realised in a cross-curricular way through the subjects of the curriculum and ethos of the school.

The educational theme that has attracted most public attention and proved most difficult for schools is education for mutual understanding (EMU), combined into a single theme with cultural heritage (CH) in 1992. Recent research has highlighted two major criticisms of EMU and CH: first, that EMU was initially presented as consisting largely of cross-community contact, which was strongly resisted by some sections of the community; second, that the themes are so abstract or ill defined that teachers have had difficulty with them. Many feel that the minister who introduced EMU overemphasised contact and that by doing so he set back the building of real understanding.

Assessment

There is a statutory assessment in specified subjects for all pupils aged eight, 11 and 14. Teachers are required to make formal assessments of pupils' work at ages eight and 11 in English and mathematics (Irish and mathematics in Irish-medium schools). Assessment Units, developed by CCEA to help teachers to confirm their assessment of pupils' progress on each Attainment Target, consist of short assessment tasks, involving 20–30 minutes of individual work by pupils, and may be used at a time chosen by the teacher. Pupils are not required to sit formal tests. Schools are required to tell parents which level their child has reached in these subjects. In addition to the statutory assessment at age 11, pupils may opt to take a transfer test if they wish to seek a place in a selective post-primary school.

At age 14 there is statutory assessment of English, Irish (in Irish-speaking schools), mathematics and science. This takes two forms – teacher assessment, without moderation, and end of Key Stage subject tests. Teachers assess each pupil in each Attainment Target in the above-mentioned subjects and record the assessment of their pupils on Class Assessment Records provided by CCEA. There is parallel reporting of both the teacher assessment and the test outcomes. The test and teacher assessment outcomes for English, Irish, mathematics and science are returned to schools so that they can report to parents. At the end of Key Stage 4 pupils enter for public examinations.

A baseline assessment scheme is being introduced for Year 1 pupils. It aims to identify the child's strengths and individual learning needs, to enable teachers to plan a programme that will meet the child's needs and to provide information that will inform parents about their child's skills and competences on entry to school.

Inspection

Schools are inspected by the DE's Education and Training Inspectorate (ETI). Inspections of individual schools are usually conducted by a team of at least two inspectors and a written report is published. In 1998, unannounced inspections were introduced to check schools' provision for pastoral care and child protection. General inspections and focused inspections, the most common kind, are conducted as follows. Schools are informed about the planned inspection four to eight weeks before the date. Before the inspection an inspector visits the school to explain the procedures and to meet staff, governors and parents. The duration of the inspection depends on the size of the school. When the inspection has been completed inspectors give an oral report to the governors and principal. When a draft written report has been completed the principal is given an opportunity to check it for factual accuracy before publication. The school is given the opportunity to complete an evaluation questionnaire. The most recent summary of evaluation shows that most schools find the inspectorate and its procedures good. Inspectors almost always present themselves as constructive and very professional.

Conclusion: initiatives and prospects

The Northern Ireland Bill of Rights

The Northern Ireland Human Rights Commission (NIHRC), established as a result of the Belfast Agreement, has been asked to advise the Secretary of State for Northern Ireland on the scope for a Bill of Rights for Northern Ireland to supplement the European Convention on Human Rights (incorporated into domestic law by the Human Rights Act 1998). The NIHRC has identified several priority areas for inclusion in a Bill of Rights, one of which is education. The agreement suggests that two issues, both of which have potential ramifications for education, require particular consideration in the context of a new Bill of Rights.

The first is an obligation on government and public bodies 'to respect on the basis of equality of treatment, the identity and ethos of both communities in Northern Ireland'. Any enhancement of Convention rights in this regard could have significant implications for issues such as language and religion in schools. Second, the NIHRC will consider the need for 'a clear formulation of the rights not to be discriminated against and to equality of opportunity in both the public and private sectors'. A review of anti-discrimination law would almost certainly entail a consideration of the need to extend the application of section 76 of the Northern Ireland Act 1998 (which prohibits public bodies from discriminating on the grounds of religious belief or political opinion) to cases of indirect discrimination. Because schools are so religiously segregated, potential issues of indirect discrimination abound. In particular, key questions arise in relation to school admissions, since many schools use admission criteria based on catchment area or contributory primary schools, which have indirectly discriminatory effects. A further issue for consideration might be the current exemption of education from the Fair Treatment and Employment (Northern Ireland) Order 1998, which means that religious discrimination in relation to the employment of teachers in religious schools is exempted. The exemption is in practice an endorsement of the usual employment of Catholic teachers in Catholic schools as a consequence of the understanding of Catholic education as comprising education in religious faith integrated with the education of the whole person. However, the legislation requires the exemption to be kept under review, and the consultation on the Bill of Rights might well revive this issue.

Post-primary review

The post-primary system of education in Northern Ireland is currently under review. The DE published a major piece of research into the effects of the selective system in September 2000 (Gallagher and Smith 2000). This sets out the various benefits and disadvantages of the current arrangements in Northern Ireland. In particular, it highlights the high levels of educational attainment in grammar schools and the fact that secondary schools often provide a very supportive environment for those not suited to academic study. However, the research also indicates some serious flaws in the current arrangements, including the distortion of the primary curriculum, the adverse impact on the self-esteem of those pupils who 'fail' the test and the low status afforded to secondary schools generally. Most significant of all, perhaps, is the finding that the selective system produces a disproportionate number of schools that combine low ability and social disadvantage in their enrolments, thereby compounding the educational disadvantage of both factors. The research does not recommend a specific solution to these problems but sets out five options: delaying selection until 14, as is currently the case in the Craigavon area; all-through comprehensive schools, as in Scotland; common primary and lower secondary schools followed by differentiated upper secondary schools, as in Italy and France; differentiated post-primary schools with distinctive academic and vocational routes; and the status quo. The task of producing recommendations has been left to an independent body, the Post Primary Review Body, which reported in October 2001 (see the Internet site). The review body's recommendations will undoubtedly go out for public consultation but may eventually result in the first major piece of education legislation to pass through the Northern Ireland Assembly. It is too early to say what form a revised secondary structure is likely to take. Although there is general agreement that the current system is flawed, there are equally strongly held views about whether or not to retain some form of selection by ability.

Review of the Northern Ireland Curriculum

The current review of the Northern Ireland Curriculum, which began in 1999 and should reach the implementation stage in 2003, is being conducted by CCEA on a basis of principle that can be summarised as follows: a stronger link between research and educational policy should be harnessed to give children the right start, a more relevant and motivating curriculum, enhanced opportunities to learn and think for themselves and appropriate assessment that recognises all their talents. Teachers would be encouraged to use the curriculum first and foremost to help young people to develop as persons, to be good citizens, to be more employable in the global economy and to have a responsible attitude to the environment (Gallagher and Smith 2000). Many people welcome the idea of placing values at the heart of the curriculum; others ask whether it is good to move the subjects from the centre; some ask whether the proposed values are sufficiently well defined and whether it is possible for schools to deliver them.

Three years into the review process teachers and others are becoming more discerning about the overall thrust of CCEA's proposals, particularly in relation to the post-primary level, and more critical than they were in the first two years of consultation.

POINTS FOR DISCUSSION

1 What are the differences between the Northern Ireland Curriculum and the National Curriculum in England and Wales or in Scotland? Are they significant educationally?
2 What do you think of the principles behind the review of the Northern Ireland Curriculum?

3 Where you live, is the question of comprehensive education versus selection at age 11 still an issue? What arguments can be advanced on both sides of the discussion?
4 Are Catholic schools and other church schools commonly perceived to be socially divisive or to make a useful contribution to the community?
5 Will human rights legislation in your part of the United Kingdom have implications for education and the administration of schools?
6 Some people view devolution as an opportunity to implement education policies tailored to local needs. Others consider that it will lead to the fragmentation of the United Kingdom's education system. What do you think?

INTERNET SITES

Government bodies related to education
Northern Ireland Assembly: www.ni-assembly.gov.uk
Office of the First Minister and Deputy First Minister: www.ofmdfmni.gov.uk
Department of Education: www.deni.gov.uk
Department of Higher and Further Education, Training and Employment: www.nics.gov.uk/hfe.htm
Department of Culture, Arts and Leisure: www.dcalni.gov.uk
Northern Ireland Network for Education: www.nine.org.uk
Council for Curriculum, Examinations and Assessment: www.ccea.org.uk
Education and Training Inspectorate: www.deni.gov.uk/keyinfo/inspection-reports

Education and Library Boards
Belfast ELB: www.belb.org.uk
North Eastern ELB: www.neelb.org.uk
Western ELB: www.welbni.org.uk
South Eastern ELB: www.seelb.org.uk
Southern ELB: www.selb.org.uk

Institutions involved in initial teacher education
Queen's University, Belfast: www.qub.ac.uk
University of Ulster: www.ulst.ac.uk
St Mary's University College: www.stmarys-belfast.ac.uk
Stranmillis University College: www.stran-ni.ac.uk

Others
Faith in Schools (a site supporting the Churches' Agreed Religious Education Syllabus); www.faithinschools.org.uk
Location of schools: www.deni.gov.uk/schoolmap/schoolsmap.htm
Research into selection at age 11: www.deni.gov.uk/parstu/selectionresearch
Post Primary Review Body: www.pprbsni.gov.uk

REFERENCES AND FURTHER READING

Coolahan, J. (1981) *Irish Education: Its History and Structure*. Dublin: Institute of Public Administration.

Cormack, R. J., Gallagher, A. M. and Osborne, R. D. (1991) *Religious Affiliation and Educational Attainment in Northern Ireland: the Financing of Schools in Northern Ireland*. Belfast: Standing Advisory Commission on Human Rights.

Council for Catholic Maintained Schools (1998) *Life to the Full*. Belfast: CCMS.

Council for the Curriculum, Examinations and Assessment (1996) *The Northern Ireland Curriculum*, rev. edn. Belfast: CCEA (available on the CCEA Internet site).

Council for the Curriculum, Examinations and Assessment (1996) *Northern Ireland Curriculum Review. Phase 1 Consultation*. Belfast: CCEA.

Gallagher, A. M. and Smith, A. (2000) *The Effects of the Selective System of Secondary Education in Northern Ireland. Research Papers* (two volumes). Belfast: Department of Education.

Gardner, J. and Leitch, R. (eds) (2001) *Education 2020: a Millennium Vision*. Belfast: Queen's University.

Hadfield, B. (1992) *Northern Ireland: Politics and the Constitution*. Buckingham: Open University Press.

Lundy, L. (1998) 'From Act to Order: the metamorphosis of education legislation', *Liverpool Law Review*, 20, 1.

Lundy, L. (2000) *Education: Law, Policy and Practice in Northern Ireland*. Belfast: SLS.

McGrath, M. (2000) *The Catholic Church and Catholic Schools in Northern Ireland: the Price of Faith*. Dublin: Irish Academic Press.

McKeown, P. (1997) *An Initial Analysis of the Impact of Formula Funding and Local Management of Schools on the Management of Northern Ireland's Schools*. Bangor: Department of Education.

Northern Ireland Teacher Education Committee for Early Professional Development (1998) *The Teacher Education Partnership Handbook*. Belfast: DENI.

Osborne, R. D. and Cormack, R. J. (eds) (1987) *Education and Policy in Northern Ireland*. Belfast: Policy Research Institute, Queen's University of Belfast and University of Ulster.

CHAPTER 3

Scotland

Lindsay Paterson

CHAPTER SUMMARY

This chapter makes four main points:

- Scottish schooling has been distinctive throughout the period of Union with England, and its distinctiveness is widely believed to be a fundamental part of the nation's identity. There has never been a 'British' system of schooling.
- In the second half of the twentieth century, Scottish schooling evolved into a fairly simple and standard pattern – neighbourhood-based, non-selective schools, modified at the margins by parental choice.
- Scottish educational autonomy has rested on local governance, overseen closely by the national Scottish Education Department.
- The advent of the Scottish Parliament in 1999 – assuming full legislative responsibility for schooling – will raise unprecedented questions about the governance of the system, but probably not about its structure. Local diversity, less intrusion from the centre and greater professional autonomy and responsibility are being promoted by Scottish politicians, policy-makers and inspectors, but as the means by which a system of community schools may be strengthened, not replaced. Whether this school autonomy overseen by the national Parliament leaves any significant role for local authorities remains in serious doubt.

Introduction

Scottish school education has long been structurally distinctive. A national system of schooling is of greater longevity than in the other parts of the UK – or indeed, in comparison to many other countries in Europe – and has been shaped primarily by the legacy of the Protestant Reformation of 1560. The influence of the reformers took over a century to be thoroughly felt, but, by the time of the parliamentary Union between Scotland and England in 1707, their vision was well on the way to being established – a school in every parish, a high school in the large towns and universities in the main cities. The long nineteenth-century campaign for a national system of state-sponsored schooling –

achieved after 1872 – was, in Scotland, as much an attempt to restore this much older national structure as the wholly new departures that were represented by the 1870 Education Act in England, by the educational reforms following 1789 in France, by the extension of the Prussian system of schooling to the rest of Germany after 1870 or by the schooling reforms that various nationalist movements inaugurated in other small European countries in the early decades of the twentieth century. This sense of Scottish educational priority continued to shape the structure of schooling throughout the twentieth century, sanctioning – as we will see – some fairly radical interpretations of common international concerns. The Presbyterian legacy in Scotland was a familiar kind of communitarianism – a sense of common schooling as the underpinning of a common citizenship, but also a feeling that these required national autonomy in education, national centralisation of control. This was overseen throughout the twentieth century by the Scottish Education Department, part of the central government, which was respected and powerful but provided at best only limited space for experimentation and dissent.

This chapter describes the important features of the structure of Scottish schooling, tracing their origins, the interrelationships of the different sectors and the prospects for school education now that almost the whole of educational policy has come within the remit of the new Scottish Parliament.

Key structures and organisational features

The starting point for any description of Scottish schooling today is the relative simplicity of its structure (SEED 2000). Nearly all the 2,364 primary schools are of one standard type, lasting seven years from age five to 12 years, and organised in age-related stages. At around age 12, children move to one of the 452 mainly standard types of secondary school, and stay there potentially for six years, although with the option of leaving at age 16, which about one-quarter of them do. There is no selection in the public sector at age 12: in principle, all children attend the neighbourhood comprehensive. Even at ages 16–18, almost all people who are in full-time education are in school: there are no analogues to the English sixth-form colleges, and only about one in 20 of the age group enters a further education college at this stage.

Within the school system, there is little structural variation. Ninety-six per cent of pupils attend public sector schools, known as public schools in Scotland in the same manner as in the USA. The main segmentation in the public sector is by religion. Around 16 per cent of pupils attend Catholic schools, wholly governed within the public sector, but with significant influence reserved to the church. There are also a few schools attached to the Scottish Episcopal Church and to the Jewish faith. In some sparsely populated rural and island areas in the north-west of Scotland, the pattern is slightly different at secondary level, the neighbourhood school being of four or even just of two years' duration, so that pupils have to move as weekly boarders at ages 14 or 16 to the full secondary school in the nearest large town. But even this pattern is reducing in extent, as electronic technology and the beginnings of new population growth in many rural areas allow full secondary schools to be established in districts that could not previously have sustained them.

Although the independent sector educates about 4 per cent of Scottish pupils nationally, this is heavily concentrated in the city of Edinburgh, where the proportion is nearly one in four pupils, and to a lesser extent in Glasgow and Aberdeen, where the proportion is one in eight.

How did this relatively uniform pattern come about, and what organisational principles has it inherited? In one sense the answer is straightforward: providing a common system of schooling was the legacy of the Reformation (Anderson 1983, 1995; Withrington 1988). But that explanation needs refining for the increasingly secular context of the twentieth century. The answers for primary and for secondary schools are somewhat different, although merging into each other in ideology and social purpose.

The modern primary sector was formed in the couple of decades after the Education (Scotland) Act of 1872. The first concern of the reformers was to extend decent schooling to the mass of the population, and a programme of new school building was the main means to that end. Along with that came attempts to standardise what was taught, through regular inspection and the tying of teachers' pay to the results their pupils achieved in tests administered by school inspectors. This controversial matter had been postponed in Scotland until after 1872, and was objected to on the grounds that the elementary schools had never restricted themselves to the basics, but had always had teachers who were capable of taking the academically more able children to a level that would equip them for direct entry to the university. Elementary schools were also viewed increasingly as agencies of social welfare, especially after an Education (Scotland) Act of 1908, which sanctioned school meals and school medical inspections. Attendance at school between the ages of six and 12 did grow steadily, so that by the first decade of the twentieth century well over nine in ten children at these ages attended. But there was less success at age five, and much lower attendance at ages over 13, even though from 1901 schooling was officially compulsory until age 14.

From the First World War until the mid-1960s, Scottish primary schooling was remarkably stable. It grew to consolidate the 1872 system – for example, by the slow amalgamation of small schools into larger ones, or by the steady extension of proper teaching qualifications to the increasingly female teaching force – but not to modify it significantly. Even the 1960s brought change to the content of the curriculum and to teaching styles rather than to structures. The most important moment was the so-called Primary Memorandum of 1965, a circular from the Scottish Education Department that sought to inaugurate child-centred teaching methods. These were introduced only slowly in Scotland, with little of the radical experimentation that could be found in parts of England or the USA (Boyd 1994). There were structural changes internally to schools, sometimes literally in the move to open-plan teaching areas, but no change to the structure of schooling.

Rather more structurally visible changes took place in the 1980s and after, with the Conservative government's legislation to allow parents much greater freedom than hitherto to choose the school to which they would send their children. This was introduced in a radical form in Scotland from 1981 – allowing almost no grounds for refusing these parental 'placing requests' – and by the 1990s about one in five pupils entering primary school were attending their non-local school (SEED 2001). This movement was concentrated in the cities, where the proportions were mostly around one-third. But, important though this change was, it did not interfere with the overall pattern of mainly seven-year, neighbourhood primaries developed since 1872.

One consequence of this was a sense of attachment of communities to their local school. That helped to sustain the Presbyterian communitarianism of the nineteenth century, and also to shape the much more turbulent debate about the structure of secondary schooling. In one sense, indeed, the controversies about primary schooling really belonged entirely to the decades before 1872, and the twentieth century was the century of secondary reform (McPherson 1993). The starting point in the 1870s was only about 60 secondaries, mostly in the cities or the pre-industrial burghs. But developing secondary education was believed to be the only way of responding educationally to the economic and military challenge posed by Germany, France and (later) the USA. This was firmly the view of Henry Craik, the secretary of the new Scotch Education Department that was founded in 1885, and he and his successor from 1904 to 1921, John Struthers, set about building up a national system of post-elementary schooling. By the First World War, they had achieved a great deal, insofar as the old secondaries had been supplemented by a couple of hundred 'Higher Grade' schools, offering mainly technical courses of three years' duration to pupils who were judged capable of progressing beyond elementary schooling. In a few of these, and in the older schools, a full five years of secondary schooling were available, leading to the new leaving certificate examinations that had been established in 1888. In this creation of a national system of public examinations, Scotland was well ahead of many of its educational rivals.

On the other hand, the extension of secondary schooling was accompanied by lengthy and fierce controversy over selection. The Higher Grade schools were not allowed at first to do the same as the full secondaries, and the 'advanced divisions' of the elementary schools – taking pupils up to age 14 – made only very limited intellectual demands. Craik, in fact, believed that only some 5–10 per cent of the population was capable of benefiting from a full secondary schooling. Against that were various shades of interpretation of the principle of secondary education for all, R. H. Tawney's slogan of 1922 that was being promulgated at the same time by such radicals as William Boyd, head of the education department at Glasgow University (Paterson 1996). These views had early success in the 1918 Act, which established the principle of free secondary education, which outlined a system of compulsory, part-time education for people who had left school at age 18 and which – of most lasting significance – made provision for the Catholic schools to transfer to the public system (as almost all of them did within a few years). The most restrictive interpretations of the 1918 Act by the Education Department were resisted, for example their views of the educability of children other than Craik's most academic 10 per cent. And so, by the 1930s, a new structural compromise had emerged. There was free secondary education for all, and in principle proper post-primary courses were made available even for pupils who left school at age 14, but this new system was divided into junior secondaries and senior secondaries. The latter took pupils to the leaving certificate, and hence to university. The former – after the leaving age was raised to 15 in 1947 – offered three years of general education and no public certification.

That bipartite selective system preceded the 1944 system in England and Wales, and underwent more profound change than the latter during the 1950s. By the end of the decade, 40 per cent of Scottish pupils were in the senior secondaries, in contrast to one in four in England and Wales, and four times Craik's 'secondary' proportion. This opened up strong pressures for further change, which first took the form of a new examination at age 16, the Ordinary Grade, introduced in 1962. More radically, however, the main response was the ending of selection between types of secondary school after 1965; the resulting system of comprehensive neighbourhood schools was fully in place in Scotland in the late 1970s.

So the history of secondary provision is of its steady extension, often achieved by means of radical resistance to the mostly conservative interpretation of educability that dominated thinking in the national Education Department. Nevertheless, even this leadership class was not undifferentiated, and the philosophy underlying the eventual outcome was most eloquently articulated in a report of the official Advisory Council on Scottish Education in 1947, which proposed a comprehensive system as the essential educational underpinning of democracy (McPherson and Raab 1988; McPherson 1993; Paterson 1996). In parallel with the delays in achieving a national, public elementary system in the middle of the nineteenth century, a comprehensive secondary system took a further three decades to be fully implemented, but the communitarianism of the 1947 report then became the basis of Scottish attitudes to their public system of schooling from age five to 16, and increasingly to 18 too. As in the primary sector, the placing requests legislation of 1981 slowly altered the relationship between secondaries and their communities: by the 1990s, one in eight pupils in secondary school had been the subject of a placing request, a proportion rising to around one-quarter in the cities. That did lead to some increase in social segregation among secondaries (Paterson 1997), although Scotland retained lower levels of segregation than England or Northern Ireland, and much the same as in Wales (Croxford 2002). But the philosophy remained intact, and support for a reintroduction of academic selection remained strikingly lower in Scotland – at around 25 per cent of the population – than in all parts of England and in Wales, where it was at 40 per cent or over (Paterson 1998; Brown *et al.* 1999: 96). That may partly have been because the Scottish system seemed to be more educationally effective, reducing social-class inequality, increasing attainment and – by the late 1990s – getting about one-half of young people into higher education (McPherson and Willms 1987; Paterson 1997, 1998).

So if there is a simple answer to the question we asked earlier about why there exists a common structure of community schooling in Scotland, it lies here. However modified at the edges by parental choice, the experience first of a national system of neighbourhood elementary education, and then of the slow introduction of a national system of comprehensive secondary education, has underpinned an educational philosophy of common schooling as the basis of common citizenship and hence of democracy. This is the secular legacy of four centuries of Presbyterianism, significantly modified in the twentieth century by an infusion of Catholic communitarianism and of social democracy.

Local, national and devolved governance

Not surprisingly, this system has been mainly locally governed and administered, although the new Scottish Parliament may lead to significant changes to that, as we will see. The 1872 Act set in place a system of 987 elected school boards to govern the new elementary schools, and it was they who raised the finance (mainly through rates) for the expansion of school building. They were a supreme instance of Victorian middle-class philanthropy. Because the franchise was wider than for parliamentary elections, they brought middle-class women into official public affairs for the first time, and female leadership was central to the development of the welfare role of schooling (Corr 1990).

The principle of local control was the main political legacy of the Union with England. Although it is often said that the Union guaranteed Scotland a distinctive education system, in fact education is not mentioned in the Treaty itself. Educational autonomy was a by-product of the guaranteed independence of the Church of Scotland and of the royal burghs, the two institutions which at that time ran the schools and had a strong influence on the universities. As the school system developed in the eighteenth century, it was firmly under local control, and its success encouraged people to believe that local management of education was a crucial part of Scotland's autonomy within the Union.

That principle was maintained throughout the twentieth century, even though the local school boards were superseded (Fairley 1998). One fixture that remained intact was the national department, renamed the Scottish Education Department in 1918. The first major simplification of local governance was also in 1918, when the boards were replaced by 38 education authorities, directly elected by a system of proportional representation. These lasted only until 1929, when schools came under the aegis of general local government, in the form of the county councils and the councils of the cities and the large burghs. That in turn lasted until 1975, when schools in most parts of the country became the responsibility of the nine large regions that formed the upper tier of a two-tier system of local government. Schools in the northern and western islands were governed by three single-tier island authorities. In 1996, the two-tier system was replaced, and schools are now managed by 32 all-purpose local authorities. As Fairley (1998) has pointed out, this means that, for the first time, all local councils in Scotland have an interest in school education, which makes up about 40 per cent of their budget.

On the whole, local administration of schools has been popular, or at least acceptable, to people in Scotland. The Conservative government of 1979–97 did increase the financial autonomy of schools, but – in contrast to the changes in England and Wales – this devolution was to headteachers, not to parents, and followed a scheme that had been piloted by the Labour-controlled Strathclyde Region. Indeed, it was not until an Act of 1989 that Scottish schools had anything resembling the boards of governors elsewhere in Britain, and the school boards that were inaugurated in that year quickly became supporters of the headteacher rather than forces for assertive parental rights. For example, the boards of primary schools led a campaign in 1991–2 to boycott the government's programme of compulsory and standardised tests, the outcome being that the tests were essentially withdrawn, being replaced by formative assessment that was intended to confirm the judgements that teachers made themselves (Boyd 1994).

Even more striking was the great reluctance of Scottish parents to vote to withdraw their schools from the control of local authorities, provision for which was also contained in the 1989 Act. Eventually only three small schools did vote for this, one of which was waiting official approval of its attempted move when the 1997 general election was called. All the other ballots that were genuinely about this matter – as opposed to being attempts to forestall closure – resulted in clear defeats for opting out. The closure-related ballots had to be vetoed by the government itself because rationalising provision was rather more pressing than promoting parental control.

Full legislative responsibility for schools passed to the Scottish Parliament in 1999, following the three-to-one endorsement of Scottish self-government in the referendum of 1997. The national management responsibility for education has passed to the Scottish Executive, which is now Scotland's government as far as most domestic matters are concerned. The referendum vote seems to have been strongly influenced by people's expectations that the Parliament would have a big impact on education (Brown *et al.* 1999: Chapter 6). Yet, at the same time, the legacy of respect for Scottish school professionals remains. For example, at the time of the first election to the Parliament in May 1999, 64 per cent of people told the Scottish Social Attitudes Survey (Paterson *et al.* 2001: 152) that they believed that local authority schools were well run, a level of trust that was exceeded only by that shown in Scottish banks (78 per cent), and that was stronger than for other parts of Scottish civic life (50 per cent for the health service, 58 per cent for the legal system, 55 per cent for the press, 53 per cent for the trade unions). But this was combined with relatively low levels of respect for local government: only 41 per cent believed it was well run.

So conflict over the ultimate responsibility for school education is likely to continue, but the underlying respect for schools and for teachers is likely to mean that the conflict will be around which agencies – local or national – are best able to guarantee the autonomy of educational professionals. We return to this in the final section of the chapter.

Teaching and learning

The structures of the Scottish curriculum, of the public examination system and of the inspection framework are all distinctive, a legacy of the autonomy the system has enjoyed throughout the period of Union. The inspectorate predates even the setting up of the national education department, having been founded in 1840 to supervise the distribution of government grants to schools. In the twentieth century, it became a strong influence towards standardisation across Scotland, despite the parallel tradition of local administration, and often on the grounds that only Scottish unity could prevent English encroachment. The inspectorate lay behind every significant educational innovation in the second half of the twentieth century, in its capacity as advisers on policy as well as evaluators of it. Providing advice was always particularly influential in Scotland, where governance was at a distance from the politicians in London, and especially after 1979 when the Scottish political majority was increasingly at odds with the policies of the Conservative government. Tory ministers in charge of Scottish education relied on the inspectors to advise them on what would be professionally acceptable, as a means of avoiding unnecessary political controversy. Often that took the form of allowing inspectors to decide how to reconcile Conservative ideas with Scottish practice.

Probably the clearest instance of that relates to the curriculum at ages five to 14. Some such framework was unavoidable politically because the Conservative government was keen on the idea of a National Curriculum in England. But the five to 14 curriculum was developed by the inspectors in consultation with the relevant quangos and with selected members of the teaching profession; there seems to have been little interference by ministers. In principle, the framework is not compulsory at all, although no public sector school has deviated significantly from it. The flexibility is most relevant in how it is interpreted, it being less prescriptive of details than is the National Curriculum in England and Wales.

Other reforms in teaching and learning are best interpreted as legacies of the introduction of comprehensive schooling, rather than as Conservative initiatives. The new Standard Grade courses and examinations at age 16 aimed to cater for a wider range and type of abilities than the old Ordinary Grade, and have attracted none of the controversy over quality that bedevilled the GCSEs in their early years. The subsequent reform of courses and certification at ages 16 to 18 – so-called Higher Still – was widely interpreted as the next logical step, aiming to combine academic and vocational qualifications in one framework, and to provide meaningful courses in the final two years of school for students of at best moderate academic ability. Again, there has been little controversy over these principles, in contrast to the enormous heat that is generated by proposals to reform A levels in England. The Scottish controversies have been about the levels of funding of the new system, the speed of its introduction and the capacity of the national examination body to manage it (Paterson 2000).

On the whole, these changes have been introduced by the inspectorate in cooperation with the system, not against its wishes. Harsh criticism of schools is eschewed, and there has been nothing resembling the prominence of Chris Woodhead and Ofsted. When, in early 1999, some segments of the right-wing press interpreted the four-yearly inspectorate report on standards and quality as showing unacceptable levels of failure, the official response after the Scottish Parliament had been elected and the new Scottish Executive had been formed was that 'it is a matter of regret that undue attention was given in public reporting to areas of weakness. . . . [The inspectorate's] report gives the Scottish Executive every confidence that any areas of weakness can be addressed and overcome and action is already in hand to do so' (Scottish Executive 1999: 11).

Conclusion: initiatives and prospects

Some things can be said with fair certainty. The normal pattern of schooling in Scotland will remain the non-selective, neighbourhood-based primaries and secondaries, although with growing erosion of the neighbourhood principle through parental choice of school. These will remain within the public sector, but with increasing devolution of responsibility to headteachers. The overall style of learning and teaching will be far more learner-centred than it was just three or four decades ago; this will be encouraged rhetorically by fashionable ideas on 'multiple intelligences', but in fact will be merely continuing a process that started in the 1960s. And the whole system will continue to be seen as a distinctive part of Scottish civic identity, the responsibility for which rests firmly in the Scottish Parliament and not even partly at Westminster or in Whitehall. It has never been accurate to talk about a British education system, and the inadequacy of doing so is now glaring. I do not expect, however, that this will deter many media and not a few academic commentators in England from continuing to ignore the diversity of UK education, notwithstanding the attempts of books such as the present one to clarify the complexity.

Even more predictable are the structural changes that follow from social change rather than from conscious, political initiative. Increasing proportions of young people will stay on at school beyond age 16, and will proceed to higher education by age 21. As a result, the final stages of school will become more diverse, and the current reforms to curriculum and assessment there will be seen as necessary to cater for this.

Where there will be changes, however, will be in governance and the degree of central control. The political tension is between the national education department, now presided over by powerful and omnipresent politicians, and the 32 education authorities. Public opinion trusts the schools in the sense of admiring their profession-alism. So the political battle will be won by whichever level can most plausibly argue that they have the best interests of school and professional autonomy at heart. And, at present, that victory seems to be going to the national level, where both main political parties – Labour and the Scottish National Party – are vying with each other to promise local flexibility and what they tend to describe as a return to professional discretion. The most important change in that respect is a new agreement on teachers' pay and condi-tions, which offers higher pay and more teacher autonomy in return for a willingness by teachers to work more flexibly. This package was endorsed by some 85 per cent of teachers in a ballot in February 2001, and so seems to form the basis for a radical shift of power away from the national centre.

In the same vein is the education minister's separation of the inspection from the policy-advisory role of the inspectorate with effect from April 2001, and the ensuing indications from the inspectorate that they will reduce the extent to which they expect schools to comply with national norms (*Sunday Herald*, 29 April 2001: 3). How true diversity can be reconciled with the inspectorate's continuing policy of nationally pre-scribed target setting remains to be seen (Scottish Office 1998). There will probably be the beginnings of greater diversity of approaches to learning and teaching, with some mild encouragement of specialist provision in such matters as music, the arts and sport, but there will be nothing along the lines of the selective, specialist schools that are being extended in England.

It may be that local authorities will be able to assert a claim that they are an essential part of a system of local diversity, but at present they are probably widely seen by schools as agencies mainly of bureaucratic interference. It has to be said also that the scope for local authorities to exercise such discretion will be potentially constrained by the new capacity of the inspectorate to examine their educational management. Whether schools will ever be strong enough to develop true local diversity on their own must be open to doubt: in Denmark, where diversity really is practised, the local author-ity is seen as their essential ally against the national government. But for local author-ities to assume this role, they would have to become assertively enthusiastic about school autonomy and school difference.

So it could be that Scottish schools are on the verge of a quite momentous change, unprecedented in the past century, where autonomy means school autonomy, where elected local government has only a very limited role to play and where the autonomy of the system is now firmly entrenched nationally in the elected Parliament. Local authorities were trusted to safeguard the public good in the absence of a Scottish Parliament, but that argument may well now be firmly in the past.

POINTS FOR DISCUSSION

1 Does it make any sense at all to talk of a 'British' system of schooling?
2 Why has the neighbourhood-based, non-selective school come to be so widely accepted in Scotland when it remains deeply controversial in England and Northern Ireland?
3 What is the role of local government in educational policy and management, and is it needed in Scotland now that the Scottish Parliament is in place to safeguard the school system's autonomy?
4 Can school diversity be encouraged without undermining the principle of community schooling, and does diversity need a system of elected local authorities to underpin it?

INTERNET SITES

Scottish Council for Research in Education: www.scre.ac.uk
Scottish Executive Education Department: www.scotland.gov.uk/who/dept_education.asp
Scottish Inspectorate of Education: www.scotland.gov.uk/hmie
Scottish Parliament Education Committee: www.scottish.parliament.uk/official_report/cttee/educ.htm#min

FURTHER READING

Bryce, T. G. K. and Humes, W. M. (eds) (1999) *Scottish Education*. Edinburgh University Press.
Clark, M. and Munn, P. (eds) (1997) *Education in Scotland*. London: Routledge.
Holmes, H. (ed.) (2000) *Compendium of Scottish Ethnology. Volume 11, Education*. East Linton: Tuckwell.
Paterson, L. (2000) *Education and the Scottish Parliament*. Edinburgh: Dunedin Academic Press.

REFERENCES

Anderson, R. D. (1983) *Education and Opportunity in Victorian Scotland*. Edinburgh: Edinburgh University Press.

Anderson, R. D. (1995) *Education and the Scottish People, 1750–1918*. Oxford: Oxford University Press.

Boyd, B. (1994) 'The management of curriculum development: the 5–14 programme', in W. M. Humes and M. L. Mackenzie (eds) *The Management of Educational Policy*. Harlow: Longman.

Brown, A., McCrone, D., Paterson, L. and Surridge, P. (1999) *The Scottish Electorate: the 1997 General Election and Beyond*. London: Macmillan.

Corr, H. (1990) 'An exploration into Scottish education', in W. H. Fraser and R. J. Morris (eds) *People and Society in Scotland. Volume II, 1830–1914*. Edinburgh: John Donald.

Croxford, L. (2002) 'Social inequalities, attainment and comprehensive schooling', paper submitted for publication.

Fairley, J. (1998) 'Local authority education in a democratic Scotland', *Scottish Educational Review*, 30, 61–72.

McPherson, A. (1993) 'Schooling', in A. Dickson and J. H. Treble (eds) *People and Society in Scotland. Volume III, 1914–1990*. Edinburgh: John Donald.

McPherson, A. and Raab, C. D. (1988) *Governing Education*. Edinburgh: Edinburgh University Press.

McPherson, A. and Willms, J. D. (1987) 'Equalisation and improvement: some effects of comprehensive reorganisation in Scotland', *Sociology*, 21, 509–39.

Paterson, L. (1996) 'Liberation or control: what are the Scottish educational traditions in the twentieth century?', in T. M. Devine and R. J. Finlay (eds) *Scotland in the Twentieth Century*. Edinburgh: Edinburgh University Press.

Paterson, L. (1997) 'Student achievement and educational change in Scotland, 1980–1995', *Scottish Educational Review*, 29, 10–19.

Paterson, L. (1998) 'Education, local government and the Scottish parliament', *Scottish Educational Review*, 29, 52–60.

Paterson, L. (2000) *Crisis in the Classroom: the Exam Debacle and the Way Ahead for Scottish Education*. Edinburgh: Mainstream.

Paterson, L., Brown, A., Curtice, J., Hinds, K., McCrone, D., Park, A., Sproston, K. and Surridge, P. (2001) *New Scotland, New Politics?* Edinburgh: Edinburgh University Press.

Scottish Executive (1999) *Improving Our Schools*. Edinburgh: Scottish Executive.

Scottish Executive Education Department (2000) *Summary Results of the September 1999 School Census*, Statistical Bulletin Edn/Bl/2000/3. Edinburgh: Scottish Executive.

Scottish Executive Education Department (2001) 'Placing requests in education authority schools in Scotland, 1989–90 to 1999–2000', News release, 14 February.

Scottish Office (1998) *Setting Targets – Raising Standards in Schools*. Edinburgh: Scottish Office.

Withrington, D. J. (1988) 'Schooling, literacy and society', in T. M. Devine and R. Mitchison (eds) *People and Society in Scotland. Volume 1, 1760–1830*. Edinburgh: John Donald.

CHAPTER 4

Wales

Robert Phillips

CHAPTER SUMMARY

- This chapter analyses the growth and development of educational devolution in Wales.
- Recent significant educational policy developments in England and Wales have symbolised the duality of educational policy-making, but these only represent the culmination of processes that had their origins in the 1980s.
- Over the past two decades or so, Wales has developed distinctive institutional, organisational, curricular and cultural educational frameworks, which are likely to be developed even further after the establishment of devolution. The year 2001 was significant in this respect with the publication of proposals in England and Wales, which differed fundamentally in philosophy, educational direction and priorities.
- It is no longer possible to talk in terms of an 'England and Wales' scenario as far as education is concerned; in future, consideration will have to be given to an 'England or Wales' framework.

Introduction

The year 2001 may well be regarded by future generations of historians of education as significant, ranking with 1944 (Education Act), 1976 (Callaghan's Ruskin College speech) and 1988 (Education Reform Act) as something of a major turning point in the history of education. It witnessed the publication of the White Paper in England, *Schools Achieving Success* (DfES 2001) and in Wales the Paving Document, *The Learning Country* (National Assembly for Wales (NAW) 2001). Exactly 25 years after Callaghan initiated the so-called 'Great Debate' on education, the publication of two documents symbolised the changed nature of education policy-making with regard to England and Wales following devolution and the establishment of the National Assembly in 1999 (Daugherty *et al.* 2000).

Yet the two sets of proposals were not merely discursive, symbolic representations of the change from an 'England and Wales' to an 'England or Wales' scenario as far as education policy formulation was concerned (Phillips 2001a). The two documents were fundamentally different in style, approach and in the articulation of future priorities, which in turn reflected the changed nature of English–Welsh cultural, political, social and educational life in the late twentieth century. This chapter provides a historical overview of this period and explains the circumstances that account for this duality in educational policy at the beginning of the twenty-first century.

The wasted years? Education policy, England *and* Wales, 1944–87

The nineteenth century saw the growth and development of relative autonomy as far as education was concerned in Wales. A distinctive educational structure had been established after the Welsh Intermediate Act 1889 and the setting up of the Central Welsh Board, and this distinctiveness with regard to the formulation of educational priorities continued in the decades before the Second World War (Jones 1997). However, the Education Act 1944 changed fundamentally the nature of education. The reconstruction of post-war life in Britain and the need for fundamental reform of social policy following the war meant that education policy in England and Wales became more heavily centralised around Whitehall. Thus, the Central Welsh Board was abolished in 1947 and responsibility for the administration of both England and Wales was given to the Ministry of Education, based in London: 'for the next forty years Welsh education policy was, effectively, indistinguishable in most respects from that of England' (Phillips and Daugherty 2001: 88).

Even the creation of the post of Secretary of State for Wales in 1964 and the separate Education Department at the Welsh Office in 1970 failed to break this mould. As Jones (1997) has argued, ambitious civil servants based at the Welsh Office in Cardiff were wary of granting local authorities in Wales too much autonomy, and initiatives to develop the distinctive Welsh nature of cultural and social life via the curriculum in Wales, such as the proposals put forward by the Schools Council in 1974, came to nothing.

There were two significant areas that did witness considerable degrees of distinctiveness. First, despite civil service attempts to the contrary, Welsh local education authorities (dominated, of course, by Labour councils) did build up considerable autonomy as far as the day-to-day running of schools was concerned. Jones (1992) has argued that this meant that following Callaghan's speech in 1976, Wales experienced a 'different Great Debate', which centred less upon issues relating to 'progressive' versus 'traditional' pedagogy and more upon issues to do with educational structure, including comprehensivisation. Despite some localised resistance, Wales became universally comprehensive by the end of the 1970s, a tradition that was to have a significant influence on debates over education in the 1980s and 1990s. The second educational area that witnessed considerable moves towards distinctiveness was Welsh language provision (Williams 1992; Baker 2000). Welsh language activists succeeded in elevating the issue of Welsh-medium education to new heights in the 1970s and new Welsh-speaking schools were established. Nevertheless, as long as educational politics in Wales was dominated by a predominantly English-speaking South Wales, progress in this respect was slow.

Attention focused instead upon the issue of standards in comprehensive schools, when David Reynolds and his colleagues in the early 1980s drew a rather furious response from the educational community by claiming that pupils in Wales were essentially 'schooled to fail' (Reynolds 1990). They argued that by the age of 15, an increasingly high proportion of pupils were becoming disaffected, caused by a range of factors. These included a lack of pedagogical innovation, poor school management and a concentration on high-ability pupils. Reynolds also suggested that pupils in Wales needed a more relevant curriculum, including one that reflected the cultural and social distinctiveness of Wales.

Extensive work by Gorard (1998a, b, 2000) has effectively turned the 'schooled to fail' thesis on its head. Gorard argues that when social and economic factors have been taken into consideration, performance and attainment at this time and since mean that Welsh schools have actually performed higher than could have been expected (see also Delamont and Rees 1997). The real significance of the 'schooled to fail' debate, however, lies in the fact that it had concentrated educational and political attention upon issues relating to social deprivation and an apparent lack of adequate educational provision. Moreover, by linking underachievement to the fact that there was not enough distinctiveness in terms of curriculum, organisation and management in schools, it raised the profile of the conduct of education policy in Wales. It raised the possibility that Welsh educational problems could be solved by distinctively Welsh-oriented solutions. But these solutions could only be really developed through a distinctive administrative, political and institutional framework.

Nation building, education and relative autonomy, 1988–99

Historians have for a long time recognised the important dynamics of two cultures in post-war Wales (Williams 1985): one, essentially Welsh-speaking, and centred mainly in rural North, Mid and West Wales; the other, predominantly English-speaking, and centred in industrial South Wales. These traditions were never the most natural of political and ideological bedfellows, with politicians in South Wales holding suspicions of the growth of an elitist cultural nationalism, and this may explain the overwhelming vote against devolution in the referendum of 1979. On the other hand, Welsh speakers in rural areas felt rather excluded by a political structure that favoured the industrial, English-speaking majority of South Wales.

As I have argued elsewhere (Phillips 1996a, b), this is why the industrial decline and subsequent social unrest of the 1980s was crucial in political terms, and ultimately in educational terms too, in Wales. Industrial decline, economic retrenchment and structural unemployment caused by a combination of world recession and government policies had a dramatic and catastrophic effect, particularly in mining and steel after the defeat of the miners in the strike of 1984–5. This was especially the case in South Wales and it is a legacy that is very much with us today, with unemployment in the valleys being among the highest in Britain. The period saw a gradual political shift, as Labour-dominated South Wales saw itself excluded from the political process through successive Tory electoral victories in the 1980s and 1990s. Many within the Labour Party recognised the need to develop ways of undermining the impact of Thatcherism. This involved developing policies within Wales via the existing institutional framework, but a significant proportion of Labour politicians also began to countenance the need for devolution, particularly when Plaid Cymru started to make inroads into traditional Labour heartlands in the 1980s.

In fact, Plaid Cymru had been campaigning for distinctiveness as far as education policy was concerned for some time (James 1998). Other pressure groups such as Welsh language organisations and the Institute of Welsh Affairs, as well as local authorities, intellectuals and elements within the media, now began to demand further autonomy with regard to education in Wales (Elfed-Owens 1996). This activity in the mid-1980s coincided with the existence of a fairly sympathetic Welsh Office Minister, Wyn Roberts (a Welsh speaker), and an ambitious civil service, which began to recognise some of the opportunities that greater autonomy could provide (Jones 1994). The political educational context was shifting very significantly.

Despite these factors, it still remains something of a mystery as to why one of the most centralist governments of the twentieth century afforded so much relative autonomy to Wales in the sphere of education after 1987. That year was significant not merely because of the announcement of the Education Reform Act (ERA) and the National Curriculum, but for the publication of separate consultation documentation in Wales, indicating that there would be separate subject statutory orders for some subjects in Wales (DES/Welsh Office 1987; Welsh Office 1987). This was an extremely important development, not only in educational/political terms but also because it recognised the cultural and national existence of Wales (Jones 1994). This is where nationhood, education and politics were irrevocably interlinked, and the early 1990s 'saw a transformation in the ways in which education policy in Wales was conceived, negotiated and implemented' (Phillips and Daugherty 2001: 91; see also Phillips 1996a). To what extent did education policy in Wales develop in distinctive ways after the Education Reform Act 1988? Could it be argued that Wales enjoyed a period of 'relative autonomy' (Dale 1989) in the decade after the Act?

Significantly, the Act established not only a National Curriculum in Wales but, equally importantly, the institutional framework to administer it. Thus, the Curriculum Council for Wales (CCW) was to initiate a range of distinctive curricular policies in the subsequent years (see below), and the establishment of separate working groups and committees in subjects like history ensured that the distinctiveness was maintained. Indeed, as has been argued elsewhere, what we call 'the history of history' (Phillips and Daugherty 2001) provides a useful case study of the ways in which aspects of the curriculum in Wales were formulated, negotiated and implemented. Thus, the History Committee for Wales (HCW) had to work within the statutory curriculum and assessment framework established by the National Curriculum, and was also required to take into account the proposals of its counterpart in England, the History Working Group. In the process, the HCW put forward a distinctive set of proposals that required Welsh history to be taught in schools in Wales within a British and world context (Welsh Office 1990; see Phillips 1996c, 1999 for a more detailed discussion of these issues). Other subject committees also placed their stamp on the National Curriculum in Wales in similar sorts of ways.

Institutional autonomy was afforded to other sectors of education, for example, in further education. Thus, the Education Act 1992 established the Further Education Funding Council (FEFCW), which, along with other bodies, such as Fforwm, the Association of College Principals, the Further Education Development Association (FEDA) and the Education and Training Action Group for Wales (ETAG), ensured that institutional and administrative frameworks were established to provide the potential to develop policies on training and skills, which in the context of high youth unemployment was particularly important in Wales (ETAG 1998; Jephcote and Salisbury 2000). There were similar developments in higher education, including the establishment of the Higher Education Funding Council for Wales (Rees and Istance 1997; Williams 2000), and in lifelong learning, with Wales having its own policy documents (Welsh Office 1998), its own distinctive initiatives such as the Community University of the Valleys (Elliott *et al.* 1996; Humphreys and Saunders 2000) and a separate policy agenda on the teaching of Welsh to adults (Morris 2000).

The aim, role and purpose of the inspection system in Wales also developed in significantly different respects from that in England. According to Thomas and Egan (2000: 149), 'the reform of inspection exemplifies the way in which policy-making in Wales in the 1990s was conducted'. Thus, although in their words inspection-related initiatives taken in England were 'foisted on Wales', differences in orientation and interpretation were allowed. For example, the Education Act 1992 created not one but two non-ministerial government departments to oversee inspection: the Office for Standards in Education (Ofsted) in England, and the Office of Her Majesty's Chief Inspector (OHMCI) in Wales (later changing its name to ESTYN: Her Majesty's Inspectorate for Education and Training in Wales). Thus although OHMCI handbooks for inspection borrowed heavily from the corresponding documents produced by Ofsted, there were some differences; for example, the inspection cycle was five, not four, years in Wales. But the real difference lay in the perceived relationship between the inspectorate and the teaching profession. Whereas in England the relationship often seemed to be confrontational, particularly after Chris Woodhead became chief of Ofsted, by contrast in Wales, as Thomas and Egan (2000) demonstrate, there seemed to be more of a consensual relationship between OHMCI and schools in Wales, especially under the stewardship of Chief Inspector Roy James.

However, to suggest that Wales enjoyed a degree of unfettered autonomy during the post-Education Reform Act period would be a gross simplification. In many ways, Welsh education was influenced and affected by the same ideological forces that were occurring in England, but in different, complex ways. As has been argued elsewhere (Phillips and Sanders 2000) teachers and schools in Wales experienced the same stress and pressure associated with the effects of marketisation that were having such an impact upon their colleagues in England. Thus, much to the resentment of the teaching profession, Wales was bound by the same clauses in the Education Act 1992 in relation to the publication of Standard Assessment Test (SAT) results. On the other hand, as far as grant-maintained status (GMS) was concerned, there was effectively no take-up of this provision in Wales, owing mainly to the close linkages between schools and local education authorities, which, as we have seen above, had developed in the 1970s and 1980s.

As in England, schools in Wales were to be monitored and held to account via a rigorous system of assessment through the National Curriculum, based initially at least on the model proposed by the Task Group on Assessment and Testing (TGAT). During the first few years after the 1988 Act, apart from some slight differences of detail over the assessment of the Welsh language, there was no distinction between assessment policy in Wales and England. This is not surprising given the priority afforded to assessment by central government, by Secretaries of State for Wales such as John Redwood and the fact that assessment policy in Wales was governed directly by the School Examinations and Assessment Council (SEAC), based in England. However, after the Dearing Review in 1994, for the first time curriculum and assessment policies were merged and administered by a new quango, the Quality, Curriculum and Assessment Authority for Wales (ACCAC). When subsequent reviews of assessment were undertaken 'the first glimmering of a distinctiveness to thinking about assessment in Wales' started to occur (Daugherty 2000: 93). Welsh documentation seemed to place great emphasis upon formative teacher assessment and whereas Key Stage 2 SAT results were published by the DfEE on every state school in England, in Wales only summaries of LEA results were published.

There were two other education policy discourses that had an important influence on Wales after 1988 and these were particularly distinctive, identified as 'cultural restorationism' and 'community' (Phillips 1996c; Phillips and Sanders 2000). Interestingly, they reflect the two distinctive traditions mentioned above. Culturally aware officials at CCW, ACCAC and OHMCI saw opportunities to develop distinctively Welsh-oriented dimensions to the curriculum, not only through some of the National Curriculum subjects but also via cross-curricular or whole-school initiatives. Thus, I have argued elsewhere that the publication of *Developing a Curriculum Cymreig* (CCW 1993) was 'an unashamed attempt to promote the distinctive culture and heritage of Wales' (Phillips 1996a: 43). It placed an emphasis upon the need for schools to use opportunities throughout the curriculum to develop distinctively Welsh elements of culture, stressing also the need to celebrate diversity. *Community Understanding* (CCW 1991), as its name suggests, recognised the other major dynamic in Welsh life and created a set of guidelines that encouraged schools to focus upon a definition of community. This was a remarkable document in many ways (Phillips 2000) because during a period of conservatism in educational politics in England it 'offered a complex, multi-faceted definition of the term "community"' (Phillips and Daugherty 2001: 93) that raised issues relating to 'diversity, inequality and prejudice' (CCW 1991: 6). In many ways, *Community Understanding* was a precursor of the Crick Report in England, published seven years later (Crick 1998). 'Policy borrowing', it seems, went in more than one direction in the 1990s.

The period after 1988 was important, as in England, for it saw a range of new policies, developments and initiatives. But to what extent had Wales developed a degree of relative autonomy by 1999? To what extent were policies initiated at Whitehall interpreted or 'recontextualised'? What role did institutional factors play here? To what extent was the collective impact of policies in Wales different from that in England?

Colleagues working on education policy in Wales (Daugherty *et al.* 2000) have concluded that during this period it was still the 'England and Wales' metaphor that dominated policy formulation. Thus, although the Education Reform Act 1988 had established a degree of distinctiveness and autonomy, the fact that it was also the biggest single piece of legislation passed during the Thatcherite era meant that in many ways it strengthened, rather than weakened, Whitehall control. However, those areas that had gained a relatively autonomous institutional framework also saw policies that differentiated most from England. This included policies on cross-curricularity, inspection, further education and lifelong learning. In short, education policy in Wales during this period was 'characterized by a complex set of policy-related dynamics, centred upon the mediation between external influences and local/regional imperatives' (Phillips and Sanders 2000: 10).

The learning country? Education policy in post-devolution Wales

By the end of the 1990s, therefore, Wales had developed a set of education policies that replicated England in many respects but in other ways were different in orientation. Yet as recently as 1998 (the year of the referendum in Wales) a publication entitled *Education Reform in the United Kingdom* (British Council 1998) could still be published without a separate section on Wales. Others have pointed to the need to consider the significance of policy differences even before 1999 (Daugherty *et al.* 2000; Phillips and Daugherty 2001). Clearly, however, the vote in favour of devolution via the referendum in September 1998, albeit by the closest of possible margins, represented (symbolically at least) a new era in education policy-making in Wales.

The perception that for much of the 1980s and 1990s Wales had, in effect, been disenfranchised from the political process was based largely upon the belief that many social and economic policies initiated during the period were irrelevant to the needs of Wales. This was obviously a major factor in convincing Labour politicians of the need for devolution as a process for change (Davies 1999). It may also account for the euphoria that greeted the Labour Party's election victory in 1997. Yet most academics agree that New Labour's 'Third Way' project in many respects has more in common with New Right than New Labour, and this is certainly the case as far as education policy is concerned (Phillips 2001b).

This has created a particularly interesting political dynamic since 1998, focusing upon the extent to which the new National Assembly of Wales could develop policies that were markedly different in the two areas for which the Assembly had been given legislative responsibility via the Government of Wales Act 1998, namely health and education. During the first year or so, this debate focused upon personality politics, with the appointment by New Labour of the Blairite Alun Michael to the position of First Minister, rather than the more popular Rhodri Morgan. After Morgan eventually gained the office he coveted, this debate took on a new relevance, with anticipation that Welsh education policy might move in more radical directions.

In a study of the National Assembly's early record, Egan and Jones (2001: 8) argue that in some respects there was little in terms of education policy outcome that was 'new, distinct and innovative and best suited to the particular needs of Wales'. Indeed, they argue that not only was there very little to distinguish between policies in England

and Wales, in some instances – for example, in relation to the funding of primary teacher education – Wales fared far worse. Similarly, as far as laptop provision, professional development grants and other educational resources were concerned, teachers in Wales complained that 'they often missed out on initiatives that benefited colleagues in England' (*Times Educational Supplement* 5 October 2001). Significantly, however, despite problems associated with lack of civil service expertise, inexperience of the processes associated with devolved governance and the inevitable 'bedding in' period of new structures, Egan and Jones (2001: 19) argue that 'in a relatively short time the Assembly has done enough to change established policy-making processes in education in Wales'. They noted in particular that the 'extensive activity' of the Assembly, particularly via its education subject committees, has 'created a public forum for educational debate in Wales' (*ibid.*: 19).

The publication in the autumn of 2001 of *The Learning Country* (NAW 2001) may be said to be the high point of this new educational climate. In many respects, the document used reference points that had become familiar since Callaghan's Ruskin speech in 1976 and repeated messages about the aims of education (see Welsh Office 1995). Under New Labour, the imperative for reform is linked to the relationship between education, economic activity and the wider benefits to the community. Thus 'training and education are equally and intimately related to successful community development, social inclusion, wealth creation and personal fulfilment. There is a close synergy between the measures necessary to sustain learning and creativity, and achieving the benefits of economic growth, community enrichment and a wonderful quality of life for individuals' (NAW 2001: 7). These sorts of statements are also to be found in *Excellence in Schools* (DfE 1997) and are justified by New Labour on the basis of international competition and, of course, the need for 'modernisation'.

However, in other fundamental respects, *The Learning Country* set an educational agenda that differed significantly from its equivalent *Schools Achieving Success* (DfES 2001) in England. As we saw above, the concept of community had an established history in Wales and was given articulation even at the high point of Thatcherite policies (CCW 1991; see also Phillips and Sanders 2000; Andrews 2001). *The Learning Country* stated that the National Assembly wanted to see an even 'closer relationship between schools and the communities they serve'. This would best be achieved through a 'non-selective, comprehensive school provision in Wales' because 'this pattern of provision serves us well'. Moreover, there would be 'real risks in a wholesale shift to extensive and untested measures delivered solely through the private sector' (p. 26). Furthermore, although it was important to give successful schools more autonomy, the document also stated that the Assembly did not want to establish a specialist schools programme because it was 'committed to a universal, publicly funded, publicly accountable education system, free at the point of delivery' (p. 26).

In further contrast to England, the document committed the Assembly to cut junior class sizes to 30 pupils by 2003 and questioned 'whether there is a need to apply national testing arrangements for 7 years olds, given the very high degree to which pupils meet what is expected of them then' (p. 19), as well as the possibility that the resources could be better used elsewhere to improve the curriculum and standards. In addition, although it recognised that performance tables on individual schools were 'introduced at a time when there was relatively little information available to practitioners, or indeed to parents, about achievement', the situation was very different a decade later. Therefore, the National Assembly proposed to 'publish aggregate data at LEA level' about performance and, equally significantly, 'this material will be supplemented in due course by value added data where that can give a fully satisfactory view of individual schools' performance' (p. 135). Finally, whereas the literacy and numeracy strategy in England was a flagship of New Labour education policy, *The Learning Country* stated that 'a common or mandatory approach to literacy, numeracy, and standards in other subjects more generally' (p. 27) was not appropriate in Wales. Moreover, in response to pressure from within Wales, it proposed to initiate a pilot programme for a Welsh Baccalaureate.

Towards utopia? Welsh education policy in the future

At the time of writing, the document has only just been released and is currently subject to consultation. However, an analysis of the press has demonstrated a very positive and favourable initial response from the educational community in Wales. Drawing attention to many of the differences over education policy emphasised above, on 2 October 2001 the *Guardian* claimed that what it called 'Great Wales' could rightly be claimed as a teacher's utopia and drew upon quotes from many in the profession in Wales to justify its use of the headline. Similarly, the *Times Educational Supplement* (5 October 2001) quoted a teacher whose 'love of teaching' had been rekindled by a move from England to Wales.

Whereas there are now clear policy differences between England and Wales, there are enough issues still to be resolved in Wales to question the references to utopian bliss mentioned above. The first relates to funding; in an analysis of educational spending between 1998 and 1999, Reynolds (2000) draws attention to some apparent disparities between England and Wales, claiming that Wales spends around 4 per cent less per pupil than in England. Unsurprisingly, these claims have been refuted by the National Assembly; in fact, when the relatively huge amount of spending on London is taken out of the analysis, Wales compares favourably to England, particularly in terms of the primary sector. Inevitably, however, there remains the perception in Wales that given its profound social difficulties, more financial support needs to be provided to education.

A second issue is the extent to which the development of a distinctive educational agenda actually benefits Wales. Reynolds himself has referred to the apparently 'meaningless blather' among education professionals about 'doing things differently in Wales because of our consensual approach'. According to Reynolds this 'prevents us from using the things in Wales that England uses to good effect' (*Times Educational Supplement* 5 October 2001). It is rather intriguing to consider how Reynolds reconciles these comments with his earlier belief that

> the gathering movement towards the generation of a distinctive set of Welsh educational policies should be furthered by a consideration of the many ways in which

the existing English policies applied in Wales are at best irrelevant to our culture and educational traditions and at worst may be positively harmful to the prospects of our pupils. (Reynolds 1995: 13)

I warned some years ago (Phillips 1996b) of the dangers of blindly rejecting educational agendas simply on the basis that they originated in England and not in Wales. Similarly, policy-makers need to proceed with caution with the development of some distinctive policies to ensure that they meet the needs of Welsh pupils in terms of national and international contexts and requirements. The Welsh Baccalaureate is a good example, for it may actually disadvantage pupils if the new qualification lacks status in the eyes of university admissions tutors and employers in the rest of Britain and beyond.

A third issue for the future concerns the nature of long-established relationships and traditions within the education policy community in Wales. It may be that the new political climate created by the Assembly means that the influence over education held by local education authorities may no longer be as relevant as it was. Teacher organisations in Wales have already registered some dissatisfaction that schools do not seem to apply the same degree of control over spending and financial management that their colleagues in England enjoy. It remains to be seen whether the National Assembly has the political courage to tackle this issue in the future. Whatever happens, there is little doubt that the past ten years or so in Wales have been very important, particularly the year 2001. It is therefore accurate to claim that it is 'difficult to overstate the significance of *The Learning Country*, not only in terms of the policy statements it contains but also in terms of its place in the history of state education in Wales' (Jones 2001: 1).

POINTS FOR DISCUSSION

1 What are the arguments in favour of the devolution of education policy?
2 Why was it that Wales gained a degree of autonomy with regard to education policy in the 1980s and 1990s?
3 What are the major differences between education policies in England and Wales?
4 What are the implications of this duality for the future?

INTERNET SITES

Qualifications, Curriculum and Assessment Authority for Wales (ACCAC): www.accac.org.uk
National Assembly for Wales: www.wales.gov.uk
Welsh Joint Examinations Committee: www.wjec.co.uk

REFERENCES AND FURTHER READING

Andrews, R. (2001) 'Citizenship education in Wales: community, culture and the curriculum Cymreig', *Welsh Journal of Education*, 10(1), 21–31.
Baker, C. (2000) 'Three perspectives on bilingual education policy in Wales: bilingual

education as language planning, as pedagogy and as politics', in R. Daugherty, R. Phillips and G. Rees (eds) *Education Policy Making in Wales: Explorations in Devolved Governance*. Cardiff: University of Wales Press.

British Council (1998) *Education Reform in the UK: Report for Overseas Offices*. London: British Council.

CCW (1991) *Advisory Paper 2. Community Understanding: a Framework for the Development of a Cross-Curricular Theme in Wales*. Cardiff: CCW.

CCW (1993) *Advisory Paper 18. Developing a Curriculum Cymreig*. Cardiff: CCW.

Crick, B. (1998) *Education for Teaching and the Teaching of Democracy in School: Final Report of the Advisory Group on Citizenship*. London: QCA.

Dale, R. (1989) *The State and Education Policy*. Milton Keynes: Open University Press.

Daugherty, R. (2000) 'National assessment policies in Wales', in R. Daugherty, R. Phillips and G. Rees (eds) *Education Policy Making in Wales: Explorations in Devolved Governance*. Cardiff: University of Wales Press.

Daugherty, R., Phillips, R. and Rees, G. (eds) (2000) *Education Policy Making in Wales: Explorations in Devolved Governance*. Cardiff: University of Wales Press.

Davies, R. (1999) *Devolution: a Process Not an Event*. Cardiff: Institute of Welsh Affairs.

Delamont, S. and Rees, G. (1997) 'Understanding the Welsh education system: does Wales need a separate "policy sociology"?', Working Paper 23, School of Education, University of Wales Cardiff.

DES/Welsh Office (1987) *The National Curriculum 5–16: a Consultation Document*. Cardiff: Welsh Office.

DfE (1997) *Excellence in Schools*. London: DfE.

DfES (2001) *Schools Achieving Success*. London: DfES.

Egan, D. and Jones, R. (2001) 'Watching the Assembly: education policy and devolved government in Wales', *Welsh Journal of Education*, 10(1), 4–20.

Elfed-Owens, P. (1996) 'The implementation of the National Curriculum in Wales', Unpublished PhD thesis, University of London.

Elliott, J., Francis, H., Humphreys, R. and Istance, D. (eds) (1996) *Communities and Their Universities: the Challenge of Lifelong Learning*. London: Lawrence and Wishart.

ETAG (1998) *An Education and Training Action Plan for Wales*. Cardiff: Welsh Office.

Gorard, S. (1998a) 'Schooled to fail? Revisiting the Welsh school effect', *Journal of Education Policy*, 13(1), 115–24.

Gorard, S. (1998b) 'Four errors . . . and a conspiracy? The effectiveness of schools in Wales', *Oxford Review of Education*, 24(4), 459–72.

Gorard, S. (2000) 'A re-examination of the effectiveness of schools in Wales', in R. Daugherty, R. Phillips and G. Rees (eds) *Education Policy Making in Wales: Explorations in Devolved Governance*. Cardiff: University of Wales Press.

Humphreys, R. and Saunders, D. (2000) 'From adult education to lifelong learning: policy, process and institutional change', in R. Daugherty, R. Phillips and G. Rees (eds) *Education Policy Making in Wales: Explorations in Devolved Governance*. Cardiff: University of Wales Press.

James, B. (1998) 'The origins, growth and development of a distinctive curriculum in Wales', Unpublished master's thesis, University of Wales Swansea.

Jephcote, M. and Salisbury, J. (2000) 'From policy to practice in further education: patterns of governance in Wales', in R. Daugherty, R. Phillips and G. Rees (eds) *Education Policy Making in Wales: Explorations in Devolved Governance*. Cardiff: University of Wales Press.

Jones, B. and Lewis, I. (1995) 'A curriculum Cymreig', *Welsh Journal of Education*, 4(2), 22–35.

Jones, G. E. (1992) 'Education in Wales: A different great debate?', in M. Williams, R. Daugherty and F. Banks (eds) *Continuing the Education Debate*. London: Cassell.

Jones, G. E. (1994) 'Which nation's curriculum? The case of Wales', *Curriculum Journal*, 5(1), 5–16.

Jones, G. E. (1997) *The Education of a Nation*. Cardiff: University of Wales Press.

Jones, G. E. (1998) *Growing Up at Last: Education and the National Assembly*. Talybont: Lolfa.

Jones, G. E. (2001) 'The learning country', Unpublished paper, Department of Education, University of Wales Swansea.

Morris, S. (2000) 'Welsh for adults: a policy for bilingual Wales?', in R. Daugherty, R. Phillips and G. Rees (eds) *Education Policy Making in Wales: Explorations in Devolved Governance*. Cardiff: University of Wales Press.

National Assembly for Wales (2001) *The Learning Country: a Paving Document, a Comprehensive Education and Lifelong Learning Programme to 2010 in Wales*. Cardiff: National Assembly for Wales.

Phillips, R. (1996a) 'Informed citizens: who am I and why are we here? Some Welsh reflections on culture, curriculum and society', *Multicultural Teaching*, 14, 41–4.

Phillips, R. (1996b) 'Education policy making in Wales: a research agenda', *Welsh Journal of Education*, 5(2), 26–42.

Phillips, R. (1996c) 'History teaching, cultural restorationism and national identity in England and Wales', *Curriculum Studies*, 43, 385–99.

Phillips, R. (1999) 'History teaching, nationhood and politics in England and Wales in the late twentieth century: a historical comparison', *History of Education*, 28(3), 351–63.

Phillips, R. (2000) 'Culture, curriculum and community: citizenship education for the new democracy?', in R. Gardner (ed.) *Citizenship, Identity and Education*. London: Cassell.

Phillips, R. (2001a) 'The great debate rolls on', *Times Educational Supplement*, 12 October.

Phillips, R. (2001b) 'Education, the state and the politics of reform', in R. Phillips and J. Furlong (eds) *Education, Reform and the State: Twenty-five Years of Politics, Policy and Practice*. London: Routledge.

Phillips, R. and Daugherty, R. (2001) 'Educational devolution and nation building in Wales: a different "Great Debate"?', in R. Phillips and J. Furlong (eds) *Education, Reform and the State: Twenty-five Years of Politics, Policy and Practice*. London, Routledge.

Phillips, R. and Sanders, S. (2000) 'Contemporary education policy in Wales: theory, discourse and research', in R. Daugherty, R. Phillips and G. Rees (eds) *Education Policy Making in Wales: Explorations in Devolved Governance*. Cardiff: University of Wales Press.

Rees, G. and Istance, D. (1997) 'Higher education in Wales: the re-emergence of a national system?', *Higher Education Quarterly*, 51(1), 49–67.

Reynolds, D. (1990) 'The great Welsh education debate', *History of Education*, 19(3), 251–60.

Reynolds, D. (1995) 'Creating an educational system for Wales', *Welsh Journal of Education*, 4(5), 4–21.

Reynolds, D. (2000) 'Education gap funding grows', *Journal of the Institute of Welsh Affairs*, Winter, 44–5.

Thomas, G. and Egan, D. (2000) 'Policies on school inspection in Wales', in R. Daugherty, R. Phillips and G. Rees (eds) *Education Policy Making in Wales: Explorations in Devolved Governance*. Cardiff: University of Wales Press.

Welsh Office (1987) *The National Curriculum in Wales*. Cardiff: Welsh Office.

Welsh Office (1990) *National Curriculum History Committee for Wales: Final Report*. Cardiff: Welsh Office.

Welsh Office (1995) *People and Prosperity: an Agenda for Action in Wales*. Cardiff: Welsh Office.

Welsh Office (1998) *Learning Is for Everyone: the BEST for Lifelong Learning*. Cardiff: Welsh Office.

Williams, G. (2000) 'Changes in government policy and the development of higher education in Wales, 1975–1996', in R. Daugherty, R. Phillips and G. Rees (eds) *Education Policy Making in Wales: Explorations in Devolved Governance*. Cardiff: University of Wales Press.

Williams, G. A. (1985) *When Was Wales? The History, People and Culture of an Ancient Country*. London: Penguin.

Williams, M. (1992) 'Ruskin in context', in M. Williams, R. Daugherty and F. Banks (eds) *Continuing the Education Debate*. London: Cassell.

PART II:

Curriculum, Assessment and Inspection

CHAPTER 5

Early Years Education

Peter Long

CHAPTER SUMMARY

This chapter makes the following points:

- Early years education provision is extremely diverse within the United Kingdom.
- Attempts to develop seamless and consistently high-quality provision for early years education have been fraught with difficulty, and the Organisation for Economic Co-operation and Development has condemned much of the UK's pre-school education.
- Because early years education is increasingly seen as foundational to children's development, a critical re-evaluation of early years education in terms of curriculum, assessment and inspection is an ongoing necessity.

Introduction

The one feature, above all others, that characterises the range of early years settings which offer education and day care in the UK is diversity. Pugh (1988) highlights this issue when she points out that 'The complexity of the range of early years services in the UK and the overall lack of co-ordination has been well described elsewhere (Pugh 1998, 1996a; David 1990; DES 1990; Ball 1994; Moss and Penn 1996).' It is not possible within the parameters of this chapter to give a detailed description and analysis of the range and quality of education and care offered by such diverse early years provision. However, Pugh (1988) offers a useful summary that falls broadly into two categories, one being the state sector and the other embracing the private, independent and voluntary sectors. State provision includes nursery schools and classes, reception classes in infant and primary schools, combined nursery centres, usually funded by the education authority and social services department, and the more recently established early excellence centres.

The early excellence centre initiative was an idea promoted by the Labour Party in its discussion paper *Early Excellence* in the run-up to the 1997 general election. The main services that these centres offer, according to the DfEE (1999) in its first evaluation of the scheme, is excellence in integrated education and care, with access extending to day and holiday childcare for children from birth. Support for families, including links to other key services such as health and affordable adult training opportunities, is another key aspect of this type of provision. Disseminating good practice to other early years practitioners, particularly through local Early Years Development and Childcare Partnerships (EYDCPs), is another salient feature of the work of early excellence centres. The EYDCPs are government funded forums which have a statutory basis outlined in the School Standards and Framework Act 1998, and 'bring together the maintained, private and voluntary sectors in a spirit of co-operation and genuine partnership, based on existing good practice' (DfEE 2001a). The early excellence centre programme has not been without its critics: concern has been voiced at the substantial sums of money being invested in such centres when, it is argued, the funding could be more effectively used if targeted at a greater number and wider range of early years settings. This is particularly the case in the voluntary sector, where minimum fees are charged to families for childcare and education to cover the cost of basic items such as resources and premises (see below for further details of this type of provision). However, the present government is determined to press ahead with the development of the centres, claiming that every £1 spent on the intervention work of such centres and the support given to families saves the taxpayer £8 which would in the longer term have been spent on other agencies, such as health and social services (DfEE 1999). The development of early excellence centres is part of a wider £600 million early years education and childcare programme initiated by the present government under the name of Sure Start to run from 2000 to 2002.

A diminishing feature of the state sector is local authority day nurseries or family centres run by social service departments and mainly for children who are considered to be 'at risk'. This particular type of early years setting now tends to be more closely linked with education-based provision, such as combined nurseries or early excellence centres.

In the voluntary sector playgroups or preschools are usually run by parents, at least half of whom must have some sort of training, often provided by the Preschool Learning Alliance (PLA). Such settings have to be registered by social service departments within the requirements of the Children Act 1989.

Within the private and independent sectors there is a wide range of groups, including playgroups, nursery schools and childminders. From September 2001 all of these groups will be registered with and inspected by the Office for Standards in Education (Ofsted).

The Labour government has indicated that this historical diversity in early years provision has not always provided the most appropriate services to meet the needs of young children and their families, and is pledged to address this through further investment in and expansion of early years education and care.

> Traditionally early years services have been delivered separately by a range of professionals working in distinct education, care and health services. However, very young children do not distinguish between care and education, and families'

needs in the modern world are best met by providing joined-up services. Our approach to early years education and care is to develop seamless services for children and families. We want to retain the best which each profession offers, but provide more integrated services which are built around children's needs rather than professional structures. All the evidence shows that joined-up services deliver both better outcomes for children and better value for the public purse. (DfEE 2001b: 18)

The current Labour government achieved a second term of office on 7 June 2001. On 10 June 2001 the *Sunday Times* featured an article under the headline 'Pre-school education condemned' (p. 28). The article refers to a report to be published that week by the Organisation for Economic Co-operation and Development, which claims that Britain has some of the worst preschool education and childcare in the Western world. In particular, the report highlights the lack of what are described as 'high-quality' nursery places, the low pay and qualifications of staff and their poor working conditions. It is acknowledged, however, that some government preschool schemes are making progress. Given this view of current early years education and care as compared to that of our international neighbours, it seems that developing 'seamless services for children and families' is going to be a challenging and demanding task. By the time the next general election occurs, it will be interesting to note what progress has been made in this pivotal phase of education.

Curriculum

The term 'curriculum' can be interpreted in a number of ways, and within the context of working with young children is often associated with the philosophy and work of the 'pioneers' of early years education. Individuals such as Froebel, Isaacs, Montessori and MacMillan have all had a very significant influence on what has come to be regarded as good practice in early years education that is conducive to effective learning and the holistic development of children. Such good practice is characterised by the importance attached to first-hand, practical experiences for children, the centrality of play and language in their learning, the use of the outdoor environment and the fact that children's social, emotional and physical development is seen to be just as important as their cognitive or academic development. The work of the early years practitioner is to promote and facilitate the development of the whole child – a holistic approach to the education and care of young children.

It is not possible within the scope of this chapter to give a detailed account and evaluation of the work of the 'pioneers' mentioned above, or the distinctive approaches to early years practice that have come to be associated with their writing and work. However, by starting with a definition of the curriculum from Her Majesty's Inspectors (1988), it is possible to trace the history of and critically evaluate the Foundation Stage and Early Learning Goals that were introduced in September 2000 for children aged from three to the end of the reception year. Most children at this point in their school career are aged four to five years and are in reception classes in state infant or primary schools.

> A school's curriculum consists of all those activities designed or encouraged within its organisational framework to promote the intellectual, personal, social and physical development of its pupils. It includes not only the formal programme of lessons, but also the 'informal' programme of so called extracurricular activities as well as those features which produce the school's 'ethos', such as the quality of relationships, the concern for equality of opportunity, the values exemplified in the way the school sets about its task and the way in which it is organised and managed.

This definition of the curriculum was published by HMI in a report titled *The Curriculum from 5 to 16* in 1988, and despite the fact that it is now dated, it remains very relevant. Although the curriculum described by HMI is applicable to children of statutory school age, the principles such a definition embraces are as relevant today as they were then. Moreover, they are particularly important when considering a curriculum for the early years. The emphasis placed on personal, social and physical, as well as intellectual, development is a strong feature of education and care in the early years tradition, promoting the growth of the whole child – a holistic approach. Further, the emphasis on ethos and the quality of relationships and the concern for equality of opportunity typify what have come to be regarded as aspects of good early years provision, and characterise what is defined as the early years curriculum by the DfEE (2000) in training materials produced for the introduction of the Foundation Stage. A key point in the training package is that the curriculum for young children is everything they experience while attending a setting, and not just the activities they may choose to undertake themselves or are encouraged to participate in by staff. However, we still have six areas of learning and experience within the Foundation Stage, the Early Learning Goals, which are essentially subject areas and are derived from a university or secondary model of the curriculum. The areas are:

- personal, social and emotional development;
- communication, language and literacy;
- mathematical development;
- knowledge and understanding of the world (incorporating the foundations of science, design and technology, information and communication technology, history and geography);
- physical development;
- creative development (incorporating music and art).

In the foreword to *Curriculum Guidance for the Foundation Stage* (Qualifications and Curriculum Authority/DfEE 2000), Nick Tate, who was the Chief Executive of the QCA at the time, states:

> The establishment of a foundation stage is a significant landmark in funded education in England. For the first time it gives this very important stage of education a distinct identity. The early learning goals set high expectations for the end of the foundation stage, but expectations that are achievable for most children who have followed a relevant curriculum. (QCA/DfEE 2000)

The term 'relevant curriculum' here is an interesting one, as it can be argued that this model of the curriculum is very much a 'top-down' one, with the imposition of subject areas and titles on the development of young children that are far from relevant. Children in the early years do not perceive the world around them in terms of compart-mentalised subject areas, and the approach to learning embodied in the Early Learning Goals appears to have more to do with preparing children for the next stage of education and the National Curriculum than with appreciating early years education and care as being important in their own right and a foundation for life.

Successful early years practitioners are, by nature, creative and innovative; this is an essential 'tool of the trade' given the nature of the work to be undertaken with young children. Many practitioners feared that the introduction of the Early Learning Goals would bring a very prescriptive dimension to their work. While it is true that the Foundation Stage has brought a degree of structure and formality to early years practice previously unknown on a national scale, it has generally been welcomed and adopted, with a particular acknowledgement from practitioners that the importance attached to play in children's learning, which the Foundation Stage guidance highlights, is a strength. Effective early years practitioners are addressing the Early Learning Goals without losing sight of the importance of the process of learning, rather than just seeing them as a set of prescriptive targets to be met with an emphasis on the 'end result' or product of learning.

Nevertheless, there remains a hierarchy of credibility within the six areas of learning embraced by the Early Learning Goals, with greater importance attached to the first three areas of:

- personal, social and emotional development;
- communication, language and literacy;
- mathematical development.

For the purposes of inspection Ofsted (2000) makes it very clear that 'Where learning and teaching in two or more of these areas are unsatisfactory, the educational provision is not acceptable whatever the quality of remaining provision.' This guidance was issued in relation to the inspection of early years practice in the private, voluntary and independent sectors, with similar information issued regarding the inspection of state provision. While it is acknowledged that personal, social and emotional development is the 'bedrock' upon which all other areas of learning and experience will be based, the continued importance attached to the acquisition of basic literacy and numeracy skills in the early years is a debatable topic. As far back as 1937 the Board of Education, commenting on nursery and infant stages of education, took up the issue of the 'The beginnings of the "Three Rs" – reading, writing and number (arithmetic)'.

> Opinions differ as to the best age for introducing the children to them [the Three Rs], and it is clear that this must depend a good deal on the development of the individual child. Rapidity of progress and thoroughness of mastery depend so much on previous preparation of a general nature that it is wisest

with the majority of children to postpone formal instruction in all three until about the age of six. (Board of Education 1937: 93)

Children in the Scandinavian countries do not start formal schooling until the age of about seven, with much emphasis in the kindergarten placed on their personal, social and emotional development rather than the development of early reading, writing and number skills. Although there is not the space within this chapter to initiate a debate about when it is most appropriate to introduce young children to early literacy and numeracy skills, the experiences of some our European neighbours and what our own Board of Education wrote over 60 years ago do raise questions about whether there are some aspects of the Early Learning Goals which are over-prescriptive, inappropriate and experienced too early by some children.

Assessment

Much has already been written about assessment in the early years. DES (1990), Blenkin and Kelly (1992), Bartholomew and Bruce (1993), Ofsted (1995, 1999), Nutbrown (1998) and QCA/DfEE (2000) are just some of the sources to which reference can be made regarding this aspect of the early years practitioner's work. However, before we proceed to examine some of the issues pertinent to the assessment of young children's progress and development, in particular the merits of quantitative or qualitative methods, it is important to establish why we undertake assessment in the first place, what purposes assessment serves and the 'audiences' that assessment addresses.

Summative assessment is an evaluation of attainment and progress at a particular point in time. This may be at the end of a term or year when a judgement is made based on observation and the collection of evidence, which enables early years practitioners to state what they think a child has achieved in that given period of time. This judgement is usually shared with parents and is often recorded in a written report. Many early years reports now have space for parents to contribute their views as written comments, allowing the 'home perspective' to be taken into account, as well as that of the early years setting.

Formative assessment is what effective early years practitioners are constantly involved in both formally and informally – the ongoing, everyday assessment of children's development and progress as they involve themselves in the activities the setting provides. Early years practitioners will be continuously making notes regarding the observations they make of children in a wide range of situations covering the six areas of the Early Learning Goals. The notes from these observations will frequently be shared with other members of the early years team at the end of teaching sessions, and will inform the formal written records that are used to monitor children's progress. On a more informal level, in the constant interaction between children and staff, formative assessment takes place as effective use is made of praise and constructive criticism. When a child is praised for a good piece of work or it is pointed out that an aspect of behaviour is inappropriate, assessment is being undertaken there and then, with immediate feedback to the child about what he or she has achieved or the impact of his or her actions.

Diagnostic assessment, as the term indicates, is used to try to establish the cause of learning difficulties that might be hindering the development of a child in one or more areas. For instance, a child having difficulties with oral communication because of physical impairment or a delay in the development of speaking skills might be experiencing problems not only in the area of language development but also in personal, social and emotional development, because of the crucial part played by language in this area of learning and experience. Effective diagnostic assessment in the early years should result in a programme being established to support children with particular needs. This may involve input from some of the aligned professions, such as the speech therapist or educational psychologist, which provide a level of expertise to support the work of early childhood practitioners.

A salient feature of each of the types of assessment outlined above should be the extent to which children are provided with opportunities to assess their own efforts and achievements. Self-assessment, even with quite young children, can be undertaken effectively and productively through the use of careful, appropriate and skilful questioning strategies, bringing the child's viewpoint to the assessment exercise, as well as those of parents and the early years setting.

It is important to remember that assessment is not just about monitoring the attainment and progress of individual children. Evaluative assessment can play an important part in enabling early years practitioners to reflect on their professional practice and the quality of provision that is offered to the children with whom they are working. In this way practitioners can evaluate the curriculum they are striving to deliver, the activities they offer the children on a daily basis and how the educational programme can be improved.

With the introduction of league tables ranking the 'performance' of individual schools and local education authorities through the publication of National Curriculum assessment results (Standard Assessment Tasks or SATs), comparative and value added assessment have gained an increasingly high profile. It is not possible to take two schools randomly and compare like with like regarding their respective SAT results because of the widely differing factors that can impinge upon the 'performance' of those schools. These can include the numbers of children attending who have some form of special educational need, those children who have English as an additional language or the very differing socio-economic backgrounds of the families the schools serve and their impact on the level of support the school receives from parents in the work it undertakes. Therefore, each year the DfES produces information whereby schools can compare their overall SATs results against national figures and against those of 'similar schools'. The 'similar schools' are grouped together using fairly crude criteria, such as the number of free school meals taken, but this does give schools the opportunity to gauge their position against the national picture and schools in similar circumstances.

Assessment in the early years is used to inform a variety of groups and individuals, not least the children themselves. Constructive feedback to children regarding their achievements and the progress they are making in all aspects of their work is a very important aspect of the early years practitioner's work. Keeping parents and carers informed and supplying colleagues involved in the next stage of a child's education with information about attainment and progress to date is another function that assessment addresses. Aligned professions working with an early years setting may require information that assessment can provide to support practitioners who are assisting children with particular needs. The increase in public accountability felt by all those working within education draws upon the process of assessment to inform proprietors, managers, headteachers and school governors responsible for early years education and care about the quality of the service they are providing. The information gained from assessment is also a useful tool to Ofsted in undertaking the inspection of settings that accommodate children in the early years.

Within the limits of this chapter it is not possible to explore all the methods that can be used to gather information which feeds into the process of assessment. However, two general principles apply. First, assessment is not some sort of 'bolt-on' activity undertaken after the planning of an educational programme and after children have completed tasks. It is part of an ongoing planning and evaluation cycle, which, as indicated above, should inform early years practitioners about the quality of provision they are offering young children, as well as highlighting individual achievement and progress. Second, what has come to be regarded as good practice in early years assessment procedures is solidly based on observing children and accurately recording their involvement in the activities they undertake. 'Careful assessment based on regular observations are key elements for ensuring that the curriculum for the under fives is based on the needs of the pupils and provides continuity and progression. . . . The quality of assessment, recording and reporting should be evaluated by: the quality and accuracy of the written observations made by staff' (Ofsted 1995). Useful, practical guidance with regard to developing effective methods for observation and recording in the early years is given by Stierer *et al.* (1993).

A contentious issue that has been the focus of much debate in recent years with respect to assessment in the early years regards the merits of what have come to be known as the quantitative and qualitative approaches to assessment. Essentially these approaches are to do with the recording of information that has resulted from assessment, completing the wider picture of assessment, recording and reporting. Quantitative methods use checklists, which may involve ticking boxes or allocating scores to children on the basis of tasks completed. Checklists are usually straightforward and quick to use. At a glance practitioners and parents can see what children have achieved; for instance, in each area of the Early Learning Goals. However, their use has been criticised (Blenkin and Kelly 1992; Bartholomew and Bruce 1993; Nutbrown 1998) on the basis that they are predeterministic and narrow in focus. In particular, Bartholomew and Bruce argue that 'Checklists do not give us the information we most need to know about children's learning.' The argument is that rather than focusing on how young children learn and how as practitioners we can best facilitate effective learning – the process involved in learning – checklists simply indicate what children appear to have learnt – the product of learning – ignoring everything that cannot be coded, scored or ticked. Obviously, it is important that early years practitioners are in a position to ascertain what knowledge, concepts, skills and attitudes young children have assimilated and are able to extend and consolidate. However, the usefulness, or otherwise, of the methods used to record this information is very debatable. Blenkin and Kelly (1992: 164) make clear their views of quantitative approaches to assessment in the early years when they write: 'Thus these forms [of assessment] have stressed the metric rather than the judgmental, the summative rather than the formative, the incremental aggregation of "scores" rather than holistic assessment, and thus attainment rather than development.'

In a review of Baseline Assessment, which is undertaken nationally, is checklist based and usually takes place several weeks after children have joined a reception class in the state education system, Nutbrown (1998) is equally doubtful about the usefulness of this approach. She points out that

> Teachers must not be encumbered with an instrument which is attributed with false validity. They must be able to trust – and adjust – their own assessments. Teachers need to be free to use a variety of ways to find out about children's learning so they can effectively develop their teaching and properly support children's learning. To require all teachers to use crude, quick, nationally imposed assessments will result in a practice of early assessment of little (or no) use to teaching and learning – its stated primary purpose.

Qualitative approaches to assessment in the early years are observation-based and much more open-ended with regard to what is recorded, although they usually have a particular focus for the practitioner, such as mathematics or language development or an aspect of these areas of learning and experience. They take longer to complete than checklists but, as Bartholomew and Bruce (1993) argue, 'Each observation contains a wealth of information, and it is efficient use of your time and energy.' Such observation-based assessment, it is argued, gives valuable insights into how individual children learn, as well as what they are learning. Not only is this a method of monitoring individual achievement and progress, it also directly feeds into assessment of provision. It tells us not only how effectively the educational programme is successfully meeting the individual needs of children, but also how challenging the activities that the setting provides are and how well children's learning is being extended and taken forward.

It is a legal requirement that all children of statutory school age must have an annual written report outlining their attainment and progress for that academic year. Parents have access to the report which is usually sent to them or taken home by the child, acknowledging receipt of the report is usually undertaken by parents signing and returning to the school a form to which they can add comments indicating how useful they have found the report. Many schools and early years settings have now adopted this type of reporting procedure for young children who, although they have still to reach school age, it is felt should have their achievements recorded and shared with parents.

In concluding this section of the chapter and considering the third stage of the assessment, recording and reporting process, it is timely to reflect on a number of questions that highlight how reports on children's achievement and progress can be written in such a way that they effectively serve the purpose for which they are intended.

A result of assessment and recording is the report. How far does the report:

• Give understandable information?
• Report constructively?
• Remain free of jargon and be easy to understand?
• Give evidence or illustrative examples of achievement and effort?
• Indicate areas for further development?
• Encourage parental involvement in children's learning and the educational pro-
  gramme offered?
• Reflect the values, aims and culture of the setting – the early years ethos?

Inspection

Prior to the 1997 general election the Labour Party, in it's discussion paper Early
Excellence, claimed that it intended to rationalise the inspection of early years education and care. This was because early years providers had been subject to no less than
three types of inspection depending on the age of the children accommodated and the
type of funding the setting received. Infant and primary schools where children are
accommodated in nursery and reception classes and maintained nursery schools, were
(and continue to be) subject to Ofsted inspections under Section 10 of the School
Inspection Act 1996. However, children in the early years accommodated in the private,
voluntary and independent sectors were subject to Ofsted inspections under what came
to be established as Section 122 of the School Standards and Framework Act 1998. In
addition to this these settings were also subject to inspection by social services departments under the remit of the Children Act 1998.

Social services inspections tended to focus on the general provision of early years
settings - the premises used, resources and staff/children ratios. However, Ofsted
inspections have a much sharper focus on the educational programme of settings and
whether or not children are effectively working towards the early learning goals, in particular personal, social and emotional development, communication, language and literacy and mathematical development. In September 2001 Ofsted established a new
Early Years Directorate, which has responsibility for a new augmented inspection
service bringing together the social services inspections and the Section 122 inspections. This new inspection system is based upon settings meeting the requirements outlined in five sets of new National Childcare Standards for the private, independent and
voluntary sectors. The Standards cover the provision offered by: Full Day Care,
Sessional Day Care, Out of School Care, Childminding and Creches (Ofsted 2001).
However, the Section 10 inspections of early years provision in state schools remains
the same and are based on The Handbook for Inspecting Primary and Nursery Schools
with Guidance on Self Evaluation (Ofsted 1999). Moreover, the Government's early
excellence centre programme has produced another anomaly in the inspection of early
years services as this type of provision is inspected by teams of Her Majesty's
Inspectors of Schools (HMI) and may on occasion be supported by social services representatives. This is because currently Ofsted are not yet in a position to inspect the

diverse range of services offered by the widely differing types of early excellence centres in the programme. Despite the Government's claim about rationalising the inspection of early years provision this has not been fully resolved and it would appear that the Government's goal of greater coherence in policy implementation and delivery through what has been termed 'joined up government', has not yet quite reached the stage of 'joined up inspection' in the early years.

Conclusion

Early years education and care is currently undergoing extensive development and expansion. New initiatives in provision, the training and professional development of practitioners, the inspection of services and the promotion of a multidisciplinary approach to working with young children and their families is taking place on a national scale not previously experienced. It is an exciting and challenging time for practitioners, as it appears that the early years are beginning to be recognised as a fundamentally important period in children's lives, and not just preparation for the next stage of education, but preparation for life. There is an increasing awareness and acknowledgement that young children's personal, social and emotional development is of crucial importance and needs to be carefully fostered through the development of attitudes, dispositions and relationships that allow children to come to terms with, and be in control of, their own emotions and feelings, and appreciate and respect those of others. We must not lose sight of this. While it is acknowledged that young children at some point in their lives will need to be introduced to early literacy and numeracy skills and begin to become familiar with other areas of learning and experience, this must not be at the expense of giving them every possible opportunity to develop as tolerant, caring, sensitive, creative, confident and respectful individuals in the early years. This period is of such importance, and has such a lasting effect on how children perceive themselves, others and the world in which they live, that they must experience learning as an exciting, pleasurable process which contributes to every aspect of their development and enables them to progress, assimilating knowledge, concepts, skills and attitudes at a rate which is appropriate for each of them as individuals. It is important that children learn from their successes and their failures and that they are not afraid of 'making mistakes' or 'getting it wrong'. However, it is even more important that we do not build inevitable failure 'into the system' through provision which does not take careful account of children's ages, natural interests, curiosity and capabilities, allowing them to develop as autonomous, competent learners, as it is this 'foundation stage' that is the basis for future success in all aspects of their lives.

POINTS FOR DISCUSSION

1 Is the government's programme of investing large amounts of public money in early excellence centres the most productive way of developing effective early education and childcare, or could the funds be better spent by resourcing a much wider range of early years settings?

2 Do the Early Learning Goals make the positive contribution to young children's learning claimed by the DfEE in *Curriculum Guidance for the Foundation Stage* (QCA/DfEE 2000)? Or are they too focused on subject areas derived from the primary curriculum and the products of learning, rather than the process of learning and development of young children in the early years?

3 Is it possible to reconcile the advantages of the quantitative and qualitative approaches to recording children's achievements and progress in the early years, to benefit children and provide access for practitioners, parents and carers to useful, informative records?

4 What essential features need to be part of the new inspection process introduced by Ofsted from September 2001 (for the private, independent and voluntary sectors) to give a clear indication of the quality of provision offered by early years settings and how such provision can be improved?

INTERNET SITES

Department for Education and Skills: www.dfes.gov.uk
Early excellence centres: www.earlyexcellence.org
National Childcare Standards: www.dfee.gov.uk/daycare
Office for Standards in Education: www.ofsted.gov.uk
Qualifications and Curriculum Authority: www.crownbc.com/qca
Schools Building on Success: www.dfee.gov.uk/buildingonsuccess
Times Educational Supplement: www.tes.co.uk

FURTHER READING

Abbott, L. and Moylett, H. (eds) (1999) *Early Education Transformed*. Buckingham: Open University Press.
Bilton, H. (1998) *Outdoor Play in the Early Years: Management and Innovation*. London: Paul Chapman Publishing.
Blenkin, G. and Kelly, A. V. (1998) *Principles into Practice in Early Childhood Education*. London: Paul Chapman Publishing.
Costello, P. (2000) *Thinking Skills and Early Childhood Education*. London: David Fulton.
Dowling, M. (2000) *Young Children's Personal, Social and Emotional Development*. London: Paul Chapman Publishing.
Edgington, M. (1998) *The Nursery Teacher in Action*. London: Paul Chapman Publishing.
Makins, V. (1997) *It's Not Just a Nursery It's Our Life: Multi-agency Early Years Centres in Action*. London: NCB.
National Commission on Education (1993) *Learning to Succeed: a Radical Look at Education Today and a Strategy for the Future*. London: Heinemann.
Nutbrown, C. (1994) *Threads of Thinking*. London: Paul Chapman Publishing.
Robson, S. and Smedley, S. (1996) *Education in Early Childhood: First Things First*. London: David Fulton.

REFERENCES

Ball, C. (1994) *Start Right: the Importance of Early Learning*. London: Royal Society for the Encouragement of Arts Manufacturers and Commerce.

Bartholomew, L. and Bruce, T. (1993) *Getting to Know You*. London: Hodder and Stoughton.

Blenkin, G. M. and Kelly, A. V. (1992) *Assessment in Early Childhood Education*. London: Paul Chapman Publishing.

Board of Education (1937) *Handbook of Suggestions for Teachers*. London: HMSO.

David, T. (1990) *Under Five – Under Educated*. Milton Keynes: Open University Press.

DES (1990) *Starting with Quality: the Report of the Committee of Inquiry into the Quality of the Educational Experience Offered to Three and Four Year Olds*. London: HMSO.

DES (1998) *The Curriculum from 5 to 16: the Responses to Curriculum Matters 2*. An HMI Report. London: DES.

DfEE (1999) *Early Excellence Centres Developing High Quality Integrated Early Years Services*. London: DfEE.

DfEE (2000) *A Training Support Framework for the Foundation Stage Ensuring Sound Foundations: from Principles to Practice*. London: DfEE.

DfEE (2001a) *Early Years Development and Childcare Partnerships: Planning and Guidance 2001–2002*. London: DfEE.

DfEE (2001b) *Schools, Raising Standards, Promoting Diversity, Achieving Results*. London: DfEE.

DfEE (2001c) *National Childcare Standards*. London: DfEE.

Her Majesty's Inspectors (1988) *The Curriculum from 5 to 16*. London: HMI.

Labour Party (1997) *Early Excellence*. London: Labour Party.

Moss P. and Penn, H. (1996) *Transforming Nursery Education*. London: Paul Chapman Publishing.

Munton, T. (1999) 'One for all', *Nursery World*, September.

Nutbrown, C. (1998) 'Early assessment – examining the baselines', *Early Years*, 19(1), 50–61.

Ofsted (1995) *Handbook for Inspecting Primary and Nursery Schools*. London: HMSO.

Ofsted (1999) *Handbook for Inspecting Primary and Nursery Schools with Guidance on Self Evaluation*. London: HMSO.

Ofsted (2001a) *Early Years Full Day Care: Guidance to the National Standards*. London: DfES.

Ofsted (2001b) *Early Years Sessional Day Care: Guidance to the National Standards*. London: DfES.

Ofsted (2001c) *Early Years Out of School Care: Guidance to the National Standards*. London: DfES.

Ofsted (2001d) *Early Years Childminding: Guidance to the National Standards*. London: DfES.

Ofsted (2001e) *Early Years Creches: Guidance to the National Standards*. London: DfES.

Pugh, G. (1988) *Services for the Under Fives: Developing a Co-ordinated Approach*. London: Paul Chapman Publishing.

Pugh, G. (1996a) *Contemporary Issues in the Early Years*, 2nd edn. London: Paul Chapman Publishing.

Pugh, G. (1996b) *Education and Training for Work in the Early Years*. London: National Children's Bureau.

Pugh, G. (1998) 'Early years training in context', in L. Abbott and G. Pugh (eds) *Training to Work in the Early Years*. Buckingham: Open University Press.

QCA/DfEE (2000) *Curriculum Guidance for the Foundation Stage*. London: QCA.

Stierer, B., Devereux, J., Gifford, S., Laycock, L. and Yerbury, J. (1993) *Profiling, Recording and Observing: a Resource Pack for the Early Years*. London: Routledge.

CHAPTER 6

Primary Schools

Liz Laycock

CHAPTER SUMMARY

- This chapter begins by contextualising primary education within a historical perspective.
- The impact on primary schools of changes in both curriculum and pedagogy is considered, from the implementation of the Educational Reform Act in 1988 to the revisions of National Curriculum requirements in 2000.
- Discussion of assessment and inspection issues focuses on the growing emphasis on summative assessment and accountability.

The primary curriculum

Introduction: a historical perspective

Perceptions of what primary education is about have changed radically since the introduction of the concept and the term in *The Primary School* (Board of Education 1931). This report (known as the Hadow Report) is where we find the first rationale provided for primary education, following the establishment of the notion of two distinct stages of education, primary and secondary, to replace elementary education. In Hadow we find a reasoned rationale for the curriculum, teaching, organisation and staffing of the primary school, drawing on what was known about children's development and learning. The language used is not at odds with what many primary teachers believe now:

> the curriculum in the primary school is to be thought of in terms of activity and experience rather than of knowledge to be acquired and facts to be stored . . . the primary school can do nothing more useful than to help children gain a thorough command of the mother-tongue, to use books freely as a source of information and pleasure, and to express their ideas readily in writing. (Board of Education 1931: 96)

Similarly, the report spoke of 'the great and special virtues' of whole-class teaching, while acknowledging the 'limits to its flexibility and therefore its usefulness' in meeting the 'varying needs of children'. The report's underlying philosophy, focusing on the needs of young learners, is striking.

It was not until after the Second World War that the two separate phases of education were formally established in the 1944 Education Act – though the process of replacement of 'all through' schools was not completed until much later. In the newly established schools, some of which were primary and some of which were 'infant' or 'junior', the curriculum was influenced by developmental approaches to teaching and learning, and new practices and organisation were implemented. In many infant departments the rigidities of the timetable were removed, classrooms were reorganised along more informal lines, work was related to centres of interest or themes and children were given greater choice and supported in taking some responsibility for their own learning. This was less apparent in junior departments where, in classes of 40 or more pupils, the demands of the 11-plus meant that much time was given, especially in the final year, to training and practice in reading, writing, number and 'intelligence', to ensure the school got as many children as possible into the grammar schools. There were, however, pockets of practice in junior departments where there was a similarly informal approach, with an emphasis on creativity, discovery and first-hand experience; primary schools in Oxfordshire and the West Riding of Yorkshire, under the direction of Alec Clegg, were much visited beacons at this time.

These areas of practice were among those investigated and described by the Plowden Committee in its mission 'to consider primary education in all its aspects'. The much reviled Plowden Report (CACE 1967) is remarkable for its principled approach and the clarity of its underlying values: equality of opportunity; compensation for handicaps; respect for individuality; commitment to the highest educational standards, with a stress on individual discovery, first-hand experience and opportunities for creative work. It took a stand in favour of 'the developmental tradition', advocating the expansion of nursery education, measures to improve home–school liaison and a move away from streaming. Plowden's 'progressive methods' have been much criticised and often misrepresented.

Its critics, both then and in the 30 odd years since, seized upon phrases which appeared to suggest that teachers should not teach, but allow the child to 'find out'. In fact there are also parts which state clearly that 'there must be teaching as well as learning' and that there is value in 'learning by description', 'practice of skills and consolidation of knowledge'. What were presented as aspirational principles were sadly misconstrued by a minority of teachers who adopted a disastrous *laissez-faire* approach – for example, in William Tyndale Junior School, which was criticised for operating an extreme, almost anarchic, version of 'child-centred' education (Auld Report 1976). Where the principles were understood, in a very few schools, the approach to teaching and learning advocated by Plowden resulted in some high-quality creative work and high levels of achievement for children who demonstrated previously unrecognised potential. In fact, as even Alexander *et al.* (1992: 9) acknowledged,

> the commonly held belief that primary schools, after 1967, were swept by a tide
> of progressivism is untrue. HMI in 1978, for example, reported that only 5 per

cent of classrooms exhibited wholeheartedly 'exploratory' characteristics and that didactic teaching was still practised in three quarters of them.

If the 1970s and early 1980s saw a decline in standards, it was certainly not due to the implementation of Plowden's approaches. The HMI Primary Survey (DES 1978) reported that 'high priority is given to teaching children to read, write and learn mathematics' and that 'the results of the surveys conducted since 1955 are consistent with gradually improving reading standards of 11-year olds'. They did suggest, however, that 'the demands of society seem likely to continue to rise'. But the common perception was that standards in schools, especially primary schools, were falling and that radical action was needed to ensure children would be able to meet the likely demands of the twenty-first century.

The Education Reform Act and the National Curriculum

Whereas Plowden's belief had been that 'at the heart of the educational process lies the child', those who created the first drafts of a National Curriculum felt that 'the school curriculum is at the heart of education' (DES 1981). The focus now shifted to *what* children should be taught and the proportions of time to be devoted to each subject. The early drafts described the curriculum in terms of subjects 'for convenience' but also commented: 'What is at issue is not the labels under which subjects appear on the time-table . . . but the place which the subjects should occupy in substance' (DES 1984).

This paper also refers to 'cross-curricular elements' as an 'indispensable part of the curriculum throughout the compulsory period'. The division of the curriculum into subjects enabled the government, later on, to invite subject groups to submit their suggestions for the content of each area, although this meant that the important cross-curricular elements were seen as added extras. The model of the curriculum offered in 1984 remained substantially unchanged in later legislation. The primary phase should:

- place substantial emphasis on achieving competence in the use of language and in mathematics;
- introduce pupils to science;
- provide worthwhile offerings which develop understanding in the area of history, geography and religious education;
- offer a range of aesthetic activities;
- provide opportunities throughout the curriculum for craft and practical work, leading up to some experience of design and technology and of solving problems;
- offer physical and health education;
- introduce pupils to computers;
- give pupils some insights into the adult world, including how people earn their living.

By 1987, it was clear that the government intended to legislate for a National Curriculum and the first 'Expert Working Groups' (Assessment and Testing, Science and Mathematics) were set up to propose content. In 1988 the Education Reform Act

(ERA) provided a legal basis for the curriculum. In the documentation for this National Curriculum, there is no stated rationale for its content or for how this relates to what we know of children's learning, beyond the requirement for schools to provide a 'balanced and broadly based' curriculum which:

> a) promotes the spiritual, moral, cultural, mental and physical development of pupils at the school and of society; and

> b) prepares such pupils for the opportunities, responsibilities and experiences of adult life. (ERA (Education Reform Act) 1988: Clause 1)

These bland statements did not contradict beliefs held by primary teachers, so, after some initial concerns, most worked long and hard to implement the requirements. The huge amount of documentation (the infamous colour-coded ring-binders, each with its Programmes of Study and Attainment Targets), gradually bringing new content on stream, was absorbed and the content taught.

For the first time there was a clear view of children's entitlement, which led, in many places, to a broadening of the curriculum for primary pupils. Equally, because teachers now had to ensure they covered the Programmes of Study, planning became more detailed and teaching and learning intentions more clearly defined. The Programmes of Study provided a clearer picture of progression and the Level descriptors a better sense of standards to be reached. Assessment and recording of children's progress became more thorough (see below). On the negative side, there was considerable concern about the erosion of time, in the earliest stages, for the teaching of literacy, as well as real curriculum overload. Many teachers struggled to implement the very detailed (and, sometimes, unclear) statutory orders, especially in Key Stage 1. Although links across different subject areas were possible, few teachers had time to explore the potential of these, so there was a tendency to teach each subject separately, even to the youngest pupils. This was despite those teachers' deeply rooted beliefs about 'holistic learning' – enabling young children to make connections and accommodate new learning across subject boundaries.

This statutory curriculum had nothing to say about learning and teaching – it was to be 'delivered' to pupils who were the passive recipients of the knowledge prescribed for them. From the start the curriculum and its assessment have been (and continue to be) concerned with performance, competition and targets, but not with children's active learning and helping them to 'make sense' of what is taught. Most primary teachers, in their training at least, spend time considering what is known about children's learning and the most effective ways in which teachers can contribute to this. Above all, understanding of the social and collaborative nature of learning informs primary teaching approaches. The adult's support and intervention at the appropriate time depends on knowledge of the child's level of understanding and needs, helping her or him to make sense of what is being taught by linking it to existing knowledge (which sometimes might be in a different 'subject'!). Research was carried out for the Teacher Training Agency (TTA) in 1995 and 1996 to find out the characteristics of effective teachers of literacy (Medwell et al. 1998) and numeracy (Askew et al. 1997). Both reported that effective teachers constantly helped children to make connections and placed emphasis on meaning, rather than adopting either 'transmission' or 'discovery' teaching approaches. Both helped children to think about what they were learning so that learning was an active process.

No sooner was the National Curriculum up and running than questions were raised about primary generalist teachers' abilities to teach the subject content of the whole curriculum, as well as about classroom organisation and teaching methodology. These issues were raised in the so-called 'Three Wise Men Report' – the discussion paper *Curriculum Organisation and Classroom Practice in Primary Schools* (Alexander *et al.* 1992). In retrospect, the conclusions about key issues in this paper were the harbingers of later developments in the teaching frameworks for the National Literacy Strategy (DfEE 1998a) and the National Numeracy Strategy (DfEE 1999) and the extensive core subject knowledge and subject specialist requirements for primary teachers in training (DfEE 1998b). The tone of many of the conclusions was seen as an attack on what many felt were the basic principles of primary teaching.

> 118 In recent decades much teaching in primary schools has suffered from highly questionable dogmas which have generated excessively complex classroom practice and have devalued the role of subjects in the curriculum. The new climate must encourage teachers to review their teaching techniques in the light of evidence about effective classroom practice and how well the pupils are making progress. . . .
>
> 121 The subject knowledge required by the National Curriculum makes it unlikely that the generalist primary teacher will be able to teach all subjects in the depth required. This is particularly the case in Key Stage 2, but is also true in Key Stage 1.

Both of these statements, and several others in the 12 key issues highlighted in the report, focus on the knowledge to be delivered to children and make no attempt to consider factors related to how young children learn or how primary classrooms might be different from secondary ones. In Alexander *et al.*'s (1993) follow-up report, written after feedback from inspections and consultation with groups of headteachers, some of the misgivings of headteachers about subject boundaries and specialist teaching are reported, and show steady support for the generalist class teacher, though with some move to semi-specialist teaching in some subjects.

There had also been much pressure, once the curriculum was in place, for immediate and far-reaching revisions to aspects of the statutory curriculum, especially the English curriculum. Right-wing pressure groups had always disagreed with the model of English presented by Cox (DES 1989) and the Language in the National Curriculum (LINC) project (1992), and reflected in the 1989 English curriculum. Because English, and literacy in particular, was so central to the control of the curriculum, the subject became a battleground from 1992, right up to the revision of the National Curriculum in 1998–9. It was a battle that many primary teachers feel was lost.

By 1998, the Dearing review of the curriculum had been completed (the final report was in December 1993), plans were made for a revision of the whole National Curriculum and the National Literacy Strategy was introduced by a new government anxious to show its commitment to raising educational standards. The primary curriculum was to be 'reduced' to make way for the increased emphasis on literacy (and later, numeracy), so the QCA produced *Maintaining Breadth and Balance at Key Stages 1 and 2* to explain how the new 'flexible arrangements' could still result in 'broad and balanced' provision for 5- to 11-year-olds. The Programmes of Study of the six foundation subjects (art, design and technology, history, geography, music and physical education) were to be 'modified' by 'prioritising, combining and reducing' the content. In many schools this flexibility resulted in a much narrower curriculum (termed by some a 'neo-elementary curriculum'), with a heavy emphasis on the core subjects (and RE and ICT), while other schools used the notion of 'combining' to provide more breadth and balance. Primary teachers were generally pleased to move away from subject teaching, which had considerable areas of overlap, and to follow the QCA guidance, which stated, 'Using this approach, unnecessary duplication or repetition of teaching points can be avoided by bringing together similar or related aspects of the programmes of study into a single teaching unit' (p. 6). Here, belatedly, there is some acknowledgement that it is possible to teach curriculum content in primary schools effectively and efficiently without insisting on subject boundaries.

The year 1999 saw the introduction of 'Curriculum 2000', the fully revised National Curriculum. Any substantial revision of the English and mathematics content had been pre-empted by the introduction of the National Literacy and Numeracy Strategies, even though these had not been working long enough for their effectiveness to be evaluated. Similarly, the increased emphasis on ICT meant that this area had to be allocated a higher profile in primary schools. The revised curriculum has been given, for the first time, a rationale, and includes the broader, non-subject area of personal, social and health education (PSHE) and citizenship, as well as a statement on inclusion. *The National Curriculum Handbook for Primary Teachers in England* (DfEE/QCA 1999) reveals the considerable emphasis and detailed prescription in core subjects, the more flexible content of all other subjects and the non-statutory nature of the PSHE framework. While some schools will ensure there is balance and breadth, just as they did in 1998, others will focus largely on what is formally assessed because there is relentless pressure to meet targets in these areas. At the same time, schools are offered the non-statutory schemes of work from the QCA for many subjects, and these are being implemented to the letter in many schools, which feel that it is best to 'play safe' with these because they come with an official stamp of approval. Although there is no formal assessment of this content, it is believed that Ofsted inspectors will wish to see the QCA schemes in place (see below).

The biggest losses of all in the primary curriculum are the creative aspects – drama, dance, music and art. Although they exist in the Programmes of Study for the foundation subjects or, in the cases of drama and dance, in the speaking and listening strand of the English curriculum or the PE curriculum, they are 'more honoured in the breach than in the observance' in many primary schools. In 1999 the National Advisory Committee on Creative and Cultural Education (NACCCE) produced an important and timely report, *All Our Futures: Creativity, Culture and Education*, which has since sunk without trace, although the intention had been for this report to inform the revision of the National Curriculum for 2000. In his Foreword to the report David Blunkett welcomed its proposals for 'this vital part of a balanced and rounded education'. Throughout the report we are reminded of the relevance of the creative elements of a curriculum in raising academic standards:

> Every child has capabilities beyond the traditionally academic. Children with high academic ability may have other strengths that are often neglected. Children who struggle with academic work can have outstanding abilities in other areas. . . . The key is to find what children are good at. Self-confidence and self-esteem then tend to rise and overall performance improve. High standards in creative achievement require just as much rigour as traditional academic work. (NACCCE 1999: 13, para. 2)

The report presents a powerful argument from all sides, the scientific and technological communities as well as the arts, for restoring the balance in the curriculum and for reasserting the place of 'creative and cultural education within and beyond the National Curriculum'. For Key Stages 1 and 2 in particular, there is evidence that 'there is a positive correlation between good provision/performance in the arts in schools and higher standards of literacy and numeracy, according to Ofsted inspection statistics' (*ibid.*: 77, para. 140).

Assessment

The forms and uses of assessment have been debated from the very start of the National Curriculum. It is probably true that assessment, record-keeping and monitoring of pupils' progress had not been an area of strength for most primary teachers in the decades preceding the introduction of the National Curriculum. It was an area teachers themselves were beginning to address, and initiatives such as the Inner London Education Authority's *Primary Language Record* (1988) and the later *Primary Learning Record* (1993) helped primary teachers with guidance and formats for assessment and recording that were changing practice. The emphasis in these initiatives was on ongoing formative assessment that would inform future teaching and contribute to summative statements at the end of a year. These records were designed to record not just children's knowledge of the National Curriculum content, but also their 'developing learning processes'; they identified 'children's strengths and growth points' and 'mapped developments within and between different curriculum areas'. The intention to involve parents, children and all adults who taught the children meant that the record-keeping was rigorous but also time-consuming. Faced with the burden of implementing the new requirements and recording children's achievement of the multitudes of statements of attainment, many teachers adopted the checklist approach exemplified in commercially published record booklets, containing lists of statements for each subject for each level/year, rather than more in-depth, qualitative systems.

The principles for assessment of the National Curriculum that had been given in the report of the Task Group on Assessment and Testing (TGAT) (DES 1988) were wide-ranging, attempting to go beyond simple summative testing. The problem was that this task group tried to construct a model of assessment that attempted to meet too many requirements and needs. It was impossible for the system to provide formative, summative, diagnostic and evaluative assessment (to provide evidence to be used in judging the effectiveness of schools). In the drive to use evidence for this last purpose, the principle that teacher assessments should be given equal weight with formal, external assessments has been lost. This is particularly disappointing in the primary context, where teachers' observations and assessments, over time and in a range of contexts, need to be the basis of planning. In the primary years, teachers' formative assessment must be embedded in daily practice, not added on. In the words of TGAT, 'it should be an integral part of the educational process, continually providing both "feedback" and "feedforward". It therefore needs to be incorporated systematically into teaching strategies and practice at all levels' (para. 4). Above all there needs to be a move away from 'assessment *of* learning' (i.e. assessment of what children know in order to record what has been completed) to 'assessment *for* learning (i.e. assessments made in order to inform teachers about what the next steps are) (James 1998). Because there is pressure on schools to demonstrate improvement, the emphasis now is on test results (summative assessment) and the range of formative assessments diminishes as children progress through the primary school.

The relentless pressure of SATs, and now the 'optional' tests for every year group, not just Year 2 and Year 6, have brought about, in many schools, not only a narrowing of assessment strategies, but also a narrowing of the curriculum. It is not uncommon for teachers in Year 6 and, to a lesser extent, Year 2 classes to reduce the curriculum largely to the subjects which are to be tested because these results are what count in judging the effectiveness of a school. The school's position in the league tables depends on SAT results and the percentage of children reaching the prescribed levels. Perhaps we need to be reminded of the TGAT statement in 1988: 'The assessment process itself should not determine what is to be taught and learned. It should be the servant, not the master of the curriculum' (para. 4), and 'any report of assessment results should be part of a broader report covering many activities and achievements of the school, including information that the school may or should publish about its curriculum' (para. 132). The situation has been exacerbated by assessments of teachers themselves, who must demonstrate year on year improvement in their results if they are to be considered as 'crossing the threshold' for performance-related pay increases.

What is needed now is a review of assessment arrangements to reduce the burden of testing and to reinstate the teacher's role in monitoring progress. The targets now set externally for each school to increase the numbers of children reaching a prescribed level establish pressures that are inevitably passed on to the children. Pupils as young as seven now talk about 'passing' the tests. The setting of targets can be valuable if the children themselves are involved in discussion of their achievements. When children are supported by critical feedback and reflection on what they need to do next and are guided by teachers, realistic, achievable targets can help them to monitor their own progress. Greater emphasis needs to be placed on formative assessments to feed into this target-setting, but more also needs to be done in primary schools to set up moderation exercises, especially between schools, where teachers discuss their assessments in order to agree common standards. TGAT recommended 'group moderation' as an 'integral part of national assessment systems' (para. 77).

Inspection

The inspection system provides a form of moderation, but it is one-sided and, of course, has an emphasis on external control. Her Majesty's Inspectors (HMI), who had been responsible for the inspection of schools before 1992, were generally respected by teachers and had a benign influence on schools. Inspectors were experienced in their own field (e.g. primary, secondary, special education) or specialist subject and had to undergo a period of probation when they became inspectors, so teachers in primary schools felt that their judgements had some validity. Their role was not only to evaluate but also to offer advice and guidance to schools. Ofsted's creation, in 1992, changed all this. Huge numbers of inspectors were needed for the increased emphasis on and frequency of inspection. To begin with, many of those who came to inspect primary schools were not experienced primary practitioners and they had had only a few days' training, so teachers often felt that their assessments lacked understanding of the context. It was not uncommon for a knowledgeable subject specialist, who did not fully appreciate the generalist role of primary teachers, to be very critical of teachers teaching that inspector's specialist subject.

Ofsted inspections were initially seen as threatening, despite the clear criteria against which judgements were made. Teachers knew that their schools could be judged as failing their pupils on the basis of a four-day visit, so the lead-up to the actual inspection put enormous strain on them. As the new inspection arrangements have settled down, more primary inspectors have been appointed and teachers have become more accustomed to the expectations, some of the pressures have reduced and it is possible to see the positive effects of regular inspections. Surveys have shown that the vast majority of primary schools accepted their inspection team's judgements and believed that their inspection report was fair and accurate. Reports provide a detailed analysis of a school's strengths and weaknesses and highlight key issues that need to be addressed in the future; this has often provided the catalyst for increased support from LEAs. The process of inspection has ensured that schools review their policies and schemes of work, and that a school development plan and clear targets are in place. For individual teachers, written planning, careful assessment and record-keeping, and increased reflection on their teaching have become the norm. Since 1997 individual teachers have been given feedback and grades on lessons that have been observed, and most have welcomed this change.

There remain, however, even following the revised framework for inspection (Ofsted 1999), some concerns for primary teachers. There is a greater emphasis now on self-evaluation, but this depends on both strong leadership and clear vision from the headteacher. A major issue of concern to primary teachers relates to the inspection of the whole curriculum, including PHSE. There is a requirement for all teachers to be observed teaching literacy and numeracy, which reduces the time available in a four-day inspection for observation of all other aspects of the curriculum. Although inspectors must make judgements about children's achievement on the basis of outcomes, and adherence to the teaching methodology in the National Literacy Strategy and National Numeracy Strategy Frameworks for Teaching is not statutory, many teachers and head-teachers believe that they will be judged less kindly if they are not following these frameworks and following the QCA Schemes of Work for other subjects.

Regional variations

It has been suggested that the National Curriculum should more accurately be termed 'The Statutory Curriculum' because requirements are not the same for the whole nation.

It is, for example, open to independent schools, wherever they are, to decide whether they wish to adopt all or part of the National Curriculum, and the Scottish curriculum differs considerably from that operating in England and Wales. The regulations for England and Wales were the same (with the addition of the Welsh language in Wales) at the beginning of development in 1988. Differences in emphasis and approach began to emerge as curriculum revisions came on stream (e.g. the revisions of the English curriculum in 1993, when the Welsh Curriculum Council did not adopt such sweeping changes), and have developed a more distinctive character with the devolution of power to the National Assembly for Wales. The statutory framework, however, remains very similar.

The approach in Scotland has always been different and rather less prescriptive than that in England and Wales. The Scottish Office Education Department (SOED) launched the 5–14 Development Programme in 1987 and subsequently produced National Guidelines on the different aspects of the curriculum and *The Structure and Balance of the Curriculum 5–14* (1993; revised 2000). The main difference in approach, which is very important to primary schools, is the highly principled rationale and division of the curriculum into areas rather than subjects:

- language (including a modern language no later than P6);
- mathematics;
- environmental studies (society, science and technology);
- expressive arts and physical education;
- religious and moral education with personal and social development and health education (SOED 2000: 11).

ICT, with separate guidance provided, is a 'cross-curricular aspect'.

Teachers are reminded that 'pupils do not all learn in the same way' and that 'teachers need to use a wide range of teaching styles that are appropriate to the task in hand and to the context in which learning can best be achieved'. The broad guidelines show awareness of the importance of teachers' professional judgements in interpreting the guidance in ways that are tailored to meet the needs of pupils.

The framework for assessment, too, recognises the importance of teachers' judgements in assessments. There are six levels of attainment (A to F); using these, teachers initially assess the level at which an individual is working. When the teacher feels the child is ready, a formal test for that level is administered to confirm that she or he has attained that level. There are no end of Key Stage national assessments and no published tables of schools' results. The level of attainment is assessed for each individual, which means that, whatever a child's age, teachers must differentiate work to match these levels.

Conclusion

All schools in England have undergone a turbulent reassessment and have absorbed huge changes in the past two decades. Primary schools, though, have been in the forefront of increasing control and direction from central government, not only of the curriculum and assessment, but also of teaching methodology. Despite serious misgivings sometimes, primary teachers have complied with directives which were driven by a view of education as a commodity to be delivered to customers, by accountability and political expediency. The barrage of directives, requirements and regulation has left many primary teachers feeling undermined and stripped of their professionalism. Most had become primary teachers because they believed primary aged children had huge learning potential and wished to be able to contribute to this. They see children's needs in terms not only of acquiring assessable knowledge and skills, but also of developing the young learner's confidence, self-esteem, independence, individuality, creativity, skills of collaboration and cooperation, and respect for others. If their belief in their own professionalism is to be restored they must be trusted to make professional judgements based on their extensive knowledge, not just of curriculum content, but also of children's individual strengths and needs, and on an understanding of how learning can best be brought about.

POINTS FOR DISCUSSION

1 What might a balanced curriculum for contemporary primary aged children consist of, and how might it differ from the current National Curriculum?
2 What would be needed to ensure that primary schools are able to nurture the 'whole child' from five to 11?
3 What is the role of teachers' assessments in the assessment and reporting process? Is regular summative assessment/testing the best way to ensure increased levels of attainment?
4 How can primary teachers reconcile the competing demands of delivering stage-specific subject knowledge and responding to individual needs?
5 Do a subject-oriented curriculum and the frameworks for teaching literacy and numeracy militate against linking different areas of knowledge and using understanding from one area to develop new knowledge in another? Is there a way of ensuring such links are made?

INTERNET SITES

Department for Education and Skills (DfES): www.dfes.gov.uk
Qualifications and Curriculum Authority: www.qca.org.uk
Ofsted: www.ofsted.gov.uk
Department of Education for Northern Ireland: www.deni.gov.uk
Learning and Teaching Scotland: www.LTScotland.com
Awdurdod Cymwysterau Cwricwlwm Asesu Cymru (Qualifications, Curriculum and
    Assessment Authority for Wales): www.accac.org.uk

REFERENCES AND FURTHER READING

Alexander, R., Rose, G. and Woodhead, C. (1992) *Curriculum Organisation and Classroom
    Practice in Primary Schools – a Discussion Paper.* London: Ofsted/DfE.
Alexander, R., Rose, G. and Woodhead, C. (1993) *Curriculum Organisation and Classroom
    Practice in Primary Schools – a Follow-up Report.* London: Ofsted/DfE.
Askew, M., Brown, M., Rhodes, V., Johnson, D. and Wiliam, D. (1997) *Effective Teachers
    of Numeracy.* Final report to TTA. London: School of Education, King's College.
Auld, R. (1976) *The William Tyndale Junior and Infant School: Report of the Public Enquiry.*
    London: ILEA.
Barrs, M., Ellis, S., Hester, H. and Thomas, A. (1988) *The Primary Language Record
    Handbook for Teachers.* London: CLPE/ILEA.
Board of Education (1931) *The Primary School* (Hadow Report). London: HMSO.
Central Advisory Council for Education (1967) *Children and Their Primary Schools*
    (Plowden Report). London: HMSO.
Curriculum Council for Wales (1993) *Review of National Curriculum English.* Cardiff:
    CCW.
Dearing, R. (1993) *The National Curriculum and Its Assessment: Final Report.* London:
    School Curriculum and Assessment Authority.
DES (1978) *Primary Education in England: a Survey by HM Inspectors of Schools.* London:
    HMSO.
DES (1981) *The School Curriculum* (Mark Carlisle). London: HMSO.
DES (1984) *The Organisation and Content of the 5–16 Curriculum.* London: HMSO.
DES (1988) *The Task Group on Assessment and Testing: a Report.* London: HMSO.
DES (1989) *English for Ages 5–16: the Cox Report.* London: HMSO.
DfEE (1998a) *The National Literacy Strategy Framework for Teaching.* London: DfEE.
DfEE (1998b) *High Status; High Standards.* London: DfEE.
DfEE (1999) *The National Numeracy Strategy Framework for Teaching Mathematics from
    Reception to Year 6.* London: DfEE.
DfEE/QCA (1999) *The National Curriculum Handbook for Primary Teachers in England.*
    London: HMSO.
Hester, H. with Ellis, S. and Barrs, M. (1993) *Guide to the Primary Learning Record.* London:
    CLPE.
James, M. (1998) *Using Assessment for School Improvement.* London: Heinemann.

Learning and Teaching Scotland and Scottish Executive (2000) *The Structure and Balance of the Curriculum 5–14 National Guidelines*. Dundee: Learning and Teaching Scotland.

LINC (1992) *The LINC Materials for Professional Development*. Nottingham: University of Nottingham English Department.

Medwell, J., Wray, D., Poulson, L. and Fox, R. (1998) *Effective Teachers of Literacy*. Final report to TTA. Exeter: School of Education.

National Advisory Committee on Creative and Cultural Education (1999) *All Our Futures: Creativity, Culture and Education* (Robinson Report). London: DfEE.

Ofsted (1999) *Handbook for Inspecting Primary and Nursery Schools, with Guidance on Self-evaluation*. London: The Stationery Office.

QCA (1998) *Maintaining Breadth and Balance at Key Stages 1 and 2*. London: QCA.

Scottish Office Education Department (1993) *The Structure and Balance of the Curriculum 5–14 National Guidelines*. Edinburgh: SOED (revised 2000).

CHAPTER 7

Secondary Schools and Sixth Forms

Jacqueline Nunn

CHAPTER SUMMARY

- The emphasis in this chapter is on the development of the National Curriculum for secondary schools between 1988 and 2001 in three major versions. It considers the shifting approaches to vocational education, and the significant changes within technology.
- Discussion of assessment focuses on the more recent concerns over assessment in the secondary phase of education.
- The impact of inspection on secondary schools and the uses of inspection and assessment evidence are considered, as well as some of the key respects in which the system in England and Wales differs from those in Scotland and Northern Ireland.

Introduction

An understanding of the current shape of the secondary curriculum requires an understanding of how it has come into being. Indeed, it is hard to recall just how controversial the introduction of the compulsory curriculum was and the impact that it has had on schools. The National Curriculum was introduced in the Education Reform Act 1988, but had its genesis at least 12 years earlier in the speech at Ruskin College Oxford by the then Labour Prime Minister James Callaghan. This speech initiated the so-called 'Great Debate' on the state of education in the UK. The concerns he raised were twofold. One can be characterised as entitlement: were our schools failing a majority of children in achieving the standards of which they were capable? Second, was the education system endangering the economy, by failing to produce a workforce with the skills and knowledge needed at the latter end of the twentieth century? These concerns were developed by successive Conservative governments between 1979 and 1997 into a systematic overhaul of all aspects of the education system. A significant turning point was the Education Reform Act 1988. This Act, introduced by Kenneth Baker as Secretary of State for Education, was arguably the most radical piece of education legislation since 1944. The National Curriculum was its centrepiece and was to deliver improved standards for all and to increase the ability of the nation to compete in the international economy.

The secondary curriculum

For the secondary phase the concerns around the curriculum derived from a number of sources. With the comprehensive school becoming the organisational unit for the majority of local authorities, the 1970s saw the merging of aspects of the grammar and secondary modern curriculum models. Following the introduction of the Certificate of Secondary Education in the late 1960s, and increasingly in the period following the raising of the school leaving age from 15 to 16 years in 1974, the secondary curriculum expanded to incorporate a broader range of subjects. These included some that were quite new to the compulsory school age curriculum, such as media studies, sociology, environmental studies, business education and computer studies. Alongside these changes, increasing amounts of curriculum time were given over to cross-curricular themes, including careers education and personal and health education. The outcome of these changes was that option choices became increasingly complex for students embarking on examination courses. This led to the perception, endorsed by Callaghan, that not all students were being given access to certain essential areas of learning and that the increase in programmes of vocational learning and work experience meant that large numbers of youngsters were failing to realise their full academic potential, through being channelled into non-academic or occupational options at an early stage.

The debate continued throughout the 1980s. The climate became increasingly hostile. Ranged on the government side was the evidence of a series of critical HMI reports, the publication of a series of 'Black Papers' by prominent right-wing educationalists and the beginnings of a radical review of the role of the local authorities and their control of schools and the curriculum. Set against them increasingly were the teacher unions, the subject associations and left-wing commentators anxious to retain room for multicultural perspectives and personal and social development among the other claims on curriculum time. The confrontational mood of the time is reflected in the speech made by Angela Rumbold, then Minister of State for Education, at the conference of the School Curriculum Development Committee, the forerunner of the National Curriculum Council.

> Why therefore can we not leave curriculum development in this country to be carried out through the varied and diverse LEAs within that framework of principles? Because the government has decided that the widely recognised need to raise standards, and the objective of cutting out clutter, are too important to leave to chance. Diversity can be a blessing and stimulation. But random divergence from what is expected of our schools is no longer acceptable. (O'Connor 1987)

The tone was prescriptive and dismissive of the concerns, expressed by teachers through subject associations and elsewhere, that important areas of learning and experience would be lost. The view of the government of the time was that this was a curriculum that would safeguard the essentials. Therefore, the National Curriculum that was introduced in secondary schools in 1991 established the now familiar pattern of core subjects – mathematics, science and English – and foundation subjects – technology, history, geography, modern languages, music, art and physical education. Religious education remained a statutory subject, although not technically an element of the National Curriculum. This, then, was the 'broad balanced and relevant curriculum free from clutter', in the words of the minister. There were those who suggested that in safeguarding the essentials, the National Curriculum in the form in which it was launched for secondary schools in 1991 was not dissimilar from that laid out in the Board of Education regulations for secondary schools of 1906. The elements were substantially the same, apart from the innovation of technology. On the other hand, it was argued that although the curriculum was prescribed and traditional, there still remained scope for teachers to devise their own schemes of work and to interpret the requirements in ways that would match the interests and aspirations of individual students.

The Dearing review

These hopes were modified in practice, so that by 1993 the government had commissioned Sir Ron Dearing with a full-scale review of the National Curriculum, long before a single cohort had passed through the secondary phase of education having experienced it throughout. It quickly became clear that the new curriculum, free of 'clutter', left time for precious little else. It was not only the new subject areas whose academic credibility had been challenged that were squeezed out by the demands of the new curriculum orders. English literature as a separate subject could no longer be accommodated, nor could two foreign languages at GCSE level, and many schools found that the timetable would not permit the teaching of three science disciplines. Ironically, the curriculum which had set out to ensure entitlement for all was beginning to be seen as a curriculum which for too many constrained choices, sometimes for the more able and academic students. On the other hand, there was increasing evidence of growing disaffection among large numbers of young people. The traditional content of the curriculum and the heavy burden of assessment had little to offer a significant minority of students, and there was little curriculum time left for vocational education, which had provided a significant motivation for some of these students. Despite the fact that students were permitted to drop art and music at the end of Key Stage 3, at the age of 14, and that short courses were available in history and geography, the volume of material to be covered remained immense. Each subject area occupied its own A4 sized folder. The requirements for assessment remained formidable. This was the context for the full-scale review of the National Curriculum carried out under the chairmanship of Ron Dearing in 1993.

The review was guided by the need to:

- reduce the volume of material required by law to be taught;
- simplify and clarify the programmes of study;
- reduce prescription so as to give more scope for professional judgement;
- ensure that the orders are written in a way which offers maximum support to the classroom teacher (Dearing 1994).

A significant strand of the framework for the review was the recognition of the clear concerns of the teaching profession that their ability to construct a curriculum appropriate to the needs of their students had been curtailed. Additionally, there was considerable concern that teachers had been undermined as a result of the demands of the curriculum and its assessment arrangements. Indeed, the review itself was initiated in part by the refusal of secondary English teachers to participate in the assessment arrangements for Key Stage 3, which led to a wider boycott and made the need for a reappraisal more urgent.

The revised version of the National Curriculum for England and Wales was implemented progressively from 1995. The review was generally welcomed for the reduction in content. Once each of the subject advisory groups had completed its work the new curriculum could be contained in one A4 volume, rather than the ten of its predecessor. A distinction was made between statutory and non-statutory elements of the curriculum. However, there was residual concern that some important areas of content had been lost at Key Stages 3 and 4. Above all there was little account of the principles underlying the new version of the curriculum. The revision was at best a pragmatic approach to a series of practical problems and it met with criticism from both advocates of traditional and more liberal approaches to the curriculum.

At Key Stage 3 the suggestion was that the prescribed content should occupy no more than 80 per cent of the available time. A shift in emphasis in the technology order gave information technology greater prominence, although it remained open to schools to deliver it across the curriculum. At Key Stage 4 greater flexibility was offered through the recommendation that the curriculum be slimmed by introducing short courses in modern foreign languages, this to be a minimum requirement in view of the fact that 'Britain's economic prosperity will depend increasingly on our relationships with our trading partners in both Europe and the wider world' (Dearing 1994). Technology too was distinguished as a strand of the nation's economic competitiveness: 'We have suffered from an inability to translate scientific discovery into wealth-generating industrial and commercial products.' For this reason technology remained a compulsory short course for all students, despite resistance from some quarters. This emphasis on international competitiveness was to become a recurrent theme of debates surrounding the evolution of education policy for the secondary phase throughout the 1990s. Allied to this was perhaps the most significant element of the Dearing review. He suggested that, unlike curricula in many other European countries, the curriculum for England and Wales had no vocational element and a strong recommendation of the report was that such a pathway be developed, in order to provide a progressive route to post-16 education and training. The final promise, widely welcomed, was a period of stability, with the firm proposal that the new curriculum would remain in place for a full five years. For a teaching profession that had had to adapt to a series of radical innovations with little time to prepare, this was a welcome commitment.

'Education, education, education'

The third version of the National Curriculum was published in draft form in 1999 under the aegis of 'New Labour', following the election of 1997. It set out initially to give an explicit account of the purposes of education:

Education must enable all students to respond positively to the opportunities and challenges of the rapidly changing world in which we live and work. In particular, they need to be prepared to respond as individuals, parents, workers and citizens to the rapid expansion of communication technologies, changing modes of employment, and new work and leisure patterns resulting from economic migration and the continued globalisation of the economy and society. (QCA 1999)

This is the underlying principle behind the commitment to 'education, education, education', which was the theme of the new administration. It also sets out clearly the purposes and concerns of that education, if only by omission. There is limited reference to the aesthetic, spiritual, moral, cultural and affective dimensions of education. The individual is of significance principally in relation to the economy and insofar as he or she may be economically active. Four key functions of the curriculum were articulated:

1 Establishing an entitlement.
2 Establishing standards.
3 Promoting continuity and cohesion.
4 Promoting public understanding.

To this extent, then, the new curriculum was underpinned by the guiding principles of the earlier versions. There were, however, some shifts in emphasis. The importance of technology, which has been a feature of all of the versions of the curriculum, is now focused formally on information and communications technology (ICT). This was in line with other ICT initiatives, including the National Grid for Learning, which set out to link all schools to the 'information highway', and a considerable investment in training practising teachers in the use of ICT through the New Opportunities Fund. If this was a new emphasis, a quite fresh element of the revised National Curriculum was the introduction of citizenship as a subject in its own right, and a statutory element of the secondary curriculum as from September 2002. The values underpinning the new school curriculum were articulated in this way:

Foremost is a belief in education as a route to: the well being and development of the individual; equality of opportunity for all; a healthy democracy; a productive economy; and a sustainable environment. Education should reflect the enduring values that contribute to these ends. These include valuing ourselves, our families, our relationships and the wider groups to which we belong, together with virtues such as justice, truthfulness and a sense of duty. (QCA 1999)

These sentiments could be interpreted as containing a new direction for the National Curriculum. They sit alongside a statement in each of the subject orders, which requires a more inclusive approach to the curriculum, one that would be less prescriptive and more flexible. However, other policy initiatives were introduced at around the same time that might compromise these aspirations.

Beyond curriculum policy there have been parallel developments in the structure and organisation of secondary schools. The City Technology Colleges (CTCs) were established in the early 1990s. Supported to some extent by private finance (although to nothing like the extent that had been planned by central government), these schools were intended to lead the way in curriculum development and in the use of technology as a basis for teaching across the curriculum. If there were only a handful of CTCs many more schools opted to become grant-maintained (GM). This was a route to diversity as it freed schools from local control; local authority schools were permitted to specialise in a particular curriculum area. Under New Labour these changes were consolidated, and the predicted abolition of GM status did not take place, although GM schools were in most cases redesignated as foundation schools. Curriculum specialism was encouraged through additional central funding for specialist colleges, with strengths in such areas as languages, performing arts, science and sport. All of these developments were part of the policy agenda, which set out to encourage diversity and parental choice.

'Education with character'

The Green Paper *Building on Success* (DfEE 2001) is a strong predictor of further change. It sets out 'to build on achievements to date to secure a step-change in secondary education'. The implication is clear, if regarded askance by those who feel that secondary education has changed considerably in the past decade. The new emphasis is on replicating the improvement in standards that has been achieved at Key Stage 2 through a fresh emphasis on Key Stage 3. There will be targets set for end of Key Stage outcomes and a focus on narrowing achievement gaps between schools in different circumstances. Above all, the aim is to achieve 'education with character', heralded more controversially at the launch of the paper as 'the end of the bog-standard comprehensive'. The vision is of 'every school having a distinctive mission and ethos and contributing to the community or wider education system'. The 'bog-standard comprehensive' has demonstrated itself in the majority of cases to be responsive, adaptable and capable of meeting the needs of a wide range of students. In the near future it may have to reinvent itself.

Vocational education

Approaches to vocational education through most of the 1980s were driven by the need to address the problem of mass youth unemployment. The Technical and Vocational Education Initiative (TVEI) was introduced in 1982 and followed in 1984 by the Certificate of Pre-Vocational Education (CPVE). These initiatives were designed to meet the needs of the 40 per cent of students who had no realistic prospect of success either in the General Certificate of Education (GCE) or in the Certificate of Secondary Education (CSE) – it was not until 1986 that they were merged in the General Certificate of Secondary Education. School-based vocational qualifications were designed to develop the technical and key skills that would be necessary for the workplace. However, it was precisely such qualifications as these that contributed to the confusion surrounding the secondary curriculum and led to the introduction of the National Curriculum. A multitude of awards and awarding bodies led to confusion for parents, employers and the wider public. It was also the case that they contributed to a two-tier system in the age 14–16 stage, which was replicated and reinforced in the age 16–19 phase. Once a student had opted for either the academic or vocational track it was difficult, even impossible, to switch. In his review of the curriculum Dearing referred to this problem and set out to address it. He did not advocate a fully vocational course, although General National Vocational Qualifications were introduced in Key Stage 4, via the piloting of a new foundation stage.

Specifically, the need was to 'broaden our concept of achievement' (Dearing 1994), a statement that contained tacit acceptance that the secondary curriculum pattern, based on ten traditional subjects, was failing to motivate a significant group within Key Stage 4 or respond to their particular talents and aspirations. However, the review did not advocate a full vocational course. It would be important to avoid a student

> making a premature commitment to one pathway thereby cutting out important options for the future . . . we need to consider nevertheless whether a vocational and/or occupational element in a more broadly based education post-14 is an option which will serve better to develop some young people into capable and sensible men and women than an education that does not offer that possibility. (Dearing 1994)

This approach went some way towards meeting concerns about a curriculum that was perceived by many teachers to be failing to meet the needs of the less academic students and failing to engage those who were disaffected. Recognition of this has come relatively late in the evolution of the curriculum, but it is currently being addressed. Under the most recent statutory orders secondary schools are permitted to disapply aspects of Key Stage 4 for identified pupils. Such pupils may spend part of the week, for instance, at a local further education college pursuing subjects such as vehicle maintenance and training in the building trades, or on other forms of work experience. But the review did not recommend a full occupational route in Key Stage 4 for a number of reasons.

First, and in addition to the concerns expressed about narrowing the range of options for some students, some aspects of the context had now changed. Technology as a subject had reinvented itself, it 'leavened a subject-orientated curriculum' (Graham 1993). The initial impetus was 'to remove the grip of woodwork and metalwork for boys and needlework and domestic science for girls' (*ibid.*). Furthermore, this new subject would be taken by all, whereas in the past able students had not chosen the craft subjects. Newly defined, technology required that students would: 'identify a problem or a need, design a solution, make whatever was required, and then evaluate the outcome in aesthetic, commercial and environmental terms' (Graham 1993). The process of redefining technology as a subject area was immensely controversial, as it cut across the work of teachers who had previously identified themselves as working in discrete subject areas of home economics, woodwork, metalwork and technical drawing. In its new formulation it drew on the skills of all these areas of the curriculum, but craft and production were no longer at the heart of the subject.

Technology no longer set out to prepare students for specific occupations, not least because of the changing nature of employment, from manufacturing to the service economy, and the demise of traditional craft apprenticeships. The 1980s saw very high levels of youth unemployment. Schemes such as the Youth Opportunities Scheme and Youth Training Scheme were designed to meet the needs of school leavers. In addition to the formal elements of the curriculum, work experience became a staple of Key Stage 4 for all students, who were expected to begin to develop the skills needed in the workplace. Ultimately, however, the recognition that contemporary circumstances demanded higher skill levels and a better qualified workforce led to the expectation of much higher participation in post-16 education and training than had been the case. Inevitably this led to a redefining of the 16–19 curriculum.

The 16–19 curriculum

Prior to the introduction of the National Curriculum, 16–19 education was defined in terms of advanced level GCE. The model was one that successively filtered out the less academic. Until the mid to late 1970s only 20 per cent of any given cohort would take ordinary level GCE, 15 per cent would progress into the sixth form to take A level and 10 per cent would go on to university. Following his work on the 5–16 curriculum Dearing was asked to follow up with a review of 16–19 provision. His report (1996) was not a curriculum review but a review of the qualifications framework for 16- to 19-year-olds. The difference is significant. It reflects the concern over the proliferation of hundreds of awards. There is no such thing as a 'curriculum' for the post-compulsory age range. Provision is dictated to an extent by individual choice and defined by sets of subject frameworks, a statutory 'core' for A level and sets of specifications for a wide range of vocational and occupational awards. The Dearing review was the forerunner of Curriculum 2000, and attempted a more systematic account of the provision post-16.

The review was significant in that it applied not just to schools but to all the institutions that young people move on to after compulsory school age, including further education and sixth form colleges and government sponsored training. It applied to those in employment and those not in any form of education or training. The Labour government adopted the principles of the review. It defined three broad pathways for the 16–19 phase. They were the traditional academic route leading to A and AS levels, a vocational route and an occupational route. These routes were to be integrated into a scheme of National Awards at foundation, intermediate and advanced levels. The aim was to achieve greater transparency and wider understanding of the range of awards and to introduce greater flexibility for students. In what is a radical move, Curriculum 2000 incorporates key skills, these skills to be certificated separately from subject qualifications.

In summary, Curriculum 2000 consists of:

• New A level syllabuses, structured into six units. They may be taken in 'linear mode' or in modular form according to whether the assessment is at the end or staged across the course.

- A new AS (advanced subsidiary) qualification. This consists of the first half of the content of a full A level or three units. The aim is twofold, to make a smoother transition from GCSE to A level and to discourage early specialisation. Students will be encouraged to take four AS levels in the first year of a two-year course.
- New extension papers aimed at the most able of the cohort but designed to be accessible to more students than the former S level papers.
- A revised GNVQ to be available at foundation, intermediate and advanced levels. The new GNVQ advanced level will consist of six units.
- Key skills qualifications in communication, application of number and the use of information technology.

The aim of these changes is to break down the divide between the academic and vocational pathways. The new six-unit GNVQ permits students to pursue a mixed programme of A level and GNVQ courses, which has been constrained before by the fact that GNVQ has occupied a full 12 units or two A level slots on the timetable.

Early indications are that these approaches have created fresh problems. Teachers working in the 16–19 phase had very little time to prepare for the new AS levels, as the syllabuses for some subjects were published only weeks before the first students began their programme in September 2000. There are concerns that the new broader curriculum contains too much content and that time for individual study and for the extracurricular activities that have enhanced the learning experience of sixth form study has been lost. There is little evidence to date that large numbers of students have taken advantage of the option of following a mixed programme of academic and vocational courses. Above all, the load of assessment with the modular schemes being introduced wholesale, alongside the new AS courses, has given rise to the criticism that students spend disproportionate amounts of time being tested, at the expense of being taught.

Further curriculum change is heralded the consultation document '14–19: Extending Opportunities, Raising Standards' (DfES 2002) which proposes significant change to the secondary curriculum. The rationale for the proposals is the need to give belated recognition to vocational qualifications. The argument is supported by international comparisons which show lower levels of participation in the UK in education and training than in France and Germany. Key features of the consultation are the introduction of a Matriculation Diploma to be achieved by the age of 19, and individual learning plans as a means of monitoring progress. Possibly the most significant proposal is that GCSE should become a 'progress check' rather than an end in itself. In order to achieve significant progress a coherent approach involving schools and colleges will be needed throughout the 14–19 phase.

Assessment

A major underpinning argument for the very existence of a National Curriculum was the need to raise standards. Many claims have been made subsequently about the improvement in standards at each of the Key Stages. However, it is hard to discern what the nature of that improvement might be without better comparative data. The amend-

ments and reviews of the curriculum that have taken place over the decade of its implementation in secondary schools mean that there is little reliable evidence as to just how
things have improved. Certainly the numbers of passes at A to C at GCSE have risen
year on year. However, there remains considerable discussion about comparability of
standards over time. What is unquestionably the case is that more is being measured.
Indeed, one of the prime criticisms of the curriculum and its assessment has been that
it is reductive, limiting learning to areas of knowledge that can be readily assessed.

The Task Group on Assessment and Testing (DES 1988) carried out the initial work
on assessment within the National Curriculum. This document (the TGAT Report)
placed considerable emphasis on a variety of assessment methods and the importance
of formative teacher assessment. However, this emphasis was to shift in the implementation and as National Curriculum assessment began to be used to compare
school performance as much as to inform learning. The framework is relatively simple.
Compulsory secondary schooling falls into Key Stage 3 (age 11–14 years) and Key
Stage 4 (age 14–16 years). This was established during the consultation phase and has
not been controversial, since it matched the common pattern of primary/secondary
transfer in most (although not all) authorities, as well as the pattern of GCSE courses.

Each subject of the National Curriculum is divided into Attainment Targets (ATs).
Each AT was arranged hierarchically on ten levels. In the early version of the National
Curriculum each level had its statement of attainment, broken down into sub-
statements. To progress from one level to the next required that all elements contained
within the statement had to be met. This proved in practice to be cumbersome and
bureaucratic. The refusal of secondary English teachers to carry out the statutory
assessment at Key Stage 3 was one factor that led to the Dearing review. In the revised
version, level descriptors were introduced with the concept of a 'best fit', whereby a
student could be assigned to a level. After 1995 the problems of reconciling GCSE performance with Levels 9 and 10 of the new curriculum were recognised and the scale
became an eight-point one, with GCSE accounting for performance in Key Stage 4.
These moves were welcomed, but concerns remained.

Some of these are general and apply to both primary and secondary schools. For teachers they have to do with the broad issues of what it is that is being tested and the uses to
which assessment outcomes are put, in the form of league tables and other measures of
quality. For pupils there are issues of motivation, especially for pupils with specific learning difficulties who may only progress one or two levels during their secondary career.
However, there are some factors of particular significance to the secondary stage. At the
lower end, there is increasing pressure from central government to review progress in
Key Stage 3. There is a perception that the improvement in standards achieved in Key
Stage 2 is being lost in secondary schools. One approach to this is to introduce further
tests, at the end of Year 7, to assess the extent to which progress is being maintained in
the secondary phase. This suggestion has been met with caution by teachers in view of
the increasing burden of assessment on the system, particularly in the secondary years of
schooling. At the upper end of the range the concerns are even stronger. Most students
are now being tested formally in every school year from age 14 to 18. This is having a
considerable impact on curriculum time and the ethos of secondary schools through loss

of teaching time and teaching space, as gyms and assembly halls are taken out of use for examination purposes. Although the National Curriculum for secondary schools is an established fact, its assessment continues to be controversial.

Inspection

Inspection and assessment have been closely linked as controversial elements of the changes in the secondary system since the Education Reform Act of 1988. One of the most disputed uses to which assessment outcomes have been put is the ranking of schools' performance in league tables according to pupils' performance at the end of Key Stages 3 and 4. This, in combination with the publication of Ofsted reports, has been a central feature of successive governments' attempts to raise standards and to ensure that all schools reach the standards of the best.

Prior to 1992, school inspection was carried out by local authority inspectors, and by Her Majesty's Inspectors (HMI). However, as the complement of HMI at the time was 480, a secondary school might expect to be inspected only once every ten years at the most. This situation changed with the creation of the Office for Standards in Education (Ofsted) in 1992, which was charged with the duty of a regular inspection programme for all maintained schools. The relevant section of the Education (Schools) Act 1992, which established Ofsted, requires inspectors to report on:

- the quality of the education provided by the school;
- the educational standards achieved in the school;
- whether the financial resources made available to the school are managed efficiently;
- the spiritual, moral and cultural development of pupils in the school (Ofsted 1995).

Inspections follow a standard framework and are supported by analysis of quantitative data, using a standard set of criteria. Subsequently a full report is produced, which must be circulated in summary form to all parents of pupils in the school and which:

- evaluates the school according to the framework;
- identifies the strengths and weaknesses of the school;
- gives the appropriate authority for the school a clear agenda for the action needed to improve it.

The new requirements led to a major recruitment drive to train inspection teams to carry out the massively expanded workload. In practice, the work was carried out extensively by former HMI and local authority inspectors, who, once trained, tendered for individual inspection contracts. The initial inspection cycle was for each secondary school to be inspected once every four years, with schools being given five terms' notice of an impending inspection. Each inspection team is led by a registered inspector, and each member is responsible for the inspection of different aspects of the curriculum and other areas, such as special educational needs provision.

In themselves the aims of Ofsted inspections appear sound. They were, however, contentious from the start. This was partly due to concern in the teaching profession about the nature of inspection teams. The inclusion of lay inspectors was an innovation that many teachers felt was intended to denigrate their professionalism. Anxieties were also heightened due to the shift in the focus of the inspection model. Whereas LEA inspections had tended to combine an advisory role with that of inspection, Ofsted inspectors were specifically precluded from offering advice. Professional dialogue was replaced by what many perceived to be externally imposed and punitive inspection. Individual teachers felt threatened and there was substantial evidence of high levels of stress in schools in the lengthy preparatory stages and during the week of the inspection itself. Because the framework was centrally decided and administered objectively, a further concern was that it failed to take into account local conditions, such as those in areas of high social deprivation. Finally, the personality of Her Majesty's Chief Inspector of Schools, Chris Woodhead, was a significant factor. His public pronouncements on the inadequacies of the profession contributed to a public perception that education was indeed failing, and undermined the morale of teachers.

If teachers hoped that the incoming Labour government would replace him in 1997 they were disappointed. However, there were developments in inspection and review of school performance. It was suggested that fairness of inspection might be enhanced by taking into account 'value-added' measures to assess the extent to which a school is enhancing the outcome for its pupils, no matter their ability. Such moves have met with a degree of approval, although they are problematic in themselves. They raise issues about the validity of the baseline assessments on which they are based. They can also be invalid for schools that have transient populations, which is the case in many inner-city areas. Conversely, some schools that have demonstrated high achievement at the end of Key Stage 3 have found it hard to add significant additional value in Key Stage 4. After two initial rounds of inspection, after 1999 there has been a move towards longer periods between inspections, a shorter period of notice (now two terms) and a focus on progression against the action plan developed after the previous inspection.

Models of inspection have shifted in line with overall policy. Schools that have 'failed' the inspection are put on special measures and given specific targets for improvement to be achieved within strict time limits. The local education authority (LEA) and the Department for Education and Skills (DfES) will review the action plans, and if no progress is made then the school can be subject to 'Fresh Start' procedures that include the appointment of a new headteacher, governors and staff. These measures come under the remit of the Standards and Effectiveness Unit of the DfES. The unit is charged not only with improvement of failing schools but with a range of measures designed to secure school improvement. They include standards at Key Stage 3, Beacon Schools, Specialist Schools, the National Literacy Strategy and the National Numeracy Strategy. The resignation of Chris Woodhead in 2000 saw the beginning of an improvement in relations between teachers and the inspectorate. In addition, it is recognised that Ofsted has generated useful data on a range of topics, including attainment by girls and boys in the secondary phase and language across the curriculum, that have informed planning and policy development. After nearly a decade of confrontation and mutual recrimination it is possible that a new phase is beginning, when schools might begin to be able to use their external reports alongside the range of other data and material available to them to foster a culture of self-evaluation.

Regional variations

Secondary schools in England and Wales are covered by almost the same version of the National Curriculum, which is managed by the QCA in England and by ACCAC in Wales.

In Northern Ireland the Department of Education has a policy of encouraging integrated education. The system is broadly selective, with a system of grammar and high schools. Grant-maintained schools receive grant aid and must demonstrate that they set out to achieve a balance of students from Catholic and Protestant backgrounds. The secondary curriculum includes English, maths, science, technology, the environment and society, creative and expressive studies, religious education and language studies. There are also cross-curricular themes, which reflect the particular circumstances of Northern Ireland. They are 'education for mutual understanding', cultural heritage, information technology, health education, economic awareness and careers education.

The Scottish system differs most markedly from that for England and Wales. Transition from the primary to the secondary stage is at 12. Most schools are comprehensive, although there is an independent sector, as elsewhere in the UK. In the Standard Grades S3 and S4, which cover the 14–16 age range, the curriculum is organised not by subjects but through eight 'modes': language and communication studies; mathematical studies and applications; scientific studies and applications; social and environmental awareness; technological activities and applications; creative and aesthetic activities; physical education; religious and moral education.

The tone of the curriculum documents for Northern Ireland and for Scotland differs markedly from that for England and Wales. While sharing the concerns for breadth, balance and progression that underpin the curriculum for England and Wales, the Scottish curriculum, for example, makes explicit reference to the importance of partnerships and successful good practice within individual schools and across local authorities. The tone is collaborative rather than prescriptive.

Welsh schools are inspected on a five-yearly cycle by ESTYN (previously OHMCI). In Northern Ireland schools are inspected every seven years by the Education and Training Inspectorate, which advises the Department of Education for Northern Ireland on each school's quality. In Scotland inspections are managed by HMI on behalf of the Scottish Executive Education Department. The outcomes or 'evaluations' are published and are supported by material for schools, parents and governors, titled 'How Good Is Our School?'. The emphasis is on self-evaluation.

POINTS FOR DISCUSSION

1 What are the essential components of a National Curriculum for secondary age students at the start of the twenty-first century?
2 How might vocational education be incorporated progressively into statutory education between the ages of 11 and 18?

3 One of the proposals to decrease the burden of assessment in the secondary phase has been to do away with GCSEs. What is your view of this proposal? What alternative suggestions do you have as to how assessment might be rationalised?

4 Would it be desirable for some elements of the curriculum models for Northern Ireland and for Scotland to be adopted in England and Wales?

INTERNET SITES

Department for Education and Skills (DfES): www.dfes.gov.uk

Qualifications and Curriculum Authority: www.qca.org.uk

Ofsted: www.ofsted.gov.uk

Department of Education for Northern Ireland: www.deni.gov.uk

Learning and Teaching Scotland: www.LTScotland.com

Awdurdod Cymwysterau Cwricwlwm Asesu Cymru (Qualifications, Curriculum and Assessment Authority for Wales): www.accac.org.uk

REFERENCES AND FURTHER READING

Dearing, R. (1994) *The National Curriculum and Its Assessment: Final Report on the Review*. London: Schools Curriculum and Assessment Authority.

Dearing, R. (1996) *Review of Qualifications for 16–19-year-olds: Full Report*. London: Schools Curriculum and Assessment Authority.

DES/Welsh Office (1988) *National Curriculum Task Group on Assessment and Testing: a Report*. London: DES.

DfEE (2001) *Schools: Building on Success*. London: DfEE.

Graham, D. (1993) *A Lesson for Us All. The Making of the National Curriculum*. London: Routledge.

National Curriculum Council (1993) *A Curriculum Perspective: 14–19 Education in Schools and Colleges*. London: NCC.

O'Connor, M. (ed.) (1987) *Curriculum at the Crossroads: an Account of the SCDC National Conference on Aspects of Curriculum Change*. London: School Curriculum Development Committee.

Ofsted (1995) *Guidance on the Inspection of Secondary Schools*. London: The Stationery Office.

QCA (1999) *The Review of the National Curriculum in England: the Consultation Materials*. London: QCA.

Wragg. E. (1995) *The Ted Wragg Guide to Education*. Oxford: Butterworth-Heinemann.

CHAPTER 8

Further Education

Linda Merricks

CHAPTER SUMMARY

This chapter assesses:

- The further education sector in Britain today.
- The changes that result from the Learning and Skills Act 2000.
- The creation of the Learning and Skills Council and the Adult Learning Inspectorate in England and Wales.
- Regional variations in further education provision.

Introduction

Further education (FE) is currently higher on the agenda of the government and the funding agencies than it has ever been before. Traditionally the poor relation of the higher education (HE) sector, FE is viewed as increasingly important because the provision it offers is seen to fit closely with the government agenda of improving the attainment of basic skills for all the community, improving the skills and competences of those in work and providing the unemployed with the skills and training to enable them to find work. The FE sector provides education and training in these areas, as well as many others, and changes in funding and organisation over recent years are providing opportunities for growth and development.

The FE sector includes many 16- to 19-year-olds and all post-compulsory education except that undertaken in universities, which is described as the HE sector. However, some HE takes place in FE colleges and some non-HE work occurs in HE institutions, especially in continuing education departments. In this chapter an attempt is made to navigate through the essential distinctions between different agencies, even if some more complicated areas are simplified. The sector consists of colleges of further education, tertiary colleges, sixth form colleges and specialist colleges (of agriculture, art and design and designated). Post-19 education also takes place in local education authority (LEA) adult and community education, in university continuing education departments (CE) and through the Workers' Educational Association (WEA). There are also a number of private training providers. Increasingly, work-based learning of different kinds provides opportunities for study. There are differences of scale and curriculum throughout these institutions and courses, and some work in partnership with each other.

FE providers

The provision and funding of further and continuing education have been complicated because of the numbers of providers and of funding agencies. There is overlap in what is provided and in many instances differences and divisions of responsibility are the result of historical events rather than any strategic planning.

Further education colleges provide training and education for those over 19 and in some cases over 16. They provide a wide range of courses that can lead to qualifications in academic and vocational fields. These are described below.

Since the Further and Higher Education Act 1992, FE colleges have been incorporated and their funding comes from a number of sources, of which the most important are tuition fees and the Further Education Funding Council (FEFC). The funding methodology of the FEFC was complicated but tried to reflect the real costs of the students. It was based on the 1992 FEFC Report *Funding Learning*. This report suggested that funding should be related to three separate stages of learning. The first is the recruitment and guidance of students on entry, the second is the teaching and guidance throughout the course and the third is the achievement of defined learning goals, normally a qualification. The funding regime attempted to remove regional differences in funding, some of which were very longstanding, and to impose a national standard. Convergence could only take place over time and complex mechanisms were developed to speed the process as far as possible.

Although the funding of FE colleges has become a part of the duties of the Learning and Skills Council (LSC) – described in detail below – it is anticipated that no major changes will be made in the system immediately. However, there is concern that the colleges will face greater local competition for funding under the new system from other educational providers and that LSC members may not initially have the expertise to understand the needs of the sector.

Courses provided by the LEA are mostly what are familiarly seen as 'evening classes'. They take place in adult education institutes of many kinds and provide a range of leisure courses, taken primarily for interest only, and vocational courses leading to various different awards described below. They were, until April 2001, funded primarily by the FEFC and by tuition fees. As with the FE colleges, this changed with the introduction of LSC.

The Learning and Skills Act 2000 removes the distinction between Schedule 2 and non-Schedule 2 courses for adults. Schedule 2 courses were described as 'vocational', or leading to a qualification, while non-Schedule 2 courses were 'non-vocational' or 'leisure' courses. The difference was enshrined in the Further and Higher Education Act 1992, which stipulated that vocational courses and those leading to a qualification should be funded by the FEFC, while the other courses should be funded by the LEA.

The removal of the division is welcome, as it created artificial barriers between different courses, especially when they were directed at adults whose primary aim was to learn, not necessarily to achieve a qualification.

The WEA was founded to provide university level courses for working-class people in 1903. These aims have proved difficult and in many ways the WEA has provided adult education very like that of the LEAs. Since 1992 its courses have been brought closer and the remaining substantive distinction, WEA branches run by volunteer members, has been in danger of erosion.

Like the LEAs, the WEA has come under the FEFC for most of the funding for its courses as one of the outcomes of the Further and Higher Education Act 1992, and as a result has come under pressure to conform more closely to the requirements of the FEFC. This funding is also transferred to the LSC.

Continuing education also takes place in universities, usually in specific continuing education departments, which are often the old extramural departments. Until 1992, these departments provided courses very like those of the LEAs and WEA, appealing to the interests of adult learners and aiming to provide a liberal adult education, but funded through the Higher Education Funding Council for England (HEFCE). The provisions of the 1992 Act demanded that, to continue this funding, the courses should lead to awards at HE level, and that this should be demonstrated by accreditation. Since then, many departments have not only accredited their courses, but have also developed awards, normally certificate (level 1), diploma (level 2) and degree (level 3). Many courses at level 1 are still designed to appeal to the interests of adult learners. The HEFCE and tuition fees fund CE courses.

There are myriad other courses in what may loosely be called continuing education, including specialist courses within or alongside the FE colleges. In addition, work-based learning is growing in importance. This description applies to courses of study taken within the workplace and leading to a qualification related to that work. There are many, and growing, ways in which this can be done, but most courses are seen as complementary arrangements between a university or college and employer. Funding depends on the precise nature of the course.

The development of the *Learning and Skills Council* is designed to simplify much of this maze of funding and other regimes. The LSC was established as the result of plans set out by the government in June 1999, in the *Learning to Succeed* White Paper, and formalised in the Learning and Skills Act 2000, to modernise and radically to reform the management of post-16 education and training provision in England. It formally undertook powers in April 2001. David Blunkett (then Secretary of State for Education and Employment) said at its launch, 'The Council has a huge agenda to make a powerful and sustained effort to raise levels of skills and knowledge to world class standards.'

The remit of the LSC is the provision of proper facilities for education and training (other than higher education) for those aged 16–19 and of those over 19. It is also responsible for the encouragement of education and training for these groups. Its creation will affect 417 FE colleges, 1,800 schools and over 2,000 private training providers. It will also affect the delivery of 17,000 qualifications from 4,000 awarding bodies. These figures reflect both the scale of the task and the complexity of further education in England. The LSC is represented by 47 local Learning and Skills Councils, each of which is responsible for its own area.

A welcome new development in the organisation of FE and HE is the inclusion of advice and guidance within the remit of the local LSCs, so that it can be seen as an important aspect of teaching, especially as increasing numbers of adults with a variety of qualifications are seeking education and training. The Information, Advice and Guidance (IAG) initiative was launched by the DfEE in 1999 to coordinate the services already available around the country, in association with the Careers Service, the Employment Service and voluntary and community bodies. It became the responsibility of the local LSCs on 1 April 2001.

Curriculum

The definition of 'curriculum' needs to be addressed, as the word can be seen as misleadingly simple. At its broadest, it can stand for almost everything that happens in the educational setting, containing all the elements of the learning process that the student experiences. While this definition can become so broad as to lose its value, it is a convenient place to start the discussion, as it guards against too narrow a view. A more useful broad definition stands for an educational, or educationalist's, view of learning, and so represents the professional's role in the organisation of students' learning. This points to recent developments in theoretical models or ideologies of curriculum that emphasise student-centred learning models. There is a wide literature on the subject of curriculum, which will not be addressed here. Instead, we will concentrate on a narrower definition that refers to the body of knowledge or skills that the teacher or institution intends to be transmitted. This definition focuses on the formal provision of courses, gives some indication of teaching and assessment methods and reflects the intention of bringing about specific learning outcomes.

The range of subjects covered in the FE sector is vast and leads to a wide range of qualifications and awards.

- FE colleges cover a very wide range of subjects and qualifications, including both academic and vocational courses. They lead to GCE, GCSE and GNVQ and other vocational qualifications.
- Sixth form colleges were designed to teach academic subjects. However, their scope has been broadened to include a similar range of subjects, so their courses too can lead to the award of GCE, GCSE and GNVQ.
- As their names suggest, the specialist colleges have a more limited remit. In addition to agriculture and arts and design, they also cater for working men and women, women only and other groups of adult learners.
- LEA courses are more varied. They cover the subjects offered by the colleges, but in addition provide leisure and recreational courses in subjects from art appreciation to zoos. Again, the course can lead to the awards listed above, but the leisure courses do not normally lead to any qualification or award.

- CE departments teach only academic subjects at HE level. These courses can lead to certificates and diplomas of higher education and to bachelor degrees.
- WEA courses did not, traditionally, lead to an award. However, one of the effects of the shift in funding to the FEFC, described above, has been an added emphasis on classes either with a vocational outcome or addressing specific educational needs, like basic skills or access classes.
- Other, often private, providers can offer a wide range of awards, which are too numerous to list here.

This range of qualifications requires equally broad curricula. However, there are certain elements that are common to all providers. These are increasingly based on outcomes models of learning and normally include a description of the aims and the objectives of the course.

The *aims* are the general descriptions of the intentions of the course, and have been criticised for this generality. They are normally couched in the language of 'to develop', 'to encourage', 'to raise awareness', 'to familiarise', and may refer to an increase in knowledge, an improvement of skills and competences, personal growth and reflective practices. The balance of these aims will vary according to the kind of qualification at the end of the course. A levels, or HE work, will tend to contain more emphasis on subject knowledge, access courses on personal growth and NVQs on competences. Aims might be:

- to develop the ability to evaluate critically;
- to encourage reflectivity;
- to be familiar with critical views of the development of the novel.

In contrast to these, the *objectives* are what the student can actually do, or has achieved, after the course. It should be possible for the student to demonstrate, through the assessment procedures of the course, that the objectives have been attained. Objectives are normally expressed in terms like 'describe', 'distinguish', 'identify', and relate closely to the subject knowledge and specific subject skills of the course. For example, behavioural objectives to be achieved at the end of a course on the history of the 1960s might include the student being able to:

- give examples of changes in youth culture during the 1960s;
- distinguish national patterns of behaviour;
- identify major shifts in attitudes to questions of race during the period.

Cognitive objectives could be to:

- review the accounts from different historical perspectives;
- discriminate between the different ideological positions;
- be familiar with the explanations given for the causes of the changes experienced during this decade.

To ensure that these learning outcomes are achieved, appropriate assessment methods are needed. These are discussed below.

Assessment

Assessment describes the process by which the achievement of students can be judged. It can take a number of forms, but will involve measurement against three kinds of references:

- where the measurement is against explicit, absolute standards, as in, for example, NVQ programmes, it is described as *criteria referencing*;
- where the measurement is relative to the achievement of all who took part in the assessment, as in GCSEs, it is called *norm referencing*;
- where the comparison is with earlier work by the learner, and measures the progress of the individual, as in some parts of access courses, it is referred to as *ipsative assessment*.

However, the three are not mutually exclusive and on occasions all three kinds of assessment may be found in the same course.

There are three main reasons for assessment. These are:

- to diagnose learning needs by identifying existing capabilities and setting realistic learning goals for the learner. An important part of the process should be to recognise additional learning support and to ensure that this is available. It should also confirm existing capabilities and competences.
- to select for progression. This is most often seen when potential students are applying for HE courses. The results of previous assessments play an important role in selection for university. It can also be used when learners move from one level to another within a system.
- to certificate achievement. The accreditation of a learner's achievement demonstrates the attainment of a particular standard.

Assessment can be formative or summative. *Formative* assessment is designed to provide supportive feedback on the learner's progress and achievement, and often will not lead to a formal grade. Formative assessment is normally used most during the early stages of a course or programme of learning. *Summative* assessment provides the formal grading of the learning experience and may offer little if any feedback. Formal, unseen examinations are probably the clearest example of summative assessment. The distinction between the two kinds of assessment need not be as stark as this suggests. For instance, many students request grades even from formative assessments, while feedback may be given on examination performance.

For some formal qualifications, the examining body imposes summative assessments; for example, in the three most common qualifications found in FE. NVQ assessment is against performance criteria set by national training organisations. While there is flexibility in how the learner demonstrates the attainment of the criteria, the criteria themselves are inflexible. This reflects the criteria-referenced model described above. GNVQs are similar. They are awarded by City and Guilds, by the Royal Society of Arts and by Edexcel. The final awards are criteria-referenced like NVQs, but there is an emphasis on formative assessment during the earlier part of the courses, when a portfolio of evidence is assembled by the learner. Guidance on this is an essential part of the process. GCSE and GCE A level assessments are somewhat different. Assessment consists of internal assessment of course work and external assessment of examinations. The internal assessment is moderated, and the examinations marked, by one of the six examining bodies. The balance between the internal and external assessments is set by the Qualifications and Curriculum Authority (QCA), which also provides guidance on subject content, assessment and grading of the courses. Where the assessment for these qualifications differs most markedly from the vocational qualifications model is in its emphasis on norm-referenced grading.

For all learners, a learning outcomes model of learning needs assessment methods that reflect the achievement of those outcomes. As described above, the learning outcomes model may be varied, comprising subject knowledge, skills and personal development. It is not sufficient merely to set examination questions and essays to cover all outcomes. Assessment strategies to reflect learning outcomes need to be varied and imaginative, and may well comprise group and individual work, learning journals, interactive presentations and the more familiar written and verbal accounts of learning. For these innovative assessment methods, evaluation demands careful thought. Self and peer assessment may play an important role, and feedback will be essential. These kinds of assessment are particularly appropriate for adult learners, some of whom will have unhappy memories of conventional assessment methods.

Inspection

The inspection regimes for the sector are different for the various parts, and, like funding, have changed with the establishment of the Learning and Skills Council, which is responsible, with the Office for Standards in Education (Ofsted) for future inspections. Before April 2001, the system was:

- The FEFC inspectorate, established by the 1992 Act, visited the FE colleges. The inspectorate visited FE colleges over a four-year cycle. The first of these was September 1993 to July 1997, and in this period all colleges in further education were visited.
- LEA provision came within the responsibilities of Ofsted.

After April 2001 the system is:

- There is a new unified inspectorate with responsibility for inspecting all provision for adults in colleges, adult education and training, the Adult Learning Inspectorate (ALI). The remit of the Inspectorate is described in its prospectus as 'inspecting a wide range of learning activities'. These include: (a) work-based learning provided to people aged 16–18 and all adults; (b) education in colleges provided to people over 19; (c) learning activities accessed through the University for Industry, *learndirect*; (d) adult and community learning; (e) learning in prisons; (f) training delivered by the Employment Service under the arrangements of the New Deal.

- The ALI works with Ofsted on joint inspections of education in FE colleges and on inspections of particular geographical areas. Ofsted inspects provision for 16- to 19-year-olds in colleges.
- All university departments, including CE, are the responsibility of the Quality Assurance Agency (QAA) and will be visited in the cycle beginning in 2002.

In the new structure there is an emphasis on local planning, which the outgoing FEFC 'considered would be of benefit to colleges', but within a common inspection framework. In their visits, the external agencies are looking for similar indications of the quality of teaching and learning within the institution and across institutions. These indications include support for students, general resources, quality assurance, governance and management.

Agencies for the development of teaching, while not strictly inspecting bodies, will also have an increasing role in assuring and developing the quality of provision in the sector. At present, there are two main agencies, the Further Education National Training Organisation (FENTO) and the Institute for Learning and Teaching in Higher Education (ILT).

- *Standards for teaching and supporting learning in further education in England and Wales* was produced by the Further Education Staff Development Forum (FESDF), a predecessor of FENTO, in 1999. The purpose of the standards is: (a) to provide an agreed set of standards that can be used to inform the design of accredited awards for FE teachers; (b) to provide standards that can be used to inform professional development activity within FE; (c) to assist institution-based activities, such as recruitment, appraisal and the identification of training needs.
- The ILT was set up in 1999 and is committed to: (a) enhancing the status of teaching; (b) improving the experience of learning; (c) supporting innovation in higher education. There is ongoing debate about the role of the ILT and how its aims can be achieved, with considerable resistance from the HE sector to any kind of external regulation of its staffing procedures. Despite these difficulties, the ILT has claimed a successful beginning, with 5,400 members and a further 6,000 applications awaiting processing in July 2001.

It is too soon to judge how effective these new bodies will be. However, the general move towards uniformity across what has been a widely disparate sector, with what has seemed to be an equally disconnected range of inspection systems, is a welcome beginning.

Regional variations

As explained in the previous section, there is a strong impetus within the LSC to remove regional anomalies and to develop a common inspection framework across England. However, there are some differences between the countries of the United Kingdom that already existed and will remain.

The Scottish Further Education Funding Council (SFEFC) took up its responsibilities on 1 July 2000. The functions of the SFEFC include:

*   responsibility for funding Scotland's 47 FE colleges;
*   monitoring the financial health of the sector;
*   offering guidance to colleges;
*   advising the First Minister on funding matters and supporting his duty to secure adequate and efficient provision of further education in Scotland.

The SFEFC is, with the Scottish Higher Education Funding Council, supported by three directorates. These are Funding, Financial Appraisal and Monitoring, and Strategy and Corporate Affairs. The latter comprises four branches: Corporate Affairs, Human Resources and Corporate Services, Strategic Planning, and Quality and Learning Innovation. Quality assessment and improvement in teaching and learning is the main area of responsibility for the Quality and Learning Innovation branch. Quality assurance in the colleges will, for the first three years at least, be carried out by Her Majesty's Inspectorate.

In Northern Ireland, responsibility for FE and HE lies with the Northern Ireland Executive Department of Higher and Further Education, Training and Employment, Further and Higher Education Division. It acts in consultation with the Further Education Consultative Committee. Its key objectives are:

*   to develop a culture of lifelong learning;
*   to promote wider access to and greater participation in further and higher education, particularly from groups previously underrepresented;
*   to promote the provision of educational programmes that meet the needs of individuals, employers and local communities;
*   to improve quality and performance in the further and higher education sectors;
*   to enhance the contribution of the further and higher education sectors to the regional economy;
*   to ensure the effective administration of the student awards system.

Conclusion

Any conclusion to this chapter can be only tentative at this time. The changes currently taking place should lead to a more coherent system and to improved educational provision. However, there are also dangers and these could challenge some areas of work, especially where new competitors appear to share what will remain limited funding. Despite these anxieties, the initial signs are at least optimistic. Perhaps by the spring of

2002, when the regional LSCs begin to apply new funding systems and methodologies, some sense of the future direction can be assessed. For now, in the summer of 2001, only questions about future developments can be posed.

Regional institutions are at present at an early stage. Until decisions on funding are taken by the LSCs, comparisons are impossible.

However, a common purpose can be seen in the emphasis on the importance of the FE sector, on vocational courses and on contributions to the economy.

POINTS FOR DISCUSSION

1 The picture painted of funding is complex and the effects of the establishment of the LSCs are not, at the time of writing, clear. Discuss your experiences of the changes and compare them with what has been described.
2 Do learning outcomes models of curriculum development clarify what is to be learnt? What effects do these methods have on the reflectivity of the teacher?
3 How can learning outcomes be assessed by (a) formative assessment and (b) summative assessment?
4 What are the effects of external inspections? Do they support teaching?
5 The essential point for discussion on regional variations is how the models have developed during the period between the writing of this chapter and your reading it.

INTERNET SITES

Adult Learning Inspectorate: www.ali.gov.uk
Department for Education and Skills: www.dfes.gov.uk
Further Education Development Agency: www.feda.ac.uk
Further Education Funding Council: www.fefc.ac.uk
Learning and Skills Act: www.hmso.gov.uk/acts
Learning and Skills Council: www.lsc.gov.uk
Learning and Skills Development Agency: www.lsagency.org.uk
Lifelong Learning: www.lifelonglearning.dfes.gov.uk
National Institute of Adult Continuing Education: www.niace.org.uk
Northern Ireland Executive Department of Further and Higher Education: www.nics.gov.uk/mainhfe
Office for Standards in Education: www.ofsted.gov.uk/indexa.htm
Qualifications and Curriculum Authority: www.open.gov.uk/qca/
Quality Assurance Agency: www.qaa.ac.uk
Scottish Further Education Funding Council: www.sfefc.ac.uk
Workers' Educational Association: www.wea.org.uk

FURTHER READING

Since the LSC is very new, little analysis of its progress has been possible. Therefore the websites and the educational press are essential sources of information. They include:

Times Educational Supplement
Guardian Education
Adults Learning

Although the Further Education Funding Council has been superseded by the LSC, it has published a vast number of materials on teaching in FE that is of great value.

REFERENCES

Dearing, R. (1996) *Review of Qualifications for 16–19-year-olds: Full Report.* London: Schools Curriculum and Assessment Authority.

Department for Education and Employment (1998a) *National Training Organisations: Prospectus 1999–2000.* London: DfEE.

Department for Education and Employment (1998b) *The Learning Age: a Renaissance for a New Britain*, Green Paper, Cm 3790. London: DfEE.

Department for Education and Employment (1999) *Qualifying for Success.* London: DfEE.

Fieldhouse, R. (1996) *A History of Modern British Adult Education.* Leicester: NIACE.

Further Education Funding Council (1992) *Funding Learning.* London: FEFC.

Gray, D. (2000) *Training to Teach in Further and Adult Education.* Cheltenham: Stanley Thornes (Publishers) Ltd.

Jarvis, P. (1995) *Adult and Continuing Education: Theory and Practice*, 2nd edn. London: Kogan Page.

Kelly, A. V. (1999) *The Curriculum, Theory and Practice.* London: Paul Chapman Publishing.

CHAPTER 9

Special Educational Needs

Chris Lloyd

CHAPTER SUMMARY

This chapter focuses upon:

- Trends in policy and legislation for special educational needs in England and Wales as symptomatic of trends throughout the United Kingdom.
- Patterns in the development of special educational needs epitomised by the Warnock report and its redefinition of handicap.
- Models of inclusivity or education for all.

Introduction

The policy provision and practice of education for those pupils identified as having special educational needs (SEN) in the UK has undergone a vast amount of change since the late 1970s. This change was inspired by a recognition in the mid-1960s and early 1970s of the need to evaluate and reform the whole area so that handicapped (the term used at the time) children and young people could have a proper education. The impetus for this can be attributed to a number of sources: the move during the 1960s towards a comprehensive system of education; a recognition of the basic human right to an education for all, enshrined for the first time in the Education Act 1970; and, of course, the need to ensure economic viability of provision. The Education Act 1976 affirmed the right to a full educational opportunity for all by stating in section 10 that all handicapped pupils should be educated in ordinary in preference to special schools. Influenced by all these pressures, Margaret Thatcher, then Minister for Education, set up the Warnock Committee in 1976 to enquire into the education of handicapped children and young people. The results of this enquiry were finally reported back in 1978 in what has become known as the Warnock Report (DES 1978).

The findings and recommendations of the Warnock Report

Although the Warnock Report has been severely criticised subsequently for its failure to tackle the underlying social factors and causes of special needs and for its simplistic presentation of what are in fact highly problematic and controversial issues (Adams 1990; Lloyd 1994, 1997, 2000), it certainly acted as a very powerful awareness raising tool and can be seen as the catalyst for all the changes and developments that have taken place in this area of education since. It is necessary for this examination of SEN in the UK, therefore, to spend some time looking carefully and critically at the findings and recommendations of the Report and assessing their implications for and influence on subsequent policy and practice.

There were 250 recommendations arising from the Warnock Report but for the purposes of this chapter it is necessary to concentrate on the broader themes and issues, rather than the detail of the recommendations themselves.

The redefinition of handicap

Perhaps the most fundamental of these issues is the redefinition of handicap. Warnock shifts the term away from the child so that she or he is seen as being handicapped by the degree or seriousness of the disability. The handicap is not rooted in the child but is the result of barriers created because provision for the child's particular disability is inadequate. The social context and the environment are seen as factors that might influence the handicapping effects of the child's disabilities, and the ever-changing nature of all these factors is constantly referred to throughout the Report. Thus emphasis is placed on the dynamic nature of disability and on the potential of the home and school environment to exacerbate or reduce its handicapping effects on the child.

> Whether a disability or significant difficulty constitutes an educational handicap for an individual child and if so to what extent will depend on a variety of factors. Schools differ, often widely, in outlook, expertise, resources, accommodation, organisation and physical and social surroundings, all of which help to determine the degree to which an individual is educationally handicapped. (DES 1978: 3.5)

This is a very different view from the traditional, medically influenced notion that handicapped children were in need of some kind of treatment or remedy to cure their problem, rather than a full educational opportunity, which was the dominant view found by the committee in the investigation leading to the report.

The Report also makes clear that in the light of the difficulty of establishing what exactly constitutes an educational handicap it is unproductive to think of children as fitting into categories of handicapped and non-handicapped, the former requiring some kind of special, often segregated, education, while the latter receive education in ordinary schools. Instead the concept of special educational needs is introduced, to be seen 'not in terms of a particular disability which a child may be judged to have, but in relation to everything about him, his abilities as well as his disability – indeed all the factors which have a bearing on his educational progress' (*ibid.*: 33.6). SEN, then, are complex and differ for each child according to her or his disability and according to the handicapping factors created by the educational and social context in which she or he operates. Another factor in Warnock's redefinition is the need to recognise a 'continuum' of need. Obviously if the context has a bearing then changes in that context may mean that the child's need will also change. Similarly, if the child's disability is physical, the degree of seriousness might change over a period of time. For others needs might arise at particular points in time and then be addressed and met, and cease to exist. The 'continuum' has yet another aspect, which refers to the span of time over which education takes place and the maturation process of the child, which will inevitably add to the changing nature of the child's educational needs.

Many subsequent criticisms of the Warnock Report arise from this attempt at redefinition and the resultant change in the language of special education. The concept of need and provision made in response to the identification of need is seen as a deficit model and patronising, implying helplessness or a lack of something. Barton (1989) and Roaf and Bines (1989) point to the problematic nature of need as the basis for achieving goals in education. The assessment of need by professionals is also seen as problematic, since value judgements are inevitably made that might be influenced by social interest, power and control and the vested interests of the professionals themselves. In addition, needs can also be generated by the valuing of some aspects of development more than others, and might even be constructed by factors that seek to define the nature of people in terms of abilities and behaviours which relate to socially created norms. In these ways the term SEN can be seen as reinforcing a deficit view of disability that seeks to portray disabled people as powerless and weak, as not fitting in and as dependent on others to provide for them (Barton 1989; Oliver 1992). Thus the new language introduced by Warnock is seen by some as failing to redefine handicap and as simply introducing a new label for old practices.

Planning and provision for SEN

Irrespective of the criticisms above, the change in concept from handicapped children to children experiencing SEN led the committee to review the organisation of the provision of special education. The Report is probably most famous for its assertion that 'the planning of services for children and young people should be based on the assumption that about one in six children at any time, and up to one in five at some time during their school career, will require some form of educational provision' (DES 1978: 3.17). This recognition that as many as 20 per cent of children may have SEN at some time, together with the redefinition of handicap, led to a number of far ranging recommendations about planning and provision for special education. In particular, a strong recommendation was that where possible pupils with SEN should be educated in mainstream rather than in segregated provision. Provision should be planned in response to the needs of the child and should be flexible and sensitive to allow for change and modification in the light of the 'continuum' of children's needs.

These recommendations led to the introduction of a policy for the integration of children with SEN into mainstream schools and to the disbanding of the majority of segregated special provision throughout the country.

Assessment and identification

In Chapter 4 the Warnock Report makes clear its view of learning, the learner and assessment. There is a recognition of the need for formative, ongoing, curriculum-based assessment procedures, involving all the agencies associated with the child and the child herself or himself. Four main requirements for effective assessment are distinguished:

* the importance of involving parents/carers and the need to take account of the home context;
* the need to observe and assess the whole child in a variety of contexts and to take account of the educational context in that assessment;
* the need to know how the child learns and the need for assessment to be underpinned by a developmental model of the learner;
* the need for specific, specialist, professional assessment with a multidisciplinary team approach (DES 1978: 4.29–4.32).

There is also a clear recommendation that assessment and identification should be part of a broad profiling system used with all children in order to eliminate the notion of handicap and non-handicap.

Warnock's recommendations for the assessment and identification of SEN were taken up in part by the Education Act 1981, and are discussed in more detail below. However, far from the assessment of SEN developing as part of a wider scheme designed to ensure that the needs of all children are appropriately addressed, the resultant procedure, Statementing, is concerned with a small minority of the total number identified by the Report as having SEN, and can be seen as a very poor response to the recommendations cited above (Lloyd 1994, 1997).

The curriculum

The Report makes a clear statement that the aims of the curriculum are the same for all children and that it should be planned according to individual need. The changing nature of educational needs makes flexibility and continuous review, modification or possibly the use of a different methodology of vital importance to ensure effective learning in the case of those children identified as having SEN. The essential message is that every attempt should be made to ensure that provision for all children, irrespective of ability, is of the same scope and quality. There is also a reminder that many learning or behaviour difficulties result from, or are created by, inappropriate and irrelevant curricula.

The chief criticisms of the Warnock Report relating to the curriculum centre on its failure to address sufficiently the whole area of the curriculum in mainstream schools. In asserting that the aims and goals of education should be the same for all children the Warnock Report was affirming the right of all children, irrespective of ability, to an equal educational opportunity. What it failed to do was to investigate fully the potential of the education system and mainstream curriculum to create failure and to preclude access to some children. Nor were issues raised about the way in which a system based on competition and selection gives rise to a certain view of ability and success (Lloyd 1994, 1997, 2000). Mary Warnock, the chair of the Committee of Enquiry, herself admitted: 'We assumed that a special need would be defined in terms of help a child might have if he was to gain access to the curriculum . . . only occasionally did we think that the curriculum itself must be changed to suit the child' (Warnock 1982: 56). This failure to recognise the role of the curriculum itself in creating and exacerbating SEN, while at the same time recommending that the majority of children should be educated in the mainstream, can be seen as one of the greatest failures of the Warnock Report.

Parents as partners

There is great emphasis in the Report on the need to develop partnership with parents in the process of educating the child. Particular reference is made to the vital importance of this partnership in the early years of education and in early identification and assessment of children's SEN.

While it is clearly laudable to involve parents in all aspects of their children's development, the Report has been criticised for presenting the development of partnership as non-problematic. It is possible, for example, that what the parent views as in the best interests of the child may be in conflict with the views of professionals. Parents may be overprotective of, or overambitious for, their children. The whole structure of family relationships has changed in recent years so that there are many single parents, unable to spare the time to be partners in their children's education, who may find that the notion increases pressure and stress and leads them to feelings of inadequacy as parents. These criticisms should not, however, detract from the importance of making every effort to involve parents at all stages of their children's educational development; they simply emphasise the problematic nature of establishing effective partnerships.

Implications of the Warnock Report

There is no doubt that the findings and recommendations of the Warnock Report have had enormous implications for the policy, planning and organisation of provision for special education since it was published in 1978. Until 1978 a large segregated special school sector existed, with provision arranged according to categories of handicap (laid down in the 1944 Education Act). There were no national guidelines about the assessment and allocation procedures, which led to inequalities in provision. The Warnock Committee found that children receiving education in segregated special schools in some parts of the country might have exactly the same assessment and diagnosis as children in other parts who were receiving their education in mainstream schools. The redefinition of handicap and recommendations about flexible assessment procedures and the 'continuum' of need raised issues about the designation of special provision and about labelling children according to their disabilities. There was a clear recommendation that children should be educated wherever possible in mainstream schools, and where there might be a case made for retaining some segregated special provision, it should be redesignated to more flexible categories that recognised the complex nature of children's SEN.

The recommendation to adopt more flexible child-centred approaches to the assessment and diagnosis of children's SEN using multidisciplinary teams and involving parents and the children themselves had major implications for practice in the area, as did the notion of parents as partners in their children's education. Indeed, the findings and recommendations of the Report required a complete overhaul of policy, provision and practice in special education, with far reaching ramifications for mainstream schools as well as special schools, for education services and, indeed, for the whole education system.

The Education Act 1981

The Education Act 1981 introduced legislation, inspired by the findings and recommendations discussed above, that would begin the process of reform in special education. However, coming, as it did, at a time of economic restraint and cutbacks on public spending, the provisions of the Act were regarded as extremely disappointing and as having failed to address or incorporate the more far reaching recommendations of the report. No extra money was provided by the government to enable the enactment of the legislation, and responsibility was placed firmly on local education authorities (LEAs) to finance the changes and reforms.

Nevertheless the Act is important because it introduced:

- a new language for special education;
- a new system of assessment and identification of SEN, the Statementing procedure;
- a new system for resourcing some children identified as having SEN;
- the right and responsibility of parents to be partners in their children's education;
- the integration of children with SEN in the mainstream of education as an imperative.

The new language for special education, much of which remains in current use, was intended to assist in the redefinition of handicap. The term SEN was introduced and defined as a learning difficulty requiring some special provision, and a learning difficulty is defined as a problem greater than those of the majority of children of the same age. New categories of SEN were introduced relating to these definitions, such as moderate or severe learning difficulty (MLD, SLD), emotional and behavioural difficulty (EBD), sensory impairment and physical disability.

The new system of identification and assessment of SEN, the Statementing procedure, through which extra resourcing was to be allocated to those children identified as having particularly extreme SEN, fell very short of the processes recommended by the Warnock Report. The safeguarding of extra resourcing was inspired by the Report's recommendation that while the 20 per cent of children identified as having SEN at some time should be educated in the mainstream alongside their peers, about 2 per cent of the 20 per cent would probably need some extra funding in order to make this possible, and a proportion of this 2 per cent might even require separate special provision. The Statementing procedure was intended to identify the 2 per cent and to ensure that they received the extra funding necessary to meet their needs, either in the mainstream or in segregated provision. It also took account of the recommendation that assessment and identification should be by multidisciplinary teams of professionals and that parents and the children themselves should be involved. The Act lays down the procedures that LEAs must follow and their duties and responsibilities with regard to the involvement of parents. The assessment and identification process results in a Statement of SEN, which clearly states the needs of the child and recommends how these should be met and the necessary resources to meet them. The LEA is responsible for ensuring that these needs are met.

Major criticisms of the procedure rapidly emerged as LEAs began to develop procedures for enacting the policy. These included:

- The emphasis on 2 per cent of the 20 per cent for extra resourcing failed totally to address adequately the resourcing of SEN in general and the resourcing of SEN in mainstream schools in particular. The procedure also individualises the funding of SEN, rather than catering effectively for the needs of all children, and fails to recognise Warnock's 'continuum' of need adequately.
- The Act did not specify the length of time the Statementing procedure should take, nor did it give details of how it should be carried out, which led to confusion and inequality of experience between LEAs.
- LEAs were responsible for funding the Statementing procedure and this led to great regional variation according to the economic constraints placed on it by different LEAs.
- The procedure was complicated, bureaucratic and professionally biased, so that parents found it exclusive and inaccessible.
- Because in extreme cases Statementing could mean the removal of a child to segregated provision, in some cases teachers/schools and even parents were encouraged to seek for children, especially those with difficult behaviour, to be Statemented rather than attempting to address their needs within the ordinary classroom.
- A Statement of SEN carried with it a negative stigma.

Despite these criticisms the Statementing procedure continues in much the same way today. Modifications and reforms have been made through subsequent legislation (Education Act 1993) in an effort to address some of the issues raised above, but in essence additional resourcing for SEN is allocated through the same statutory process.

The role of parents and their right to be involved in the assessment of their children's SEN, enshrined in the 1981 Act, has continued to be a central issue in subsequent education debate and policy. Schools are required to ensure that parents are informed and involved and most have policies for enabling the process.

Perhaps the most controversial and difficult outcome of the 1981 Act was the imperative to move towards integration for the majority of children with SEN. LEAs were required to develop policies for integration and to reform the provision of special education to facilitate integration. The 1980s saw a wide variety of responses in provision for integration, including:

- children with SEN fully integrated into the ordinary class with support;
- partial withdrawal into special classes or special units, either in the same school or elsewhere;
- special units attached to mainstream schools;
- part-time attendance at the mainstream school, with the majority of work in a segregated special school;
- full-time attendance at a day or boarding special school.

The process of moving towards integration was not, however, easy. Many teachers in the mainstream of education felt unprepared and were reluctant to deal with the SEN of the pupils they now found in their classes. Teachers in special schools felt threatened and undervalued. Units attached to mainstream schools sometimes became segregated schools within the school. Pupils with SEN in mainstream classes sometimes felt isolated or stigmatised. Many of these problems continue to exist and are still hotly debated by teachers. There is no doubt, however, that since 1981 there has been a dramatic shift in the provision of special education from segregated schools to the mainstream. Some segregated special schools still exist, as do many special units, but the majority of children with SEN in the UK receive their education in mainstream schools.

From integration to inclusion

In addition to leading to a plethora of responses in terms of provision the imperative to move towards integration also inspired a debate about the concept itself and about the adequacy of the responses to provide a genuinely equal educational opportunity. Many of those who have joined in the debate have identified integration as a means to exacerbating inequality and perpetuating the status quo in education (Tomlinson 1982; Barton 1989; Oliver 1990, 1992; Lloyd 1994, 1997, 2000; Slee 1995, 1996). Integration is seen as merely tinkering around with current provision, rather than providing the radical impetus for the change necessary if equal opportunities are to be ensured. Oliver (1992) makes a powerful case for reconstructing what he calls the 'old view' of integration, where people are fitted into existing structures, which themselves remain unchanged, and provided with a few additional resources to enable them to function within those structures, into a 'new view' informed by a notion of full participation, as a right. Integration is seen as reinforcing the inequalities in the system because it is underpinned by compensatory measures aimed at normalising those identified as having SEN. The 'new view' of inclusion

> rejects totally any ideas about normalisation or compensation . . . the demand is for an inclusive approach to planning and provision. There is recognition too of the value of celebrating and capitalising on the enrichment of difference and

diversity rather than the impoverishment of provision through the process of fitting it to a narrow set of artificially produced concepts of what is normal. (Lloyd 1994: 187)

A great deal has been written about inclusion and it is beyond the scope of this chapter to enter fully into the debate. What is important to note, however, is that integration and inclusion are very different concepts, leading to very different views of education, provision and organisation. Unfortunately this has not been recognised by official policy-makers. At some point during the 1990s official documentation referring to SEN and its provision began to replace the word integration with the word inclusion. Nowhere in that documentation can any real attempt be found to define the concept or to recognise the very fundamental differences discussed above (Lloyd 2000). There is no recognition that genuine inclusion requires a very different set of practices and approaches to planning, organisation and provision. Indeed, the policy and practices that have continued can clearly be seen as integration and are underpinned by models of compensation and normalisation. However, official policy continues to demand that children with SEN are *included* and that schools and teachers strive towards *inclusion*. The development of policy for integration, now called inclusion, throughout the UK required far more than organisational change. It made demands on teachers and schools to address issues about how to provide access to the mainstream curriculum for an ever-widening range of ability. This resulted in a range of variable practice, some of which has been severely criticised as perpetuating segregated practices and further disadvantaging children with SEN (Oliver 1990; Barton 1993; Slee 1996). In addition to changes in policy for special education, the whole education system has undergone massive change since the early 1980s. Inspired by a competitive market ideology, large-scale changes have taken place in the curriculum, testing procedures, funding arrangements and procedures of inspection and accountability. A severe impediment to the development of genuine integration, and certainly to the development of inclusive practice, is that many of these changes seem to have taken little or no account of the needs of children with SEN, except to address them as an afterthought (Lloyd 2000), and this is seen most clearly in the changes to the curriculum.

The National Curriculum and the Education Act 1988

The Education Act 1988 is best remembered as the legislation that introduced the National Curriculum. For the area of SEN it was doubly important because it enshrined in legislation for the first time the right of all children, irrespective of ability, to a broad, balanced, differentiated curriculum, including the National Curriculum. The Act also, however, makes provision for modification or even exemption from the National Curriculum for some children with SEN, implying that entitlement was used as a relative term, and that far from genuinely positive legislation there was, as in the past, a deficit attitude towards SEN.

Much has been written about the inadequacies of the National Curriculum as a curriculum for all. Dyson sums up many of these criticisms:

> Despite the rhetoric of 'breadth, relevance and differentiation', it is difficult to imagine how it could have been more narrowly conceived and retrospectively academic, more exclusive in its emphasis and more inaccessible in its demands. What children were entitled to, therefore, was not participation in meaningful educational experiences so much as confinement within a rigid and inappropriate hierarchy of knowledge. (Dyson 1997: 154)

Certainly the National Curriculum seems to take little account of the issues raised by the Warnock Report about the potential of the traditional academic mainstream curriculum to exacerbate or indeed create SEN. It is a very traditional content-based curriculum, which places emphasis on academic subjects and cognitive skills and relies on standardised, age-related tests to assess success and achievement. It takes little account of the Report's recommendations about the need to develop flexible, child-centred, accessible, inclusive curricula and assessment procedures that take account of individual differences. A full critique of the Education Act 1988 and the National Curriculum is not possible or appropriate within the remit of this chapter, but there is no doubt that the reorganisation and restructuring of education that has taken place as a result of it has had far reaching consequences for educational practice in the area of SEN.

The implementation of the National Curriculum and at the same time the continuing policy of integrating the majority of children into the mainstream of educational provision produced a great deal of tension. A range of policies and practices have developed to address the difficulties of providing genuine access and, in the best practice, the opportunity to participate fully in the curriculum for children with SEN. These include:

* setting and banding children according to ability within mainstream classrooms and schools;
* learning support units and classes within, or attached to, mainstream schools that children with SEN can attend for part of the time;
* learning resource and support centres, within schools or as separate provision;
* individual, or group, in-class support from a support teacher or a learning support assistant;
* differentiated materials and teaching methods;
* adapted and modified curriculum content and special programmes;
* the use of a range of information and communication technology (ICT) and other aids to support children with SEN.

This list is not intended to be exhaustive but it indicates some of the major strategies that have been employed. The one that has perhaps most changed practice in SEN is the introduction into schools of learning support assistants (a variety of different titles may be employed to describe this role) to work with individuals or groups of children and to support the teacher within the ordinary classroom. This growing band of largely unqualified assistants is now responsible for ensuring that those children identified as having SEN have maximum access to the curriculum. It should be noted that a number of courses and a range of professional qualifications and development opportunities

are currently being developed for learning support assistants. In examples of best practice teachers work closely with learning support assistants to plan, monitor and evaluate children's progress and achievement, and to ensure that they participate fully in all
aspects of learning. At the other end of the spectrum poor practice can result in the
isolation of the child within the classroom. What is clear, however, is that this model of
support for learning is here to stay. Current government initiatives and policy for education make continuous reference to the importance of learning support assistants and
of increasing their numbers (DfEE 1997).

Assessment

A Code of Practice for SEN

The implementation of the National Curriculum and the growing concerns expressed
by teachers about the lack of guidance and national policy for SEN resulted in the
development of a Code of Practice on the Identification and Assessment of SEN
(DfEE 1993), introduced in the Education Act 1993. The Code of Practice, clearly
inspired by the recommendations of the Warnock Report, introduced:

- A five-stage model of assessment and identification of SEN – with the first three
  stages school-based and the responsibility of the school, and stages four and five as
  a redefinition and refining of the Statementing procedure. These latter stages are the
  responsibility of the LEA and intended to ensure, except in very exceptional cases,
  the continued education of the child within the mainstream setting, but with additional, appropriate support provided as a result of the Statement of SEN.
- A whole-school policy on SEN within every school. This is to be published and to
  contain all information about the school's strategies for meeting children's SEN and
  for the assessment and identification of SEN.
- The role in every school of a Special Educational Needs Coordinator (SENCO) to
  be responsible for the day-to-day operation of the school's SEN policy, coordinating provision for pupils with SEN, advising colleagues, liaising with parents and
  outside agencies, maintaining a school SEN register and pupil records, contributing
  to staff training and professional development. (This role has subsequently been
  expanded and further defined in the National Standards for SENCOs (DfEE 1998),
  and is now well established in all mainstream schools.)
- The use of individual educational plans (IEPs), to be drawn up to address the needs
  identified by the staged assessment process. The IEP is used to set targets for learning, and where necessary behaviour; these are implemented, monitored and reviewed
  regularly together with the child. IEPs are the responsibility of the teacher, together
  with the SENCO.

The Code of Practice also spelt out, in detail, the involvement of parents in the processes of assessment and identification and introduced the idea of a SEN Tribunal to
ensure parents' rights and to allow for challenges to LEA decisions. Every school was

also to have a named governor responsible for SEN. The importance of involving the child in the process of assessment and identification is also emphasised, and the Code is underpinned by the imperative to educate children with SEN in the mainstream except in very exceptional circumstances.

The Code of Practice is now well established in practice in all schools and has brought about significant changes and raised awareness of the whole area of SEN by placing responsibility with the school and with teachers. It is at the time of writing (June 2001) being revised in order to address criticisms about the additional bureaucratic workload created by the five-stage model, IEPs and the review process. What is emerging in drafts of the new code are stages of *School Action* and *School Action Plus* rather than the five-stage model, and the notion of a continuum of need with thresholds at which intervention in terms of support may be necessary. The Statementing procedure will continue and there is a recategorisation of SEN into areas of:

- cognition and learning;
- emotional, behavioural and social difficulties;
- communication and interaction difficulties;
- sensory and physical difficulties.

Once again the imperative for children's needs to be met in the mainstream of education is emphasised, together with the need to involve parents and children themselves.

Inspection

One of the most influential changes to have taken place in education since the late 1980s is the introduction of the national policy for the inspection of schools. Much debate has ensued and there are conflicting views about the model and indeed the value of the inspection process, and it would be inappropriate to enter into a discussion here about those issues. What is important to note with regard to SEN is that while initially it was not a major focus for inspection it has now been recognised as having significance, and Ofsted inspectors have received guidance and training in order to enable them to identify areas of strength and weakness and focus on the implementation of the Code of Practice in schools when they inspect them.

The most significant recent guidance issued in this area is *Evaluating Educational Inclusion: Guidance for Inspectors and Schools* (Ofsted 2000).

Conclusion

The Green Paper *Excellence for All Children: Meeting Special Educational Needs* (DfEE 1997) provides us with a vision of education for children with SEN for the twenty-first century:

> Our vision is of excellence for all. This inclusive vision emphasises children with
> special educational needs . . . what is not in question is the case for setting our

sights high for these children. . . . Good provision for SEN does not mean a sympathetic acceptance of low achievement. It means tough minded determination to show that children with SEN are capable of excellence. . . . The great majority of children with SEN will, as adults, contribute as members of society. Schools have to prepare children for this role. (DfEE 1997: 4)

This is indeed a laudable vision, which emphasises the rights of children with SEN to equal educational opportunities and to participate in and contribute fully to society. It can be argued, however, that the vision is flawed (Lloyd 2000), because it is simplistic and still fails to take account of a number of problematic and controversial issues: the organisation and funding of schooling; the narrow academic model underpinning the curriculum; the standardised, age/norm-related assessment procedures; the emphasis on success as academic achievement and the development of cognitive skills; the compensatory models of resourcing of SEN; and a range of other issues too numerous to list here. What is clear, however, is that SEN issues are now central to the education agenda and that they will continue to be debated and discussed and will form an important focus for education policy, provision and practice in the twenty-first century.

POINTS FOR DISCUSSION

1 The continuing UK-wide policy of integrating the majority of children into the mainstream of educational provision produced difficulties in terms of implementation. Why was this the case, and does it continue to be so?
2 Are policies designed to provide access to the curriculum effective in practice?
3 Is the use of learning support assistants the best way to enhance inclusive education in the classroom?

INTERNET SITES

Department for Education and Skills: www.dfes.gov.uk
National Curriculum Online: www.nc.uk.net.home/html
Ofsted: www.ofsted.gov.uk
Department of Education (Northern Ireland): www.deni.gov.uk/index.htm
Northern Ireland Council for the Curriculum, Examinations and Assessment: www.ccea.org.uk
Scottish Executive Education Department: www.scotland.gov.uk/who/dept_education.asp

REFERENCES AND FURTHER READING

Adams, F. (1990) *Special Education in the 1990s*. London: Longman.
Barton, L. (ed.) (1989) *Disability and Dependency*. Lewes: Falmer.
Barton, L. (1993) 'Labels, markets and inclusive education', in J. Vissor and G. Upton (eds) *Education in Britain after the Warnock Report*. London: David Fulton.

DES (1978) *Report of the Committee of Enquiry into the Education of Handicapped People and Young Children – the Warnock Report*. London: HMSO.

DfEE (1993) *Code of Practice on the Identification and Assessment of Special Educational Needs*. London: DfEE.

DfEE (1997) *Excellence for All Children: Meeting Special Educational Needs*. London: DfEE.

DfEE (1998) *National Standards for SENCOs*. London: DfEE.

Dyson, A. (1997) 'Social educational disadvantage; reconstructing special educational needs', *British Journal of Special Education*, 24, 152–6.

Lloyd, C. (1994) 'Special educational needs and the early years', in G. Blenkin and A. V. Kelly (eds) *The National Curriculum and Early Learning: an Evaluation*. London: Paul Chapman Publishing.

Lloyd, C. (1997) 'Inclusive education for children with special educational needs in the early years', in S. Wolfendale (ed.) *Meeting Special Needs in the Early Years*. London: David Fulton.

Lloyd, C. (2000) 'Excellence for all children – false promises. The failure of current policy for inclusive education and implications for schooling in the 21st century', *International Journal of Inclusive Education*, 4(2), 133–51.

Ofsted (2000) *Evaluating Educational Inclusion: Guidance for Inspectors and Schools*. London: Ofsted.

Oliver, M. (1990) *The Politics of Disablement*. London: Macmillan.

Oliver, M. (1992) 'Intellectual masturbation; a rejoinder to Soder and Booth', *European Journal of Special Educational Needs*, 1, 58–69.

Roaf, C. and Bines, H. (1989) *Needs, Rights and Opportunities in Special Education*. Lewes: Falmer.

Slee, R. (1995) 'Inclusive education: from policy to school improvement', in C. Clark, A. Dyson and A. Milward (eds) *Towards Inclusive Schools?* London: David Fulton.

Slee, R. (1996) 'Disability, class and poverty: school structures and policy identities', in C. Christensen and F. Rizvi (eds) *Disability and the Dilemmas of Education and Justice*. Buckingham: Open University Press.

Tomlinson, S. (1982) *A Sociology of Special Educational Needs*. London: Routledge and Kegan Paul.

Warnock, M. (1982) 'Children with special needs in ordinary schools: integration revisited', *Education Today*, 32.

PART III:

Denominational and Independent School Provision

CHAPTER 10

Church of England Schools

David W. Lankshear

CHAPTER SUMMARY

- This chapter provides an introduction to Anglican schools.
- It presents the position in the summer of 2001 shortly before the publication of the report on the development of the schools prepared by a committee chaired by Lord Dearing (Dearing 2001).
- The Dearing Report is likely to lead to significant development in Anglican schools, particularly at secondary level.

Introduction

It is important to state clearly that this chapter was written in the early summer of 2001. At this time the Church of England was awaiting the final report of the Dearing commission into the future of church schools. It is expected that this report will set a framework for the expansion of the number of Church of England schools within the maintained system for the first time in 100 years. This introduction to the Church of England's contribution to the maintained system must therefore be seen in the context of the changes that have happened between the date of writing and of reading.

In order to understand the significance of the above statement it is necessary to look back almost 200 years. At the beginning of the nineteenth century it began to be clear to philanthropists and to many people in the churches that there was a need to provide the children of 'the poor and manufacturing classes' with access to elementary education. A number of parishes responded to this need by creating schools for this purpose. In 1811 the Church of England found a means of coordinating and stimulating this work by the creation of the National Society. This voluntary society stimulated and supported the growth of over 15,000 schools and the colleges to train the teachers that they needed. It received grants from the government for its work, and for a while it seemed as if the National Society together with the British and Foreign Schools Society would succeed in sponsoring the provision of elementary education for all children in the country. By the middle of the century, however, it was becoming apparent that these two societies would not be able to create sufficient schools in some parts of the country, particularly the growing suburbs of the great cities. As a result the state at last decided to intervene directly in the provision of schools in those places where the churches were not able to meet the demand. To achieve this the Education Act 1870 was passed. This act set up school boards with the power to levy local rates and to create and run schools. In 1902 local education authorities replaced the school boards. Although it was not immediately apparent, this period marked the beginning of a slow decline of church schools.

Forty years later, when the government published the Green Paper that led to the Education Act 1944, it was clear that the church would need help and support to continue to provide primary schools and to develop new schools to reflect the need to provide a distinctive secondary stage in education for all pupils. This led to the introduction in the 1944 Act of a new structure for church schools, which, despite a number of subsequent adjustments, still largely shapes the pattern of the church's provision. The subsequent introduction of comprehensive schools, the National Curriculum and local financial management affected the management of church schools in similar ways to the impact in all other schools within the maintained system.

In 1997 the advent of a new Labour government that placed education at the top of its agenda for action led to a series of events in the development of Anglican schools, which paved the way for the Dearing review and subsequent development.

The churches read and interpreted the documents on which government policy was developed in 1997 as being unfavourable towards church schools. This led to a growing concern among church leaders that the government intended to create conditions in which church schools would wither away. As a result the bishops of the Church of England released a press statement expressing these concerns and their support for church schools. This led to a clarification of the government's position which was further evidenced when the text of the Bill that subsequently became the School Standards and Framework Act 1998 was published. As finally worded, this Act provided significant clarification of the position of church schools within the education system of England and Wales and gave a framework for development in the quality of education within them, and the possible expansion of the numbers of church schools.

The church was also stimulated by the events surrounding the development and passage of this Act to the extent that, during a debate in the General Synod of the Church of England in November 1998, the Synod passed a resolution, without a single negative vote, which begins: 'believing that church schools stand at the heart of the church's mission to the nation'. This resolution also set in motion the creation of the committee chaired by Lord Dearing to review church schools and make recommendations for their future development. The bench of bishops of the Church in Wales made a similar commitment to Church in Wales schools in 1999.

Distinctiveness I: administration and governance

In September 1999 there were 186 Church of England secondary schools and 4,531 Church of England primary schools (both figures include some middle schools). This represents 5.5 per cent of the total secondary provision and 25 per cent of the primary provision. Of these schools 2,035 were voluntary aided, 2,636 were voluntary controlled and 46 were foundation schools (Lankshear 2001). Each of these categories of schools has different arrangements for their governance and management, but all of them, having a legally defined 'religious character', must have an ethos statement that defines the way in which that character will be reflected in practice. The model ethos statement for Church of England schools is as follows.

> Recognising its historic foundation, the school will preserve and develop its religious character in accordance with the principles of the Church of England/ Church in Wales and in partnership with the churches at parish and diocesan level.
>
> The school aims to serve its community by providing an education of the highest quality within the context of Christian belief and practice. It encourages an understanding of the meaning and significance of faith, and promotes Christian values through the experience it offers to all its pupils.

The key features of the differences between these three categories of school, as far as the church is concerned, are summarised in Table 10.1.

School worship should reflect the religious character of the school. Therefore the policy and programme of worship in the school will include material drawn from the usual pattern of worship within the church, together with material developed by that church or others that is deemed to be appropriate to worship for the age group of the school. Within those Christian denominations where the Eucharist is central to the worship of the church, the school will have to include a section on the place of the Eucharist in its school policy document.

Voluntary aided schools are the schools in which the churches have the most direct influence because of the built-in majority on the governing body. Just under half of all Anglican schools are voluntary aided. In voluntary controlled and foundation schools

Table 10.1 The key features of the different types of Anglican school

	Voluntary aided	Voluntary controlled	Foundation
Membership of the governing body	Church nominees in majority	Church nominees in minority	Church nominees in minority
Admissions	Governors	LEA	Governors
Employment of staff	Governors	LEA	Governors
Ownership of the building	Trustees	Trustees	Trustees
Cost of building maintenance	Governors and LEA	LEA	LEA
Cost of building improvement	Governors	LEA	LEA
Religious education syllabus	Church syllabus	LEA agreed syllabus	LEA agreed syllabus
School worship	Anglican	Anglican	Anglican

the church must act in partnership with others in the community to provide the education for the children. Voluntary controlled schools are often seen as a model for the type of cooperation that should exist in areas served by only one school when that is a church school. Just over half of all Anglican schools are voluntary controlled.

The different arrangements for governance of schools in these three statuses represent a considerable challenge to the Church of England in the development of coherent policies and identities for its schools. Voluntary aided schools are more likely to pursue policies clearly in line with the church's understandings of the nature of church schools, given that the majority of the governors are church nominees. On the other hand, where a church school is the only school serving an area, it has been argued (Ramsey 1970) that the voluntary controlled school, and by implication the foundation school, represent a balance between the church and other parts of the local community. In the past ten years the advent of inspections under section 23 of the Schools Inspection Act 1996 has tended to bring voluntary controlled schools and foundation schools closer to the church structures for the support of its schools. However, there is still considerable variation in the extent to which voluntary controlled schools take account of Church of England policies for the church's schools.

The key relationship between the school and the church is focused in two distinct ways. The parish, or in the case of a few secondary schools the deanery, nominates a number of the foundation governors and the parish priest is automatically a governor. The diocese probably also nominates a number of the foundation governors and also provides support for the school through the Diocesan Director of Education and other professional members of the team employed by the Diocesan Board of Education.

Distinctiveness II: curriculum, assessment and inspection

The previous section sets out some of the principal differences between the various types of church school. This section discusses the way in which the key curriculum issues for which the church has direct responsibility are dealt with in Anglican schools.

Religious education

Throughout the 1990s the church has had a clear focus on the importance of the delivery of the curriculum in all church schools (Lankshear 1992a, b). Within this there has been a particular emphasis on the quality of religious education and school worship (Barton *et al.* 1996). There are two approaches at diocesan level to the development of the syllabus for teaching religious education in voluntary aided schools within the diocese. Some dioceses take the view that the interests of pupils are best served by all schools using the agreed syllabus for religious education, with the voluntary aided schools being provided with a diocesan supplement, in order to ensure that the elements of the agreed syllabus that focus on Christianity are well resourced. Other dioceses provide a full syllabus for use in voluntary aided schools in their area. The reasons for these differences are complex and often reflect the relationships that exist between the dioceses and the local education authorities in a particular region.

In Wales, the Church in Wales has usually provided advice on syllabus issues at provincial level.

Worship

The worship in Anglican schools should always reflect both the spiritual needs of the pupils and staff and the traditions of the Anglican church. This does not mean that Anglican schools should be using the formal services of the church, but it does imply that within every school worship policy there will be a clear statement about how the worship of the school relates to the worship of the church locally and as a whole. This will make clear how pupils will, in the course of the school worship, learn sufficient of the worship of the church to be in a position to join that worship should they choose to do so as adults.

Inspection: sections 10 and 23

In all church schools the inspections conducted by the Office for Standards in Education (Ofsted), or ESTYN in Wales, are complemented by inspections of those aspects of the religious character of the school that are distinctive. Provision for these inspections was originally included in section 13 of the Education (Schools) Act 1992. Subsequently the provisions, as amended in 1993, were incorporated in section 23 of the Schools Inspections Act 1996. In order to distinguish between the two inspections the convention has developed of referring to the inspections conducted by Ofsted or ESTYN as 'section 10 inspections' and the inspections of the religious character provisions as 'section 23 inspections'.

In response to these acts the Anglican church, working through the National Society, set up a national scheme of inspection, whose framework and training have developed significantly since it was first introduced. It will be apparent from reading the sections that precede this one that the way in which section 23 inspections impact on church schools will vary with their status. Table 10.2 is taken from the National Society's Inspection Handbook (Brown *et al.* 2000) and shows the normal situation for inspection.

Table 10.2   The impact of inspection

	Voluntary aided	Voluntary controlled	Foundation
Religious education	Section 23	Section 10	Section 10
School worship	Section 23	Section 23	Section 23
Spiritual, moral, social and cultural development	Sections 23 and 10	Sections 23 and 10	Sections 23 and 10

Note: Section 23 applies where parents have requested religious education in accordance with the religious character of the school. Section 10 inspectors will report on whether the school is complying with the law on school worship in terms of pupil attendance.

Although there is no legal compulsion to use inspectors trained by the National Society for section 23 inspections, in excess of 90 per cent of Church of England schools do so (Lankshear, J. F. 1997). This makes the National Society Inspection Handbook a very significant document for those who wish to know what standards are expected of Church of England schools.

Distinctiveness III: ethos

The ethos of an Anglican school should be reflected in every aspect of the school's life. It consists of several threads which, interwoven, make up the whole. Crucial to the development of the ethos of the school is the role of the headteacher. Even in voluntary controlled and foundation schools, where there is no provision for the governors to discriminate in favour of teachers drawn from the Christian community, there is specific legal provision for the governors to satisfy themselves that every candidate for the headship of the school has the ability to sustain and develop the religious character of the school (School Standards and Framework Act 1998). The leadership provided by the headteacher will set a standard for all those involved in the school to emulate. It is essential that every headteacher of a church school has a clear understanding of how the key concepts within Christianity should be reflected in the life of a church school. Some of these are briefly introduced in the following paragraphs.

Values

One of the key areas in which the ethos of the school will be reflected is the values that the school uses and reflects. A good introduction to the issues associated with the values that a church school should adopt is provided by the National Society publications *Values for Church Schools* (Shepherd 1998) and *A Christian Voice in Education* (Carey *et al.* 1998), the latter of which contains articles by three authors, including both current English Archbishops. In an Anglican school all the values reflected in the life of the school should be based on a clear understanding of Christian theology, particularly as it relates to childhood and to education. This represents a challenge to those responsible for the leadership of such schools, in that the time and opportunities to discuss these issues are limited within the context of the pressures on professionals to deliver the highest possible standards of general education and to administer a well organised school.

Relationships

The quality of the relationships that exist within a school is one of the key indicators of the extent to which the values that the school espouses are carried through in practice. In an Anglican school these should be based on the example and teaching of Christ. Nothing less than this could possibly reflect a Christian theology of education. The principal demonstration of these relationships will be among the adults who work in or lead the school. Unless they strive to conform their own relationships to these principles it is unlikely that the demands made on the pupils to treat each other and the adults in the school in accordance with the principles will be understood or accepted by them. No school is isolated from its local community and the wider community that it also serves. Therefore, the relationships that it maintains with members of these communities must also reflect the same principles of love, respect and service.

Stewardship

Another key concept in the teaching of Christianity is the twin threads of our involvement in creation. We are called to be both stewards of God's creation and partners with God in the continuing act of creation. This gives a particular responsibility to church schools to demonstrate a full commitment to these ideas in their teaching, their care for the environment within and outside schools, their respect for the creativity of artists, writers and musicians and the care with which they seek to develop the creativity of all those involved in the school, pupils and adults.

An Anglican school's commitment to good stewardship of its resources will also be shown in the measures that it takes to give an account of its work to the parents, the local community and the other stakeholders in the school. Openness and honesty will be the hallmark of all its dealings.

Justice

It will be clear immediately that the concept of justice must be reflected in the policies on rewards and discipline that the school develops, both for staff working in the school and for the pupils. In practice, under the pressure of running a complex institution, problems sometimes arise in ensuring that this principle is applied, particularly when it must be combined with the need to ensure the quality of relationships discussed above. In theory, of course, there is no conflict. Relationships based on love, respect and service should also incorporate justice; in practice, towards the end of a long term during a wet dinner break, the theory is easily lost in the pressures of the moment.

Justice, however, goes beyond the discipline and rewards policies in the school. If a school is to operate justly in the world then it must seek to apply the principles of justice in all its dealings with the world beyond its gates. This might present challenges to the way in which the school works with other schools in the area, to the way in which it obtains goods and services and to the way in which it accepts its accountability to the local and wider communities. The advent of the citizenship curriculum should present new opportunities for church schools to think through these issues and to explore how far the school's practices support the principles that are being taught to the pupils.

Theology

Each of the above sections has picked a single idea from Christian theology and briefly developed its implications for a church school. There are many other areas that could have been included and each of the chosen areas could have been developed more fully. The purpose in selecting these issues was not to attempt a comprehensive review of the ways in which an understanding of Christian theology interacts with the policies and management of an Anglican school, but to demonstrate that such an interaction should exist, and that all those who work in and particularly who seek to lead an Anglican school need to understand that at its heart must be the Christian faith. Christianity is not an extra to be bolted on to the school where it can be made to fit. It must stand at the centre. The difference between a church school and a community school does not lie in what the school does, but in why it does it.

Those in leadership positions in Anglican schools need to engage with Christian theology as well as with educational practice, so that within the school these ways of understanding the world are brought together and reflected in practice.

Regional variations

The previous paragraph argued strongly for the interaction of theology and educational practice in the development of a church school. A further issue for all Anglican schools is the interaction between the school and the type of community it serves. For the purpose of exploring some of the issues that this raises, three distinct types of community are considered for the issues that they raise for Anglican schools. It should be clear from this analysis that every Anglican school has to address the question: 'what does it mean to us to be the Anglican school in this place?' The need to be clear about the variety and variation among Church of England schools has been an important theme in the development of the section 23 inspection regime by the church (Brown *et al.* 2000).

Village schools

Many Anglican schools are in villages where they offer the only available primary education for the children of the village. In such circumstances the theology of service will be very important to the church school. Effectively the church school is offering the best possible education to the children who come, regardless of the faith stance of the children's parents. This offering of a service, in the name of Christ, is a long tradition in the church. It requires an open engagement with the local community and places great importance on the way in which the governors and staff of the school can sustain a Christian vision for their work, while respecting and honouring the different life stances of the parents of the pupils in the school. Church schools in villages share with all other village schools the challenges of providing a rounded education for all the possible futures of their pupils while working in a small community, which might be quite isolated from the rest of the world.

Suburban schools

Earlier in this chapter it was noted that a comparatively small number of Anglican schools were established in suburban areas. As a result of the lack of provision in these areas there is often considerable pressure from Christian parents to obtain access for the children to the school. This pressure can have two distinct results. At the level of the individual school it may result in the school adopting a policy for admissions that places an emphasis on the church attendance of the child's parents. This creates a different type of church school from the village school model. In these church schools many of the parents will share the commitment of the staff and governors to the Christian ethos of the school. This can be a strength for the school, but can also create pressures if the particular commitment to the faith among some parents does not reflect the spirit of openness and the pursuit of truth that is a longstanding tradition of Anglican schools and colleges at their best.

The second result of the pressure on the school for admission is the recurrent stories of people attending a local church for the sole purpose of obtaining a place for their child. It is important that such issues and the problems that they cause are discussed, but it must be remembered that the schools that face such problems are a very small proportion of the total number of Anglican schools. Schools have had to make their admissions policies public since the Education Act 1980. It is inevitable that, where the policy is public, a proportion of parents will comply with the steps necessary to obtain a place for their child. This would be true whatever the policy said. One of the ways of tackling the issue is to ensure that there are sufficient church school places available in the suburban areas to meet the demand of parents for them and thus to make complying with rigorous conditions to obtain entry unnecessary.

Inner-city schools

Anglican schools that serve inner-city areas are less likely than those in suburban areas to have to use their admissions policies, as the local church congregations are likely to be smaller. These schools have much in common with the village schools, in that they are offering education to children of the area, regardless of the faith stance of their parents. The difference is that in most inner-city areas parents have a real choice of schools if they wish to exercise it. In such areas a church school will attract parents either because it is the nearest school or because parents value the education that is being offered in the school, which will include taking religion and faith seriously. For this reason, in some areas it is possible to find Anglican school with a high proportion of children from Muslim homes. In such schools the need to respect the faith of the parents and pupils is particularly clear. It is also important that the staff and governors are clear about the way in which the school expresses its Christian foundation. These two imperatives are not exclusive to inner-city church schools, they apply to all church schools, but many of the Church of England inner-city schools provide examples from which others might learn in this context.

DfES regions

The three types of areas discussed above can be found in most parts of England and Wales. It is important to complete this section with a brief consideration of the national distribution of Church of England schools. Table 10.3 shows the proportion of Church of England schools, expressed as a percentage of all schools in each of the

Table 10.3 The percentage of Church of England schools by region

Region	Secondary schools	Primary schools	Total
North-east	0.61	10.14	8.31
North-west	5.38	28.32	24.97
Merseyside	2.91	13.66	11.74
Yorkshire and Humberside	3.12	21.76	18.72
East Midlands	4.08	27.58	23.73
West Midlands	6.64	25.97	22.55
Eastern	5.32	25.13	21.78
Inner London	10.61	17.85	16.74
Outer London	5.55	9.25	8.56
South-east	6.75	29.61	25.99
South-west	8.96	36.96	32.95
Total	5.51	25.04	21.85

regions used by the Department for Education and Skills. This table is taken from a paper presented to the biennial conference of the Ethos and Education Network in 2001 (Lankshear 2001), and reflects the position in September 1999. The most obvious fact from this table is the disproportionately low number of Church of England secondary schools compared to Church of England primary schools. This disproportion is one of the reasons why the church is now seeking opportunities to develop its provision of secondary schools.

Table 10.3 also shows some remarkable differences between regions. It is immediately clear that the predominantly urban areas of London and Merseyside are amongst the areas where the Church of England's provision is weakest. Perhaps most striking is the very low proportion of Church of England primary schools in Outer London, which of all the DfES regions is the most suburban. It is salutary to see that the current provision still reflects, to some extent, the problems that the church experienced over 150 years ago in making provision for the education of the children growing up in the expanding suburbs of the great cities.

Conclusion

At the beginning of this chapter reference was made to the changes that are likely to take place within Anglican schools in the next few years. It is important to return to that theme in closing. In June 2001 the Church of England published the final report of the committee chaired by Lord Dearing, which enquired into the future provision of church schools and their development (Dearing 2001). The report focused on three major themes:

- *The expansion of provision.* This chapter has indicated some of the reasons why the church should be pursuing some expansion of its provision of schools. The discussion of Table 10.3 highlighted this, as did the discussion of the problems created by pressures on admission to Church of England schools in the suburbs. The report sets a target of 100 new secondary schools within the next seven to eight years and also some increase in the provision of Church of England primary schools, particularly in suburban areas. The extent to which this is achievable will depend on a variety of factors, including the attitude of central and local government to such aspirations.

- *The continued improvement in the quality of the education being offered.* It would be quite wrong for the Church of England, or any other body, to seek or sustain an involvement in schools if it were not committed to providing the best possible education for all the pupils in its schools. To achieve this there must be a constant concern with the standards being offered and an active pursuit of excellence. For this reason if for no other the report addresses how this can be achieved, and places considerable emphasis on the professional education and development of teachers as a key factor.

- *The vocation to teach.* The report lays great stress on the contribution of teachers and challenges the church to do more to develop and support the vocation to teach among all those who have the talent to undertake the work. This will require a positive response from every local church, as well as from the bodies responsible for education at national and regional level. The report emphasises the important contribution that the church colleges have to play in developing the ways in which the nurture of the Christian vocation to teach can be sustained and enhanced during initial professional education and in continuing professional development.

One final factor that contributes to the feeling of growth and development within the Anglican church's contribution to the maintained system of education in England and Wales is the number of voluntary controlled schools that are seeking to use the provisions of the School Standards and Framework Act 1998 to change from voluntary controlled status to voluntary aided. This movement towards voluntary aided status within the existing schools seems to be a demonstration of the belief that the governors and staff of the schools have in the importance of their church identity.

This chapter has described a dynamic sector of the maintained system of education in England and Wales. It has been assumed that the next few years will see further development in the provision of Anglican schools. If this does not happen it will be important for those studying the sector to identify the reasons that have contributed to a change of mind within the church or within government. At the time of writing this chapter, however, such a change of intention seems remote and all the signs point to a period of expansion and development within the Anglican church's provision.

POINTS FOR DISCUSSION

1 What are the main reasons for the growing commitment of the Anglican church to its church schools and the expansion of their numbers?
2 What are the defining features of a Church of England school?
3 Are there any tensions between Church of England schools and 'secular' schools within the diverse social and cultural setting of the contemporary UK?

4 How far can a Church of England school maintain a Christian identity or ethos in a society that is culturally diverse and in a school setting that might be representative of many faiths or none?
5 Why are there relatively few Church of England schools in suburban settings?
6 What are the main conclusions of Lord Dearing's review of Church of England school provision (see Internet site below)?

INTERNET SITES

Church of England books and reports: www.chbookshop.co.uk
Church of England schools: www.churchschools.co.uk
The Dearing Report on Church Schools, *The Way Ahead*: www.natsoc.org.uk/ LateNews/wayahead/html
The National Society: www.natsoc.org.uk
New religious education texts: www.encounterchristianity.co.uk

REFERENCES AND FURTHER READING

Barton, D., Brown, A. S. and Brown, E. (1996) *Open the Door – Guidelines for Worship and for the Inspection of Worship in Voluntary and Grant Maintained Church Schools*. London: The National Society and Oxford Diocesan Education Services.
Brown, A. S., Lankshear, D. W. and Seaman, A. (2000) *The National Society's Inspection Handbook for Section 23 Inspections*. London: The National Society/Church House Publishing.
Carey, G., Hope, D. and Hall, J. (1998) *A Christian Voice in Education: Distinctiveness in Church Schools*. London: The National Society/Church House Publishing.
Dearing, R. (chair) (2001) *The Way Ahead: Church of England Schools in the New Millennium*. London: Church House Publishing.
Lankshear, D. W. (1992a) *A Shared Vision – Teaching in Church Schools*. London: The National Society.
Lankshear, D. W. (1992b) *Looking for Quality in a Church School*. London: The National Society.
Lankshear, D. W. (2000) *Governing and Managing Church Schools*. London: The National Society/Church House Publishing.
Lankshear, D. W. (2001) 'The religious identity of schools in England – a regional analysis', unpublished paper presented to the third conference of the Ethos and Education Network, Nymegen.
Lankshear, J. F. (1997) *Denominational Inspection in Primary Schools*. London: The National Society.
Ramsey, I. T. (chair) (1970) *The Fourth R – the Durham Report on Religious Education*. London: The National Society/SPCK.
Shepherd, P. (1998) *Values for Church Schools*. London: The National Society/Church House Publishing.

CHAPTER 11

Roman Catholic Schools

James Arthur

CHAPTER SUMMARY

This chapter examines:

- Catholic schools in the United Kingdom contextualised as part of global provision by the Catholic Church as 'the world's largest voluntary body in the provision of schools'.
- The historical role of Catholic education in England since the nineteenth century.
- The contemporary role of the Catholic Church in relation to its schools in England and Wales.
- Regional variations within Scotland and Northern Ireland.

Introduction

The Catholic Church has consistently made two principal claims in the realm of education and schooling: first, that parents have an inalienable right to decide whether or not their children should be educated in accordance with their religious beliefs; second, that political and social equity demand that the state recognises this parental right and materially assists its furtherance by the provision of denominational schools. Both claims have been accepted and met, in various ways, by numerous countries, making the Catholic Church the world's largest voluntary body in the provision of schools. The Church has been particularly successful with its twofold claim in countries where Catholics are in the minority. Consequently, we find extensive networks of Catholic schools owned and run by the Church, but aided by the state, in Australia, Canada, Denmark, the Netherlands, New Zealand and Scotland. Inevitably, state assistance has brought with it extensive state regulation. There are, therefore, disadvantages to state aid for the Catholic authorities, who continue to discuss what level of government interference is tolerable in their schools in areas such as the curriculum, building specifications, admissions, textbooks, educational philosophy and teacher training and appointments. The fundamental question arises that if government requirements seem to prejudice the deeper questions underlying Catholic educational theory and practice, then Catholic educators have to consider whether they can rightly cooperate. Generally, the Church has compromised simply in order to provide Catholic voluntary schools for its members.

This is no less so in England and Wales, where the first government grants to Catholic schools in 1847 were accompanied by specific conditions, including the right of the state to inspect schools aided from the public purse. While the Church continued to object to government regulations, it nevertheless has campaigned since 1847 for a greater share of national and local resources for the provision and maintenance of its schools, and in this it has been largely successful. By 1944 the Church could receive 50 per cent of a school's capital building costs and the Education Acts of 1967 and 1975, both under Labour governments, progressively raised this percentage to 85 per cent. In 2001 another Labour government announced that it intended to raise the percentage to 90 per cent. The Church has almost achieved its aim of equality of treatment between county and voluntary schools, while effectively being able to control some aspects of the voluntary aided schools' curriculum and management. The Church is successfully operating with a sympathetic government, as many of New Labour's policies, particularly communitarian or 'Third Way' ideas, are generally compatible with Catholic teaching (Arthur 2000). It is for the Church now to seek ways of preserving the ethos and character of its schools.

This chapter does not provide the space to do justice to this topic and therefore readers are referred to the main texts contained in the references for a more comprehensive account. This present chapter merely seeks to illustrate some selected aspects of policy and practice.

Administration and governance

The Education Act of 1944 was the cornerstone of the partnership between the Church and state, for the establishment of voluntary aided school status was largely undertaken to satisfy the demands of the Catholic Church. A spread of power and authority across interested partners ensured a degree of partnership. Today, the Catholic Church has over 2,200 voluntary aided schools in England and Wales, which are part-funded by their founding trust, normally a diocese. In return for these payments (15 per cent of major capital and maintenance expenditure, soon to be 10 per cent) the trustees are able to appoint the majority of the governors who in turn appoint and employ the staff and set admission policies. In addition, each Catholic school was free to teach within the framework of its specifically Catholic religious beliefs. Therefore, the control of education in England and Wales was commonly described as an administrative partnership, between central government, local education authorities and voluntary bodies. The partnership provided the Church with opportunities to influence the direction of education policy by means of official representation on committees, working parties and 'quangos' set up by central government. Official representatives of the Church therefore had access to many national levels of discussion and debate. While the Church actually implements policy through its own involvement as a partner in the system, it cannot escape a degree of political confrontation with the other partners – central and local government.

These structures have led to a number of well publicised conflicts and disputes within the Catholic community (Arthur 1995a, b). The establishment of grant-maintained schools in the 1988 education legislation simply demonstrated how weak the legal powers of the bishops are when they act as trustees of a group of Catholic schools within their diocese. The law treats each voluntary aided school as a separate and independent entity, with the governors responsible for the character and management of the school. The role of trustees in setting educational policies is much more limited than that of governors. While the foundation governors, those appointed by the diocese, must safeguard the religious character of their school, they do not have to follow any specific reorganisation plans suggested or proposed by the diocese. Consequently, a number of Catholic schools used the 1988 legislation to 'opt out' of local education authority funding arrangements, against the express advice of their bishops acting as the trustees of their schools. These actions served to emphasise that there are differing educational priorities within the Catholic community. The Labour government elected in 1997 abolished grant-maintained status and returned schools that had 'opted out' back to LEA funding arrangements, but preserved a degree of independence within them by creating a new status – foundation schools. In order to illustrate some of the problems with governance in Catholic schools this chapter restricts itself to looking at the employment of teachers, although other issues, such as admissions, would raise similar points.

Teachers in Catholic schools

Catholic school governors in England and Wales have traditionally managed their own staff appointments and employment relations. The Education Act 1944 established governors of Catholic schools within the maintained sector as the sole employers of teachers. Teachers in voluntary aided schools therefore had employment contracts with the governing body, which had the power to appoint, suspend and dismiss staff. Contracts of service specifically designed for teachers working in voluntary aided Catholic schools are consequently not new and they operated within a Catholic framework. This framework included a richness of 'custom and practice', coupled with broad statements of principles at the expense of precision and detail. Today, employment relations operate within a different climate and accord with very different structures and circumstances.

It is well established that certain *public* acts or activities of teachers employed in Catholic schools, which might be viewed as a facet of an individual's private life in any other type of school, can be judged by governors as incompatible with the role of a teacher. Hence, acts or activities which would not incur the wrath of an employer in any other school or profession could have major repercussions for the teacher in a Catholic school. Moreover, the standards of belief and moral behaviour expected from the Catholic teacher are even more pronounced. There is potentially a wide range of behaviour that could be viewed as breaking a teacher's contact with a Catholic school's governing body.

The Catholic Education Council produced a model contract in the 1950s for use by governors of Catholic schools, and in 1981 the Council revised this model by adding clause 4 (III)(a), to the effect that the teacher agrees 'to have regard to the Roman Catholic character of the school and not to do anything in any way detrimental or prejudicial to the interests of the same'. The clause was originally drafted by R. J. Harvey QC, a leading expert on employment law. This new clause generated some opposition from the teaching unions, but despite this the Catholic Education Council has consistently encouraged its use. Every teacher employed within a Catholic maintained school is normally expected to sign this contract. With the passage of the first School Teachers' Pay and Conditions Act in 1987, the Catholic Education Council proposed a new contract which, combined with new statutory teacher conditions, became an issue of conflict with the National Association of Schoolmasters and Union of Women Teachers. The Catholic Education Council proposed that the contract should also refer to the duties of the teacher in respect of the school's religious character, and provided the following wording for standard incorporation into all contracts in Catholic schools: 'The teacher should endeavour to maintain and develop the Catholic character of the school, in accordance with the direction of the governors, and, subject thereto, the direction given by the headteacher' (Cunningham 1988).

The clause appeared all-inclusive and met with some opposition among Catholic teachers themselves. The clause was later abandoned by the Catholic Education Council. Clearly it was an attempt to enforce by legal means the obligation of teachers actively to develop a school's religious ethos and identity under the direction of the headteacher. Case law would suggest that this is already implied in the contract of a teacher in a Catholic school, and in private discussions with a sympathetic Labour government the Churches were able to secure significant amendments to the School Standards and Framework Act 1998.

Section 60(5) of the Act reads:

> If the school is a voluntary aided school –
> (a) preference may be given, in connection with the appointment, remuneration or promotion of teachers at the school, to persons –
>   (i)   whose religious opinions are in accordance with the tenets of the religion or religious denomination specified in relation to the school under section 69(4), or
>   (ii) who attend religious worship in accordance with those tenets, or
>   (iii) who give, or are willing to give, religious education at the school in accordance with the tenets; and
>   (iv) regard may be had, in connection with the termination of the employment of any teacher at the school, to any conduct on his part which is incompatible with the precepts, or with the upholding of the tenets, of the religion or religious denomination so specified.

The Church has therefore secured in statutory form a clarification of the Education Act 1944, which was done in anticipation of problems with the European human rights legislation.

In Catholic schools, headteachers are widely acknowledged to be crucial in defining the nature and quality of the religious life. Consequently, there is a growing emphasis by governors and diocesan officials on defining the religious and moral leadership qualities of Catholic headteachers. That they are expected to promote the religious identity and life of the school is illustrated by a memorandum approved by the Westminster Council for Diocesan Affairs in 1989 entitled *Description and Responsibilities of Headteachers of a Catholic School*. Three principal responsibilities are detailed:

1 Potential headteachers need to understand the nature and purpose of Catholic education.
2 They must establish and sustain the Catholic identity of the school and safeguard the Church's teaching on a day-to-day basis.
3 They must be leaders of a Catholic faith *community* comprising teachers and pupils.

This is a definition of *community* interpreted not as a sociological term but primarily as a theological concept, and the only conditions for establishing such a faith community are achieved within a shared perspective of meaning. This represents a considerable challenge to headteachers of Catholic schools, who are charged with the responsibility for helping to prepare and form pupils for adult membership of the Church in conjunction with the wider Catholic community.

The appointment of headteachers is also the responsibility of the governors in Catholic schools in England, and the trust deed for each school will usually make it clear that a Catholic must be appointed. The governors invariably consult with officials from the diocesan education commission who represent the interests of the trustees and are almost always present at the interviewing of candidates for appointment. There have been a growing number of cases of dismissal, suspension and governor difficulties over the appointment and retention of Catholic headteachers. Some of these have reached the national press or the courts in one form or another. Catholic headteachers can certainly face a range of ethical and moral dilemmas, and the vast majority of them are loyal to the Church, but tensions can arise. It is not surprising that research among headteachers conducted by Gerald Grace (1996) concluded, 'Many of the dilemmas that the headteachers faced arose from a disjunction between official moral teaching and the mores of contemporary society.' Nevertheless, Catholic headteachers are expected to fulfil a number of requirements, not least those of being:

• headteachers who are committed, believing, and practising Catholics who pray in faith and are loyal to the Church, accepting its authentic teaching, and who can lead the school community in prayer;
• headteachers who insist on the central place of religion in the life of the school community and ensure the priority of religious education on the timetable, school worship and priestly chaplaincy;
• headteachers who establish a school community where the process of faith and moral development are integrated and where Catholic social principles are embedded in the curriculum and the life of the school;
• headteachers who can articulate the Catholic educational vision of the school and confidently expound a philosophy of Catholic education, and who can inspire in the school community a vision of what it can become;

- headteachers who see all things in the light of faith and place Christ at the centre of education, who can set the school tone accordingly and, in particular, who are sensitive to the demands of justice, love and charity.

How can the Catholic community ensure a sufficient supply of Catholic teachers with these qualities? What are required are teachers who are not simply practising Catholics but who are able to give an appropriate form of witness to Catholicism as part of their professionalism. There is clear evidence that the number of teachers willing and able to fulfil these requirements is in decline.

The respective roles of the parties concerned in Catholic education, and the relationship between them, require much clearer definition. These parties include central government, local education authorities, the trustees of voluntary schools and the governors of individual voluntary schools, together with the headteachers, teachers and parents. One of the central claims of the Church in education is that the whole Catholic community has a legitimate interest in the future direction of Catholic schooling. However, while the Church recognises that parental rights are fundamental in the choice of school, it also acknowledges that these rights must be balanced against those of the community. Catholic schools are not to function in isolation from one another or from the Catholic community in general. The present structures and governance to facilitate the Catholic community's participation in educational policy-making remain dependent on co-option by clerics. The Church remains very firmly hierarchical. Active lay involvement is essential for the survival of Catholic schools. Ultimately, after consultation and participation from the laity, it is the diocesan bishop who declares what Catholic education is to mean in practice. The only definition of what constitutes a Catholic school is that it must be one recognised as such by the diocesan bishop.

Curriculum, assessment and inspection

Section 23 of the Education Act 1944, which dealt with 'control of the secular curriculum', gave governors of Catholic voluntary aided schools control over the secular curriculum in their schools. Sections 1–4 of the Education Reform Act 1988 removed this control and returned it to the DES/DfEE, which imposed a National Curriculum on all state-funded schools. The Catholic Church opposed this move, but was completely unsuccessful. One reason for this lack of success was the basic question of whether there could be a Catholic school curriculum based on its own distinctive aims. Governors of Catholic schools had previously been responsible for their school's curriculum, but there is little evidence that they sought a curriculum different from LEA schools. The Education Reform Act did provide for 'safeguards' under section 17, which allowed for 'exception clauses' or 'specified modifications' to the National Curriculum. However, apart from changes to the 'technology of contraception' aspects of the natural science curriculum, the Catholic Church has not sought to make any changes. The theoretical principles that govern design, implementation, development and evaluation in terms of contributing towards the aims of Catholic education are almost wholly absent from debates about the National Curriculum.

It is the Office for Standards in Education (Ofsted) that inspects the secular curriculum in Catholic schools, while religious education is inspected by the diocesan authorities. Inspections by Ofsted have generally been favourable of the curriculum standards in Catholic schools, but it is still for the bishop to ensure that religious education is conducted in accordance with the rites and practices of the Catholic Church. With regard to the majority of the school curriculum the Catholic school claims to seek a Christian milieu through which the secular curriculum is delivered. This is a growing challenge for all Catholic schools.

The Catholic Education Service has produced a series of development materials to help staff and governors to define their role and to evaluate the specifically Catholic nature of the school and the curriculum it delivers. For example, the document *Evaluating the Distinctive Nature of a Catholic School* (CES 1999) affirms a Vatican II approach to Catholic Schools:

> all aspects of the Catholic school or college, the academic work, the relationships, the priorities, the aims and objectives, the pastoral care and discipline, have the potential to speak of God's loving care for each person involved in the school's life. God is at the centre of the learning process and is the ultimate purpose of schooling, as of all aspects of life. (CES 1999: A-11)

In addition, this document took into account the more recent publication of the *Curriculum Directory*, a universal document aimed at enunciating further what was to be taught formally as part of a Catholic school's classroom religious education. It addresses itself to the whole curriculum of a Catholic school and draws on *The Catechism of the Catholic Church*. The Congregation for Catholic Education in Rome also issued *The Catholic School on the Threshold of the Millennium* in 1999, which commits Catholic schools to developing the religious and moral formation of their pupils. Indeed, it is precisely the emphasis and priority that religious education is generally given in the Catholic school curriculum that distinguishes them from county schools. It is much more difficult to fulfil Groome's (1996: 107) proposal for the curriculum in a Catholic school: 'that the distinctiveness of Catholic education is prompted by the distinctive characteristics of Catholicism itself, and these characteristics should be reflected in the whole school curriculum'. The curriculum in a Catholic school should also emphasise service to neighbour and many Catholic schools are proud of their achievements in working with their local communities.

Ethos

Schools develop unique climates and lives of their own, created by means of a great many influences that affect the quality of relationships and the teaching and learning within them. The Catholic Church believes that a Christian atmosphere or tone within a school can act as a profound formative influence on the development of a pupil's faith. However, while much educational thought stresses the importance of an appropriate ethos within schools, there is little in the way of practical definition given to this elusive term. In a Catholic school the central position of religion, more particularly the

Catholic faith, is emphasised. The sum of this ethos has been defined in Church documents as being that: 'everyone agree with the educational goals and cooperate in achieving them; that interpersonal relationships be based on love and Christian freedom; that each individual, in daily life, be a witness to Gospel values; that every student be challenged to strive for the highest possible level of formation, both human and Christian'. This emphasis on a distinctive Catholic ethos is a central theme on which Catholic educational policy is founded. While the ethos in schools will differ, as a result of local traditions and successive intakes, it is what they ultimately share in belief that makes them a 'community of faith' rather than another kind of community. It is why John Haldane (1996: 135) says: 'the primary function of Catholic schools is to transmit Catholic truths and Catholic values. Everything else, no matter how important, is secondary to this.'

Catholic schools are required by the Church to be different from largely secular institutions in their philosophy, mission and actions. They will also differ from each other, while emphasising general principles that reflect the universality of the Church. The Catholic Church has a rich tradition to draw upon in developing a unique ethos for its schools. After all, parents send their children to a Catholic school voluntarily: in choosing a Catholic school they signify a willingness to join a particular community and to accept its shared practices on behalf of their children. Catholic schools seek to build a communal ethos, which is ideally an extension of the family. This communal ethos within Catholic schools 'often enhances their organisational effectiveness and in turn improves student academic performance. This communal ethos is often elusive, but it consists of a real weaving of traditions, beliefs, rituals and stories into the way people speak and act' (Arthur 2000: 115). This is why there is such emphasis on the qualities of Catholic teachers, for it is they who are responsible for ensuring that the ethos is fully developed. Nevertheless, pupils are not spectators in the creation of this ethos, but should be part of integrating gospel values into their learning. Indeed, parents must be welcomed into the school and the local church must be an active participant. Above all, the interpersonal relationships in the school should be based on love and Christian freedom.

Regional variations

There are a number of regional variations between England and Wales, Scotland and Northern Ireland. In 1918 the Scots achieved a 'final' settlement of the denominational schools question. The Education (Scotland) Act 1918 provided a solution to the same fundamental issue as in England and Wales: that there should be Catholic teachers for Catholic schools. The 1918 Act allowed the Scottish bishops a veto over the appointment of teachers in Catholic schools, and in return Catholic schools would be transferred to the local authorities, with the Catholic financial burden relinquished. A fifth of maintained schools in Scotland are Catholic, but unlike in England, these schools do not have a governing body functioning as the employer of staff. Appointments are made by the local education authority, subject to the approval of the Church as regards the religious beliefs and character of the candidate. This approval was formerly only required at the initial appointment, but as the religious practices among teachers have changed the bishops found this once-only approval inadequate for protecting the school's Catholic identity. They therefore campaigned successfully to extend this approval system by an amendment to the Self-governing Schools (Scotland) Act 1989, which refers to 'any post' being approved. This means that approval is now required for first appointments and transfers to other Catholic schools, as well as for every pro-moted post.

The Church is required to give any reasons for refusing approval to individual teach-ers, but it is not obliged to give them to anyone else. Once approval is given by the Church, it cannot be legally withdrawn. However, the Church certificate of approval includes wording to the effect that approval may be withdrawn. It therefore acts as a licence to teach in a Catholic school. The advantage of this system means that disputes do not generally arise at the appointment and promotion stages. However, the Church would find it difficult to remove a teacher who publicly departed from Church teach-ing. The Scottish bishops also appear to share the same reluctance to make judgements about non-Catholic teachers as the English and Welsh bishops. In their seven-point national system of approval they state that: 'The Church does not presume to make judgements as to the religious beliefs and character of teachers who are not Catholics.' However, the law requires the bishops to approve both Catholic and non-Catholic teachers. In the same way the distinctive religious provisions in the Catholic Teachers' Contract in England and Wales apply equally to Catholic and non-Catholic teachers. The Catholic Church's approach to non-Catholic teachers working within its educa-tional establishments has created ambiguity as to what is expected from them in rela-tion to the school's religious identity. It is therefore important that Catholic authorities scrutinise their practices for compliance with the European Convention on Human Rights, as the Convention may pose a threat unless the Catholic authorities ensure that their procedures to remedy disputes are both just and transparent (Arthur 1998).

In Northern Ireland, Catholic schools are maintained by the state, but controlled by the Catholic authorities, which ensures the appointment of Catholic teachers to Catholic schools. Northern Ireland has a 'dual system' of schools similar to that in England. There is still considerable opposition to 'segregated' schools in both Northern Ireland and Scotland (Conroy 1999) and some are arguing for 'integrated' schools (Chadwick 1994). However, the Catholic authorities in both countries are deter-mined to secure the place of Catholic schools within the state system, so that Catholic parents have the choice of a Catholic school for their children.

Conclusion

The Catholic community has made enormous sacrifices in order to establish, from its own limited resources, a national network of schools. All Catholic schools, whether publicly assisted (voluntary aided) or independent of public funds, have their founda-tion in a trust deed. These trust deeds were generally drawn up during the nineteenth century in a world very different from our own, based on many assumptions about the nature of society and the Catholic community that no longer apply. Today the Catholic bishops are responsible for over 2,200 voluntary schools in England and Wales, which comprise a major part of the activity generated by their diocesan trusts. The majority of Catholic schools are oversubscribed. Many appear high up in performance league tables and are seen to produce excellent examination results. Catholic schools often enjoy good reputations in the local community, reputations based on clear teaching doctrinally and morally, firm and fair discipline, educational support for those with identified needs and proven track records in social inclusion. This is true across both phases of education. It can be attributed to a number of factors: strong support from local parishes and parent communities; clear vision from diocesan authorities; commitment from the teaching staff; and shared values between the stakeholders. There are governing tensions within the Catholic system, but the majority of Catholic parents and teachers support their schools and seek to build them as faith communities inspired by gospel values, which are committed to serving others.

POINTS FOR DISCUSSION

1 Do Catholic parents have an inalienable right to decide whether or not to educate their children in accordance with their religious beliefs?
2 In what ways can denominational education be socially and politically divisive or a force for social order?
3 Why does the state in all parts of the UK continue to recognise and support Catholic Church schools and those of other Christian denominations?
4 What are the potential disadvantages of state involvement in the support of Catholic schools?

INTERNET SITES

The official site of the Catholic Church in England and Wales, including the Catholic Education Service, the Department of Christian Education and Formation and the Bishops' Conference of England and Wales: www.tasc.ac.uk
The Catholic Church in Scotland: www.catholic-scotland.org.uk

REFERENCES AND FURTHER READING

Arthur, J. (1995a) *The Ebbing Tide*. Leominster: Gracewing.
Arthur, J. (1995b) 'Teaching and employment conditions in Catholic schools: principles and practice', *Law and Justice: the Christian Law Review*, 124/125, 132–8.
Arthur, J. (1998) 'British human rights legislation and religiously affiliated schools and colleges', *Education and the Law*, 10(4), 225–35.
Arthur, J. (2000) *Schools and Community: the Communitarian Agenda in Education*. London: Falmer Press.
Catholic Education Service (1999) *Evaluating the Distinctive Nature of a Catholic School*. London: CES.
Chadwick, P. (1994) *Schools of Reconciliation*. London: Cassell.

Congregation for Catholic Education (1999) *The Catholic School on the Threshold of the Millennium*. Rome: Vatican.

Conroy, J. C. (1999) *Catholic Education: Inside Out, Outside In*. Leamington Spa: Lindisfarne Books.

Cunningham, R. (1988) Letter to Dicocesan School Commissioners from the Secretary of the Catholic Education Council.

Grace, G. (1996) 'Leadership in Catholic schools', in T. H. McLaughlin, J. O'Keefe and B. O'Keeffe (eds) *The Contemporary Catholic School*. London: Falmer Press.

Grace, G. (2002) *Catholic School Leadership*. London: Routledge.

Groome, T. (1996) 'What makes a school Catholic?', in T. H. McLaughlin, J. O'Keefe and B. O'Keeffe (eds) *The Contemporary Catholic School*. London: Falmer Press.

Haldane, J. (1996) 'Catholic education and Catholic identity', in T. H. McLaughlin, J. O'Keefe and B. O'Keeffe (eds) *The Contemporary Catholic School*. London: Falmer Press.

McLaughlin, T. H., O'Keefe, J. and O'Keeffe, B. (eds) (1996) *The Contemporary Catholic School*. London: Falmer Press.

CHAPTER 12

Faith and Diversity in Religious School Provision

J. Mark Halstead

CHAPTER SUMMARY

- This chapter examines religious schools in the UK outside the Church of England and the Roman Catholic Church.
- Two distinct groups are identified. The 'old' religious schools are long-established schools belonging to the Free Churches that are either voluntary aided or members of the Independent Schools Council. The 'new' religious schools are smaller, private schools established by evangelical Christians, Muslims and other minority groups in response to the growing secularism of modern society. Jewish schools are found in each group.
- Generally, the 'new' religious schools have a more pronounced religious ethos and a higher proportion of curriculum time devoted to religious teaching. A few 'new' religious schools have very recently received state funding, and this has provoked considerable debate.
- The chapter concludes with a review of some of the main arguments for and against such schooling.

Introduction

As we have seen in Chapters 10 and 11, most religious schools in the UK are either Anglican or Roman Catholic, but there is now a wider diversity of other religious schools than ever before. It is this diversity that forms the topic of the present chapter. Among the main providers of religious schooling apart from the Church of England and the Roman Catholic Church are the Methodists, the Presbyterians, the Quakers, the United Reformed Church, various evangelical Christian groups, the Seventh Day Adventists, the Greek Orthodox Church, Jews from both Orthodox and non-Orthodox traditions, the Muslims, the Sikhs and the Hindus. However, the diversity is not simply a matter of denomination: there are many different types of religious school, including voluntary aided schools, foundation schools, a City Technology College and a wide range of private, independent and other non-maintained schools. Many of the schools were established within the past 30 years, though some have a much longer history; for example, the oldest Quaker secondary boarding school dates back to 1779, and John Wesley founded a residential school in 1748 that still operates in Bath. Many of the schools are very small, though some (such as the King Fahd Academy in London) have well over 1,000 pupils.

The term 'religious school' is an imprecise one. This chapter does not deal with Sunday schools or with the supplementary schooling on which many Jewish, Muslim, Sikh and other groups rely as a way of transmitting their faith and initiating their children into the values and practices of the religious group. Nor does it deal with those community schools that as a matter of fact, if not of policy, cater for the children of a single faith community. Schools like these, such as Belle Vue Girls' School in Bradford, where 97 per cent of the pupils are of Muslim background, often perform a delicate balancing act as they seek to prepare their pupils for full British citizenship while at the same time offering opportunities for them to develop and enrich their religious and cultural commitments. The focus of the chapter is exclusively on full-time schools founded by religious groups other than the Church of England and the Roman Catholic Church. For the purposes of the chapter the schools are divided into just two groups, which I call the 'old' religious schools and the 'new' religious schools.

The 'old' religious schools are generally fairly large, well established schools that fall into one of two categories: those that receive state funding as voluntary aided or voluntary controlled schools and those that are members of the Independent Schools Council (ISC). There are 28 Methodist schools in the voluntary sector (all primary), a further 16 independent Methodist schools (all senior boarding schools), five independent schools that retain their links with the United Reformed Church, eight independent Friends' schools (Quakers), 10 independent Free Presbyterian schools in Northern Ireland, 29 voluntary-aided Jewish schools, one independent Jewish boarding school in England and another in Scotland, a small number of other Christian schools and a rather larger number of voluntary schools of mixed denomination, including joint Anglican-Methodist schools.

The explanation for the very small number of such schools compared to those of an Anglican or Roman Catholic foundation must be sought in the historical development of education in the UK. The Free Churches were at the forefront of the campaign to provide a state system of education for all children, and when this was established, most Methodist, Baptist, Presbyterian and Congregationalist schools were either closed or transferred into the state sector, becoming county (now called 'community') schools. Most of the Free Churches were satisfied with the religious provisions of the Education Act 1944, including non-sectarian religious education and a daily act of non-denominational collective worship. Thus the Baptist Church abandoned denominational schooling entirely, and the retention of schools by the other Free Churches was the exception rather than the rule. Most of the United Reformed Church schools that remain today were founded as boarding schools for the children of Congregational ministers who needed to be free to move around the country. The Methodist Church retained a small number of voluntary schools under its direct control after 1944, but its independent schools came into being with the abandonment of the direct grant system for schools in the 1970s. There is continuing debate in the Methodist Conference as to the moral and theological justification for the continued sponsorship of these schools. The history of Jewish schools is more varied: the first Jewish school in London opened in 1657, and the Manchester Jews' School was the first to receive state funding in 1853. By 1880 more than half the Jewish children in Britain were being educated in Jewish schools, but by 1939 this figure had dropped to below 10 per cent. The past 25 years have again been a time of rapid expansion, with new Jewish voluntary aided and independent schools opening (both Orthodox and non-Orthodox or 'pluralist') and the number of children attending Jewish schools more than doubling. As a group, the 'old' religious schools share many features with Anglican and Catholic schools. Sometimes their distinctive religious nature is not very prominent, though this is less true of the Jewish schools than of those established by the Free Churches.

The 'new' religious schools are generally much smaller, were all established as private schools and typically have a much stronger religious dimension (Walford 2000). Most were established within the past 30 years, and what they have in common is the desire to provide an education that is in harmony with the distinctive beliefs and practices of the founding groups and that rejects the growing secularism of modern society. Their aim is to integrate the religious perspective into the school ethos and curriculum, and to strengthen their pupils' faith so that they may grow up as well informed and committed members of the group. The 'new' religious schools fall into two main categories: evangelical or charismatic Christian schools, and schools set up by other world faiths. There are currently over 60 evangelical Christian schools scattered throughout the UK, though numbers fluctuate as existing schools close and new ones open. Most are primary schools with an average size of about 50 children. Some were established by churches, particularly independent Baptist churches, Pentecostal churches and house churches, others by groups of parents concerned that their children should receive a Bible-based education. Many of the schools are linked to the Christian Schools' Trust, which was established in 1988 (Deakin 1989; O'Keeffe 1992). In addition to the schools run by parents and churches, there are a few private evangelical Christian schools run for profit, and one City Technology College, Emmanuel College in Gateshead. Of the world faith schools, the biggest group by far is the Muslim, with an estimated 77 full-time schools in England, Scotland and Wales. About 50 of these are members of the Association of Muslim Schools (AMS), which was established in 1992 to represent the interests of Muslim schools. In contrast to the evangelical Christian schools, there are more secondary than primary Muslim schools, and since separate schooling for girls and boys is a feature of Muslim practice, there are no coeducational schools at secondary level. Among other world faiths, there are currently three Sikh schools (one in Chigwell and a primary and secondary in Hayes), two Hindu schools (the Bhaktivedanta Manor Primary School in Watford and the Swaminarayana Mandir School in North-west London) and a number of independent Jewish schools of varying persuasions, including three primary schools promoted by members of the Progressive and Masorti Movements (Akiva, Clore Shalom and Clore Tikva Schools) and three ultra-Orthodox schools that use Yiddish as a language of instruction (in Hackney, Golders Green and Newcastle). Other religious minorities with a number of small schools include the Seventh Day Adventists, with about 12 primary schools and two secondary, and in addition there are a number of individual schools with distinctive religious affiliations, such as the Maharishi School of the Age of Enlightenment in Skelmersdale, which describes itself as a non-denominational Christian school.

The most significant development in recent years involving the 'new' religious schools has been the granting of state funding to a very small number, which means in effect that their status is now on a par with the 'old' religious schools (Walford 2000). Some groups had been campaigning for state funding via the voluntary aided route since the early 1980s, but the provisions in the Education Act 1993 that allowed groups of parents and charitable, religious or independent sponsors to apply to the Secretary of State for Education in England or the Secretary of State for Wales to establish their own grant-maintained schools offered a new pathway for state funding. Several Muslim schools and evangelical Christian schools applied unsuccessfully under this new scheme, and the failure of Oak Hill School, which had led the campaign for several years, resulted in its closure in 1996. By 1997 the only schools to be accepted as grant-maintained schools under the new scheme were either Catholic (including one in Wales) or Orthodox Jewish. Within a year of coming to office in 1997, however, the new Labour government had extended the diversity of state-funded religious schools by allowing sponsored grant-maintained status to one secondary Seventh Day Adventist school (the John Loughborough School in Tottenham, which serves a largely Afro-Caribbean community), two Muslim primary schools (al-Furqan School in Birmingham and Islamia School in Brent) and two 'pluralist' Jewish schools (the Jewish Community Day School in Borehamwood and the Mathilda Marks-Kennedy School in Barnet). More recently, the Guru Nanak Sikh Secondary School in Hayes, Feversham College in Bradford (a Muslim girls' secondary school) and a Greek Orthodox school have all gained voluntary aided status, and others, including a Hindu school, hope to do so soon. The Labour government's continuing commitment to diversity of educational provision is made clear in its Green Paper *Schools: Building on Success* (DfEE 2001), which recognises the contribution made by faith schools (para. 4.13) and states:

> Schools supported by the churches and other major faith groups . . . have a good record of delivering a high quality of education to their pupils and many parents welcome the clear ethos of these schools. We therefore wish to welcome more schools provided by the churches and other major faith groups. [In addition to Church of England schools] we know other faith communities are also interested in extending their contribution to education. We intend to change the capital funding arrangements to make them more favourable to enable this to occur. (para. 4.19)

Distinctiveness I: administration and governance

Where a religious denomination has a sizeable number of schools, there is usually an umbrella organisation that performs a number of functions, including representing the interests of member schools, acting as a pressure group with local and national government, encouraging cooperation between schools, organising conferences, providing sample trust deeds and clarifying the educational philosophy of member schools. Such organisations include the Methodist Church Division of Education and Youth, the Friends' Schools Joint Council, the Association of Muslim Schools, the Christian Schools Trust and the Jewish Board of Deputies. However, there are significant numbers of schools, especially among the 'new' religious schools, that remain outside any such organisation – particularly where they have been sponsored by an individual church, mosque, gurdwara, temple or other place of worship or by a group of parents acting on their own initiative.

The instruments of government for voluntary schools were laid down in the Education Act 1986, and schools that are members of the ISC tend to have a similar pattern of governance, but the new religious schools are governed on an individual basis. Consequently there is a wide diversity of practice. Sometimes there is a separate board of trustees, sometimes governors and trustees are the same people. Sometimes the governing body is called a school council or management committee. In the case of the evangelical Christian schools, the governors may be made up exclusively of church leaders, or of any combination of parents, teachers and church leaders. The governing body is generally responsible with the headteacher for staffing, funding, admissions, discipline, curriculum, organisation and management, health and safety, religious issues and developing school policy. Meetings take place anything between once a week and once a term.

The aims of the schools are not always fully articulated, though most now produce a mission statement in line with the requirements of the Education (Schools) Act 1992. Statements usually include phrases like: 'to build a strong community based on the Sikh religion' (Guru Nanak Sikh Secondary School); 'to create a caring warm Islamic atmosphere within which pupils can develop to their full potential' (Manchester Islamic High School for Girls); 'to foster an attraction for Krishna consciousness within the children using the framework of the National Curriculum' (Bhaktivedanta Manor Primary School).

Among the diversity of religious schools, three distinct school philosophies can be identified. The first group (mainly but not exclusively 'old' religious schools) seeks to minister to the whole community, even where this is multifaith, and does not place any religious restrictions on pupil admissions; the religious dimension to the school is most evident in the provision of care and discipline based on a religious ethos. Quaker schools, for example, emphasise the qualities of community, openness, humility, peaceableness, spirituality, tolerance, respect, responsibility and growth towards truth, maturity and wholeness. The second group identifies its primary purpose as the intellectual and spiritual nurture of children in the faith; admission is open to any child ('irrespective of creed, colour, intellect or social standing'), but since there is no provision for withdrawal from any part of the life of the school, this means that anyone who does not wish to participate fully is effectively precluded from attending the school. The John Loughborough School, for example, presents itself as a school for children of all faiths even though Seventh Day Adventist beliefs and practices are at the heart of the school's ethos and curriculum. The third group restricts admission to children of members of the religious group. A number of Jewish schools, for example, make it clear that admission is restricted to Orthodox Jewish children, and some Muslim and evangelical Christian schools require parents to sign an agreement indicating support for the aims of the school when their child is admitted.

The financial position of many of the 'new' religious schools is precarious, and financial difficulty is a major cause of closure. Though one school requires parents to pay 10 per cent of their income, the fees of most schools are set at a low level that does not cover costs. The school then has to rely on donations or financial support from the sponsoring church or mosque. One result of the financial difficulties is that there is often a shortage of resources, particularly library books, computers and facilities for technology, art, science and physical education. The schools themselves are housed in a wide variety of buildings, including former school buildings, large Victorian houses, converted farmhouses and farm buildings, refurbished churches and church halls, garages, mills, theatres, factories, other converted buildings and various homes. Very few have purpose-built accommodation, and often there is a shortage of play areas.

The 'new' religious schools are often dependent on the commitment of their teachers to compensate for the deficiencies in other areas of provision. Research suggests that there is a favourable staff/pupil ratio and a very high level of qualified teachers among full-time staff in the evangelical Christian schools (MacKenzie 1994), though this pattern is not necessarily repeated in the other faith schools. There is also a high ratio of part-time staff, some of whom provide their services without pay. Staff are seen as role models for students in terms of belief and commitment, and so wherever possible they are drawn from the faith group of the school. This does not usually apply to the 'old' religious schools. One of the main strengths of the 'new' religious schools is the close positive links that usually exist between the home, the school and the sponsoring religious community. The shared purpose and commitment are made easier by the sharing of fundamental beliefs and values, and children undoubtedly benefit from the family atmosphere of many of the schools and the resulting sense of stability and coherence.

Distinctiveness II: curriculum, assessment and inspection

It is in the area of the curriculum that tensions are most apparent between the liberal framework of values which underpins most education in the UK and the religious values which are the very *raison d'être* of the schools under discussion. Four distinct approaches to the curriculum can be identified.

First, voluntary schools are required to teach the full National Curriculum, though they are free to teach religious education and organise assemblies in accordance with their own denominational teaching. Independent schools are not required to follow the National Curriculum, but City Technology Colleges and most ISC schools do so, because they would be less likely to attract pupils if they were unable to provide a broad and balanced curriculum. According to its prospectus, Emmanuel CTC in Gateshead, for example, seeks to combine a Christian ethos with a 'commitment to a rich technological and work oriented curriculum'.

Second, some of the 'new' religious schools seek to provide a more even balance between the religious and secular curriculum. In Ikra Primary School in North London, about 70 per cent of the time is devoted to the National Curriculum subjects, and about 30 per cent to Islamic subjects and Turkish culture. In Bhaktivedanta Manor Primary School, the children have a special morning programme (prasadam) from 7 to 9 a.m., and then study the National Curriculum for the rest of the day. In the Menorah Foundation Primary School the time is divided almost equally between the National Curriculum and the religious (Limmudei Kodesh) curriculum.

Third, some 'new' religious schools seek to eradicate the religious/secular divide by teaching the National Curriculum within a religious worldview, and adapting secular materials to give them a religious slant. In some Muslim and evangelical Christian schools, for example, science teaching may be adapted to bring it into line with sacred texts and to acknowledge God as the creator of all things.

Fourth, some schools attempt to provide a balanced alternative curriculum based on religious principles, using secular materials only as a supplement where necessary. The main problem here is the choice of curriculum materials. Several evangelical Christian schools use the Accelerated Christian Education (ACE) programme, an individualised learning programme developed in the USA, which covers English, maths, science, social studies and history. However, the ACE packages have been widely criticised for inculcating the uncritical acceptance of authority and a distorted worldview with a nationalist American bias. Several Islamic organisations in the UK are currently working on Muslim materials for schools, mainly following the 'Islamisation of education' principle.

Some religious schools pay particular attention to children's special educational needs (SEN). For example, there is a Jewish Special School in Cheshire which provides for pupils nationwide, and the Guru Nanak Sikh Secondary School has a well developed SEN policy. Assessment policies vary from school to school. For example, the Manchester Islamic High School for Girls places a strong emphasis on assessment, not only of learning and academic achievement but also of personality, helpfulness, a caring nature and respect for others. Muslim schools are encouraged by the AMT to engage in a regular process of self-evaluation.

Religious schools are subject to three different kinds of official inspection:

- Voluntary aided schools are subject to regular Ofsted inspection for their National Curriculum provision, plus separate denominational inspection for religious education, collective worship and the wider school ethos.
- The ISC arranges the inspection of its member schools and provides information to the DfES on their registration. A single inspection agency, the Independent Schools Inspectorate (ISI), was formed for this purpose in April 2000. This deals with just over half of the 2,204 independent schools. Ofsted in turn monitors ISI inspections.
- The remaining independent schools are inspected by Ofsted. HMI inspect provisionally registered schools to see if they are ready for final registration and other schools on a five-year cycle to see if they still meet the conditions of registration. In addition, there are full inspections of a small number of independent schools, particularly those in receipt of some public funding.

Independent religious schools often receive favourable comment from inspectors on the quality of teaching, the observed care of children and the relationships within the school. However, one key concern raised in the *Annual Report of Her Majesty's Chief Inspector of Schools: 1999/2000* (Ofsted 2001) was the lack of a broad and balanced curriculum in some schools:

> Many religious schools provide a pattern of religious instruction throughout the morning with an inevitably limited secular curriculum delivered in two hours a day in the afternoons. Even where the balance between religious and secular studies is different to this, the amount of time available for the core subjects is sometimes inadequate and this can pose severe problems to GCSE courses, for example the lack of opportunity for investigation in science. The creative and aesthetic areas of the curriculum are often poorly represented or non-existent. (Ofsted 2001: 80–1)

Distinctiveness III: ethos

If we take 'ethos' to refer to the pervasive atmosphere in a school, which may be influenced by a wide range of things, including the dominant forms of social interaction, the attitudes and expectations of teachers, school policies, discipline procedures, forms of communication, teaching and management styles, the physical environment, the learning climate, the nature of pupil involvement in the school, school–parent–community relations and even the kind of language used, then most religious schools do have a distinctive ethos. Typically, religious schools seek to provide a calm, caring atmosphere where the spiritual and moral growth of children can thrive as much as their intellectual development. They also generally have well developed discipline policies and seek to encourage a strong sense of community and commitment. Perhaps the biggest differences between the schools lie in the cultural values and assumptions on which these aims are based. In the case of the 'old' religious schools, the differences tend to be subtle ones, because many of the underlying cultural values are shared in society at large. But in the case of the 'new' religious schools, the atmosphere is likely to be much more distinctive, in line with the cultural values and practices of the sponsoring group.

Because they do not necessarily share the dominant values of the broader society, the 'new' religious schools perhaps try harder than others to ensure that the messages that children pick up through the hidden curriculum (for example, through the example set by teachers or through teacher–pupil relationships) are in line with the school's teaching and underlying philosophy. Children are kept in constant touch with the symbols and practices of their faith. Muslim schools, for example, take many steps to maintain an Islamic environment: assemblies include readings from the Qur'an and the *hadith*, Islamic feast days are observed and a strict uniform policy is enforced in keeping with Islamic teaching, including headscarf or hijab and shalwar-kameez for girls. Children are encouraged to say all the compulsory prayers which fall within the school day (*salah-al-Duhr* in summer and *salah-al-Duhr* and *salah-al-Asr* in winter), to do *wudu* each time they visit the toilet and to fast during *Ramadan* (from breakfast to lunchtime only up to the age of seven, but for the whole day after that age if they wish and their health allows it). Similar activities and requirements reinforce the religious ethos of other 'new' religious schools.

Regional variations

Apart from the preponderance of Presbyterianism in Scotland and Northern Ireland, the regional differences in religious schooling are slight compared to the denominational differences. There are evangelical Christian schools throughout England, Wales, Scotland and Northern Ireland, and Muslim schools in England, Scotland and Wales. Other schools serving world faith groups are located mainly in the big cities.

Conclusion

The 'old' religious schools are widely accepted, alongside Catholic, Church of England and ISC schools, as part of the rich tapestry of the education system in the UK, though a few groups continue to oppose all state funding for religious schools and all private schooling on principle. The 'new' religious schools, however, have proved much more controversial (DES 1985; Halstead 1986; CRE 1990; Haw 1994; Halstead 1995). In order to understand the controversy, a number of separate debates need to be disentangled. Questions concerning the freedom of minority groups to provide separate religious schooling for their own children at their own expense need to be separated from questions about the appropriateness of state funding for religious schools, and claims that religious schools are not in the best interests of children (because they may not promote the development of personal autonomy) need to be separated from claims that they are not in the best interests of society at large (because they may promote separatism and threaten the cohesion of society as a whole by damaging the chances of mutual understanding among different communities).

It also needs to be recognised that different parties come to the debate with different interests, different agendas and different fundamental values. Parents and religious groups may support such schools because they provide their children with a secure and stable environment where the beliefs and values of the school are broadly in line with those of the home; they may also judge the comprehensive school to be educationally inadequate because it does not provide a context where the faith of their children can flourish. They may have nothing in common with conservative politicians and economists who support the schools as an example of the market values of choice and diversity and because they are likely to produce honest, law-abiding citizens with a strong respect for authority. Similarly, opponents who claim that many such schools reinforce ethnic divisions (because Muslim, Jewish, Sikh, Hindu and Seventh Day Adventist schools generally serve families of a single ethnic minority group) come to the debate from a very different angle from feminists, who see such schools as bastions of patriarchal values.

At the heart of the various arguments and strands of debate, however, lie questions about minority rights in a democracy. It is often argued by liberals that the purpose of education in a democracy cannot be to confirm a minority in their own culture, and that children have the right as morally autonomous individuals to form their own conception of the good life rather than being trapped in a restrictive culture. In response, the proponents of religious schools will argue that parents, by virtue of their responsibilities in bringing up their children, have a strong claim to a major say in how their children are educated – a right, incidentally, which is contained in Article 2 of Protocol No. 1 of the European Convention on Human Rights. For children born and brought up in religious homes, there may be a danger to the stability of their development in such a radical discontinuity to their upbringing as would be involved in suddenly transplanting them into an environment in which all their parents' most cherished beliefs are subjected to close criticism and treated as of no more value than beliefs their parents totally reject (Ota 1997). Schools of their own faith are much more likely to provide this necessary security and continuity in their development, at least until they are of an age when they can assume responsibility for their own life stance.

A second anxiety is that minority faith groups might abuse the right to establish their own schools by using them for undemocratic ends, such as promoting fundamentalism and intolerance, engaging in indoctrination or supporting and justifying gender inequalities. To some extent these anxieties are based on hearsay and on a failure to understand the beliefs and practices of the faith groups concerned. Arguments about the repression of women in Islam, for example, might be countered by Muslim claims that it is in the West, not in Islam, that women are exploited sexually and economically, that it is not enlightenment but the regrettable break-up of the family that has led Western cultures to stress the social equality of the sexes, and that treating boys and girls the same may actually lead to discrimination against girls. The charge of indoctrination lacks subtlety because it does not distinguish between (a) inculcating belief in such a way that nothing can ever shake it and (b) giving children a stable moral and religious foundation until they are old enough to make up their own minds. To fail to do the latter might leave the child floundering at the very moment when he or she is most in need of moral support and guidance.

To its supporters, religious schooling is about self-determination, choice, justice, fairness, recognition, respect, personal and group identity, and above all about the freedom of individuals to make decisions for themselves about their own best interests and those of their children in line with their most fundamental beliefs and values. It is hard to see how society as a whole or inter-group relations would be improved by a more paternalistic approach that paid less attention to these basic rights and freedoms.

POINTS FOR DISCUSSION

1 Does the diversity of religious schools in the UK today damage or strengthen the cohesion of British society?
2 Is it the role of the school to help children to escape from cultural encapsulation in the values of the home and local community?
3 Should religious schools receive state funding? Are there justifiable reasons for allowing funding to some groups and not to others?

4 Are there any limits to parents' rights to make decisions about their own children's education?
5 Are religious schools by definition indoctrinatory?

INTERNET SITES

Association of Muslim Schools: www.ams.uk.net
Board of Deputies of British Jews: www.bod.org.uk/jewishschools.shtml
Centre for Jewish Education: www.knowledge.co.uk/cje
DfES: www.dfes.gov.uk/statistics/schools
Religious Society of Friends: www.quakerschools.co.uk
United Methodist Church (US, but contains some information on Methodist schools in the UK): www.umns.umc.org

NOTE

This chapter is based on the author's own visits to Muslim and other schools over a period of 15 years, as well as on a range of school prospectuses and other documents, DfES statistics, Ofsted reports, various published research reports and academic articles and advice and unpublished material kindly provided by Professor Geoffrey Walford of Oxford University, Dr Michael Shire of the Centre for Jewish Education and Dr John Shortt, co-editor of the *Journal of Education and Christian Belief*. My sincere thanks are due to all schools and individuals who have helped in contributing information.

REFERENCES AND FURTHER READING

Commission for Racial Equality (1990) *Schools of Faith*. London: CRE.
Deakin, R. (1989) *The New Christian Schools*. Bristol: Regius Press.
Department for Education and Employment (2001) *Schools: Building on Success*. London: Stationery Office.
Department of Education and Science (1985) *Education for All* (Swann Report). London: HMSO.
Halstead, J. M. (1986) *The Case for Muslim Voluntary-aided Schools: Some Philosophical Reflections*. Cambridge: Islamic Academy.
Halstead, J. M. (1995) 'Voluntary apartheid? problems of schooling for religious and other minorities in democratic societies', *Journal of Philosophy of Education*, 29(2), 257–72.
Haw, K. F. (1994) 'Muslim girls' schools – a conflict of interests?', *Gender and Education*, 6(1), 63–76.
MacKenzie, P. J. (1994) 'A critical analysis of the Christian school movement in England and Wales', Unpublished PhD thesis, University of Reading Department of Educational Studies and Management.
Office for Standards in Education (2001) *The Annual Report of Her Majesty's Chief Inspector of Schools: Standards and Quality in Education 1999/2000*. London: Stationery Office.

O'Keeffe, B. (1992) 'A look at the Christian schools movement', in B. Watson (ed.) *Priorities in Religious Education*. London: Falmer Press.

Ota, C. (1997) 'Learning to juggle – the experience of Muslim and Sikh children coping with different value systems', *Journal of Beliefs and Values*, 18(2), 227–34.

Shire, M. (2000) 'Do day schools create new ghettoes?', *Manna*, Spring, 2–5.

Walford, G. (2000) *Policy and Politics in Education: Sponsored Grant-maintained Schools and Religious Diversity*. Aldershot: Ashgate.

Weller, P. (ed.) (1993) *Religions in the UK: a Multifaith Directory*. Derby: University of Derby/Inter-Faith Network for the UK.

CHAPTER 13

Independent Schools

Alistair B. Cooke and David Woodhead

CHAPTER SUMMARY

This chapter provides an overview of the distinctiveness and diversity of independent school provision in the United Kingdom, especially in terms of:

- administration and governance;
- curriculum, assessment and inspection;
- ethos.

Introduction

There are over 2,300 independent schools in the United Kingdom educating more than 600,000 children (some 7 per cent of the total school population). They are 'independent' because they are free of local or central government control and funding; they are sometimes called fee-paying (or, more accurately, fee-charging). They are also called 'private', but this is misleading because most are not privately owned.

'Independent' does not mean isolated. Independent schools are a vital part of Britain's national education system, educating 20 per cent of its sixth-formers, for example, and consistently achieving academic, cultural and sporting excellence. But independence does mean diversity. Almost every type of school can be found in the independent sector:

- 'all-through' schools, from nursery to pre-university, including junior, or preparatory, and senior schools;
- day schools, boarding schools and many with a mixture of day and boarding pupils;
- academically selective schools and others for children of all abilities (the latter accounting for around one-half of all independent schools);
- schools catering for special educational needs and talents, including specialist schools which have no equivalents in the state system;
- coeducational and single-sex schools at all ages, and schools that are one or the other for different ages;
- traditional and progressive;

- ancient foundations and schools established within the past 20 years;
- schools in rolling acres and inner cities;
- schools with up to 2,000 pupils, others with fewer than 100.

All independent schools in the UK are registered with the appropriate government department in England, Wales, Scotland and Northern Ireland. That simply means schools have met the basic legal requirements, such as the suitability of buildings and staff. A sharp distinction exists between the 1,275 schools that are accredited by the Independent Schools Council (ISC) through its inspections arm, the Independent Schools Inspectorate (ISI) – where 80 per cent of the children in the independent sector are educated – and those, some 1,100 in number, that are outside the ISC and unaccredited by it. Accreditation means that the *quality* of a school – not just its basic provision – is assessed and confirmed by rigorous inspection under arrangements formally agreed between the ISC on the one hand and Ofsted and the Department for Education and Skills on the other.

Among ISC schools, 85 per cent of pupils are day, but they often come from a wider area than those at maintained day schools. As well as those at entirely day schools, many others are at schools with weekly or full boarders. No such details are available for non-ISC schools, which have no institution comparable to the ISC to represent them or provide detailed statistics about them. The information given in this chapter therefore relates to ISC schools.

Distinctiveness I: structures, administration and governance

The middle and primary schools in the independent sector, many of them called 'prep schools', cover Years 1 to 8. A large number are free-standing, separate schools. Some are part of a bigger, all-age school. Others are junior schools linked to senior independent schools. In most, the years from age five to seven are often called 'pre-prep'. Many schools have a nursery section for children aged three and four; some take two-year-olds.

'Prep' is short for 'preparatory', since the pupils are generally prepared for senior schools. Transfer may be at 11 plus (Year 6), 12 plus (Year 7) or 13 plus (Year 8). There is great flexibility, which means that the varying needs of individual children can be met. A typical prep or junior school nowadays is a mixed day school, but there is the widest variety of boarding and day provision, in both single-sex and coeducational schools. Children come to prep schools from all sorts of backgrounds, as do those who teach and look after them.

In recent years there has been a huge development of facilities in prep and junior schools: design technology centres, IT provision, libraries, theatres, music schools and sports centres. Many possess specialist sports facilities, which provide a rich and varied sporting life: more than 30 games and sports are played competitively and recreationally, and much time is given to physical education generally.

Prep schools employ secondary-trained as well as primary-trained teachers. Up to the age of seven, children are usually taught by class teachers. Between seven and nine there is increasing use of specialist teaching. Thereafter, secondary-trained specialist teachers are introduced. Nursery nurses and classroom assistants will often be used to give teachers support in nursery and infant classes. Teachers are fully involved in pastoral care, contact with parents and extracurricular activities in addition to their teaching commitments. Professional development is strongly encouraged by prep schools.

Pupil–teacher ratios are very favourable and class and group sizes are small. Setting by ability is frequently used for the older children, in subjects such as maths, French and science.

There are about 620 senior ISC schools. Educating around 285,000 pupils, they encompass the full diversity of the independent sector. Some are wholly or largely boarding, recruiting most of their pupils at 11, 12 or 13. Others are wholly day schools; some have a mixture of day and boarding in varying proportions. Some are very old, with religious or secular foundations going back centuries, while the newest are less than ten years old. Some 50 per cent of ISC schools have a Christian affiliation.

ISC senior schools include almost all of the most academically successful schools in the country, reflecting, in many cases, a highly selective admissions policy. Others have a much broader ability range, getting excellent results for children of all abilities by virtue of high-quality teaching and relatively small teaching groups.

Some are large: the largest ISC member school has more than 2,000 pupils and 50 or so schools have more than 1,000 on roll. Some are, by the standards of the maintained sector, very small: schools of between 200 and 300 pupils, with a distinctive family atmosphere, are relatively common in the independent sector. Increasingly, such schools may guarantee a broad and balanced curriculum by cooperative arrangements with other schools, especially at sixth form level. Typically, however, an independent senior school will have between 350 and 800 pupils, its sixth form making up a significant proportion of the roll.

Most of these schools pride themselves on the quality of their sixth forms, and rightly so: more than a third of *all* candidates in the country achieving three A grades at A level are from independent schools. The opportunity to teach one's subject to a high level to groups of able, demanding and motivated students is highly prized in these schools. But there are also schools that stop at 16, after GCSE, and concentrate on providing a sound grounding for pupils of all abilities. Schools like these (and to an increasing extent other independent senior schools) usually form part of an all-through establishment, taking pupils from nursery or pre-prep stage up to public examinations.

It is at secondary level that one of the most distinctive choices the independent sector has to offer is at its sharpest – the choice between single-sex and coeducational schools. Independent schools offer a wide choice of teaching experiences in single-sex schools. Nearly half the ISC secondary schools are single-sex: more than 220 of them are girls' schools and around 70 are boys' schools (with around a further 120 single-sex prep schools). In many areas of the country, it is only the independent sector that continues to offer single-sex, and in particular girls-only, education. In addition, a small but increasing number of coeducational schools offer separate teaching to girls and boys between certain ages.

Many single-sex schools are highly academic, but there are numerous smaller single-sex schools that specialise in developing pupils of all abilities in a supportive and caring environment. The large single-sex urban and city schools are mainly former grammar or direct grant schools; some are part of larger educational foundations, where there are boys' and girls' schools operating on adjacent sites.

Those who work in single-sex schools believe that boys and girls benefit academically and socially from being taught separately. Girls and boys mature at different ages and their approaches to learning differ. Single-sex schools aim to meet these particular needs, not only academically in the style and pace of the teaching and learning, but also in the schools' ethos and culture. Parents and pupils choose single-sex schools in the knowledge that the teachers will be expert in the teaching of girls or boys.

These schools offer their pupils plenty of opportunities for mixing with the opposite sex in sporting, social and cultural activities. Links between neighbouring single-sex schools are common and many joint initiatives take place. Most single-sex schools operate an equal opportunities policy and have men and women in their common rooms. Applications are equally welcome from male teachers to posts in girls' schools and from female teachers to posts in boys' schools.

There are many arguments in favour of coeducation and many more independent schools are coeducational than was the case in even the recent past. But the high academic results achieved by both girls' and boys' schools have guaranteed a continuing strong demand for single-sex education. While the teaching profession maintains a healthy debate about the merits of single-sex versus coeducation, there will always be a demand for it from both boys and girls.

Most ISC schools have a board of governors and a bursar, who are responsible for the school's finances. Any surplus income is used for the benefit of the school. The head is responsible to the governors but is usually given a free hand to appoint staff and admit pupils. The governing bodies of ISC schools determine the aims and overall direction of the school, while leaving the day-to-day management to the head and senior staff. Although the appointment of teaching staff is a matter for the head, the contract of employment is made with the governors, who are the legal employers.

ISC school governing bodies bring together people with experience in education, business and the professions, alongside current and former parents and former pupils. Teacher governors are relatively rare – because the charitable status of most schools requires that governors, as trustees, do not benefit from the charity – and schools adopt other strategies to ensure good communication with the teaching staff. The governors normally meet at least once every term, and much of their business is conducted through standing committees and working parties.

Distinctiveness II: curriculum, assessment and inspection

While the National Curriculum – which lays down what must be taught at stages of compulsory education between 5 and 16 – is compulsory in maintained schools, independent schools are free to observe it, either in whole or in part, as they wish. What all ISC schools strive hard to do is to provide *more* than the National Curriculum in, for example, the range of subjects and a breadth of education outside the classroom. Many prep and ISC schools have become fully involved in the National Curriculum, and all have been prepared to make adjustments to come into line with the National Curriculum programmes of study. However, the National Curriculum is seen simply as a basic entitlement, and prep schools often go beyond it, teaching French from an early age, frequently Latin and often a second modern or classical language.

Regular testing and reporting have long been a part of prep school life. Many prep and junior schools are involved in testing at Key Stages 1 and 2, and the Key Stage 2 tests are externally audited by the Qualifications and Curriculum Authority. The results achieved by independent schools speak for themselves:

- 81 per cent of 15-year-olds at independent schools (including independent special schools) gain five or more GCSEs at grades *A–C (compared with 47 per cent of maintained school pupils);
- 84 per cent of independent school A level candidates get three or more passes, compared with the national average of 63 per cent (and the national average is inflated by including *independent* school results);
- 38 per cent of all A grades are gained at independent schools;
- From a minority of A level entries in almost every subject, between 41 and 76 per cent of *all* the A grades obtained nationally in at least 11 subjects were achieved in independent schools – for example (in 2000), classics 76 per cent, French 53 per cent, German 54 per cent, economics 46 per cent, chemistry 46 per cent, biology 44 per cent, music 47 per cent, religious studies 46 per cent, physics 42 per cent, history 41 per cent, mathematics 42 per cent;
- nine out of ten independent school leavers with A levels go on to higher education degree courses, and 20 per cent of new university students coming from schools or sixth form colleges have been educated in them.

Department for Education and Skills (DfES) statistical bulletins have provided evidence of pupils *at all ability levels* in independent schools achieving better examination results than candidates at other schools. For example, a recent comparison of A and AS level grades with the GCSE scores gained by the same pupils two years earlier concluded:

> Candidates from independent schools tended to achieve higher GCE A/AS level scores than candidates from maintained schools. In independent schools, 42 per cent of candidates achieved a GCE A/AS level score of 25 or over compared with 18 per cent of candidates from maintained schools. In contrast, 8 per cent of candidates from independent schools compared with 24 per cent of maintained schools achieved a GCE A/AS level score of less than 10. (DfEE 2001: 4, para 13)

It went on to say that, *at every level of ability*, 'there was a clear tendency for candidates in independent schools to achieve higher GCE A/AS level scores than those in maintained schools'.

Some parents choose independent schools because their children have special talents or needs that they feel cannot adequately be met by other schools. These include:

- Children who are particularly gifted academically, in the arts or sport.
- Children who need a great deal of individual attention, because they suffer from dys-

lexia, are slow or backward in their work or have some other special educational need.

- Children who will benefit by being in a single-sex school. Some educationalists suggest that girls at girls' schools are more likely to study science and technological subjects.
- Children whose parents want them to grow up in a particular religious faith. Many schools have links with the Church of England, but there are schools for Roman Catholics, Methodists, Quakers and Jews, as well as Anglicans. Most denominational schools admit children of other beliefs.
- Children who want or need to be boarders. Those who need boarding education may have a parent working for a company overseas or serving in the armed forces, or both parents with full-time jobs in the UK. Only a few maintained schools have boarding places.

In surveys carried out for the ISC, the main reasons stated by parents for choosing independent schools included high standards of education and examination results, good discipline, small classes with individual attention, encouragement of a responsible attitude to school work, development of social responsibility and extracurricular activities.

Significant numbers of long-established teachers in independent schools lack a formal teaching qualification, though as the above statistics show, the excellence of their teaching is not in doubt. Indeed, there was a time when qualified teacher status (QTS) could only be achieved by those who completed a period of probation validated by the local education authority. This is no longer the case. All those who satisfactorily complete a BEd or PGCE, including teaching practice in maintained or independent schools, are awarded QTS. Under the new system of induction introduced in September 1999, QTS is confirmed on the successful completion of the required programme.

Under the regulations it is possible for someone to teach in an independent school without undergoing the induction programme, but the ISC strongly advises against this practice. Without successful induction, a teacher will not be able to work in the maintained sector, will find it difficult to transfer between schools and will not be able to register for membership of the General Teaching Council (GTC).

Some independent schools will continue to appoint directly from university those who have obtained good degrees, particularly in subjects in which there is a shortage of teachers. In many cases these recruits will be encouraged and helped to work for QTS while they are in employment. The Secretary of State has constituted the Independent Schools Council Teacher Induction Programme (ISCTIP) as an appropriate body for non-qualified teachers working in ISC schools. Full details of what is required for the successful completion of the induction programme can be obtained by writing to the Professional Officer, ISCTIP, at Grosvenor Gardens House, 35–37 Grosvenor Gardens, London SW1W 0BS. The important point to stress is that induction *can* be carried out in an independent school, despite what some teacher training institutions have been saying to the contrary. The programme is based on the needs of the individual non-qualified teacher, as set out in his or her career entry profile. The timetable of teaching and other duties should be reduced by 10 per cent to allow for induction activities, particularly meetings with the tutor and observation of lessons. The outcome of the induction is determined by the appropriate body on the recommendation of the head. ISCTIP is responsible for the induction programmes of some 650 non-qualified teachers a year in ISC schools – more than any single LEA handles.

Accreditation is required of any school seeking full membership of one of the associations of governors or heads which comprise the ISC. There are two for governing bodies – the Governing Bodies' Association (GBA) and Governing Bodies of Girls' Schools Association (GBGSA) – and five for heads – the Girls' Schools Association (GSA), Headmasters' and Headmistresses' Conference (HMC), Incorporated Association of Preparatory Schools (IAPS), Independent Schools Association (ISA) and Society of Headmasters and Headmistresses of Independent Schools (SHMIS). Another organisation, the Independent Schools' Bursars Association, includes most of the schools represented in the other bodies. All 1,275 ISC schools are members of at least one of these associations.

All associations except HMC require any school seeking membership to be inspected by the Independent Schools Inspectorate (ISI), which sends a team to visit the school over a period of several days. HMC makes its own accreditation arrangements, which involve a visit by an inspection team. A school is evaluated by ISI on:

- educational standards achieved, including attainment, learning and behaviour;
- the quality of teaching, assessment and recording;
- curriculum and extracurricular activities;
- staffing, premises and resources;
- links with parents and the community;
- pupils' personal development and pastoral care;
- the management and efficiency of the school, including its aims and ethos.

Boarding schools are also affected by the Children Act 1989, which places a duty on their governing bodies, heads or private owners to safeguard and promote the welfare of their pupils. It also requires local authority social services departments to satisfy the Registrar of Independent Schools at the DfES that welfare arrangements are adequate; from 2002 this will be the responsibility of the National Care Standards Commission.

ISC schools are required, as a condition of continued membership, to undergo rigorous inspection by ISI every six years to ensure that standards are maintained and improved. The Independent Schools Inspectorate is operationally independent of ISC and carries out inspections within a framework approved by the government and Ofsted. Inspection teams are composed of independent schools inspectors, trained by ISI and drawn from serving or retired heads and senior staff of member schools. Teams are led by reporting inspectors, also trained by ISI: they include former members of Her Majesty's Inspectorate, Ofsted registered inspectors and some former ISI team inspectors.

Inspections lead to a detailed published report, including a summary that the school must send free of charge to parents. Parents and other interested parties may also obtain the full reports. In all cases, a school must have a satisfactory report in order to remain in membership.

ISI enjoys formal government recognition and approval. In addition to its own extensive quality assurance measures, a proportion of its inspections and reports are checked by Ofsted. Since 1999 ISI has replaced Ofsted as the agency advising the DfES on whether schools meet statutory requirements for continued registration with the Department. Information in ISI inspection reports is passed to the DfES and relevant associations, who deal with any deficiencies.

This does not mean that a school outside ISC is a poor school, but the annual report for 1998–99 of Her Majesty's Chief Inspector of Schools stated that 'overall, schools in the ISC perform substantially better than schools outside its membership', and most ISC schools 'provide a good, in many cases excellent, education. The teaching is generally of high quality and pupils achieve good standards.' (Office of HMI 2000, paras 307, 304). It added that at GCSE 'ISC schools achieve significantly better than non-ISC schools on all measures.'

Distinctiveness III: ethos

Pupils at independent schools are not the 'toffs' of tabloid headlines. More than half of all children now entering them are from families where neither parent went to an independent school. Wider access is encouraged through scholarships and bursaries: over 25 per cent of pupils in ISC schools (about 156,000) receive help with their fees – most of it from the schools themselves. In boarding schools, the presence of young people from overseas creates a cosmopolitan atmosphere.

Whatever their background, pupils are encouraged to develop academically, creatively and socially. Expectations are high: encouraging the personal fulfilment of the less able is just as important as stimulating the high flyer. The fundamental expectation is that all concerned will get on with the job of teaching and learning.

The 'experts' may argue about the effects of class size on children's performance, but parents are in no doubt that the greater individual attention possible in smaller classes is a major reason for 'going independent'. Furthermore, the unusual degree of parental support in independent schools is another source of professional and personal satisfaction. The commitment to a school–home partnership is strongly embedded in the sector.

Most are mainstream schools – in which special educational needs may, nevertheless, be catered for – but there are also independent schools catering exclusively for such needs or disabilities. They include 'special schools' in the strict sense of the term and schools that specialise in helping children with a variety of learning difficulties (some of which are recognised for the placement of children 'statemented' by local education authorities).

Unique to the independent sector are the specialist music and ballet schools, which include internationally renowned centres of excellence for outstandingly talented boys and girls, and also provide a mainstream academic education. So important are they in complementing state provision that pupils are eligible for fee assistance under the government's Music and Ballet Scheme. Similarly, heavily subsidised places are offered at the 35 independent choir schools, where choristers receive a first-class academic as well as musical education.

In all schools, music, drama, sports and games, clubs and societies, activities of many kinds flourish. Staff in independent schools can gain as much satisfaction from opportunities provided by the 'informal curriculum' as from awakening and sustaining an interest in their academic subject.

Mobility between independent and maintained schools is very common. Many independent school teachers and an increasing number of heads have also taught in maintained schools. There are strong national and local links between heads' and teachers' professional associations, including shared in-service training.

Many people comment on the distinct ethos of independent schools. Some claim that exclusiveness or separateness from the national education system is the chief feature of that ethos. This is a mistaken view. What independent schools seek to inculcate is an ethos that comprises clear and well defined values.

Heads and staff encourage children to work hard and to take pride in their work, to pay attention to detail, to have good manners, to consider other people's feelings and to grow up into responsible adults who will contribute to the community. They wish to inspire in each generation of pupils an appreciation of the richness of their European cultural heritage, in music, literature and the visual arts; to lift their eyes and ears above the contemporary to more nourishing cultural experiences.

POINTS FOR DISCUSSION

1 What do some parents feel they can gain for their children through the independent sector?
2 How distinctive is the ethos of the independent school sector?
3 Are there still obstacles to achieving co-operation between the independent and state sectors of education?

INTERNET SITES

Independent Schools Council information service (ISCis)/iscis.uk.net/
The Headmasters' and Headmistresses' Conference: www.hmc.org.uk
The Good Schools Guide: www.uk-independent-schools.co.uk

REFERENCES AND FURTHER READING

DfEE (2001) *Statistics of Education: GCSE/GNVQ and GCE A/AS Level Performance of Candidates Attempting Two or More GCE A Levels or AS Level Equivalents in 1999/00: Schools and FE Sector Colleges in England*, DfEE Statistical Bulletin 02/01. London: The Stationery Office.

Guide to Accredited Independent Schools. Available free of charge from the Independent Schools Council Information Service (ISCis, formerly ISIS), Grosvenor Gardens House, 35–37 Grosvenor Gardens, London SW1W 0BS (tel. 020 7798 1500; e-mail info@iscis.uk.net/).

ISC Annual Reports. Available free of charge from the above address.

Independent Schools Yearbook. London: A & C Black.

Independent Schools in the UK. London: Burrows Communications.

Office of Her Majesty's Chief Inspector of Schools (2000). *The Annual Report of Her Majesty's Chief Inspector of Schools 1998–99*. London: The Stationery Office.

PART IV:

University Education and Initial Teacher Training

CHAPTER 14

University Education

Vaneeta-marie D'Andrea and David W. Gosling

CHAPTER SUMMARY

This chapter provides:

- An overview of the diversity of higher education provision in the United Kingdom, including the historical background to the development of the sector.
- An assessment of the pivotal importance of the Further and Higher Education Act 1992.
- A review of higher education funding for teaching and research and the quality assurance mechanism to ensure accountability in relation to the latter.
- An outline of initiatives in higher education, especially in relation to devolved governance, with prospects for the future.

Introduction: diversity of the higher education sector

Higher education (HE) in the United Kingdom is characterised by considerable diversity of mission, type and size of institution, level of specialism, wealth and status. Within such a diverse sector, generalisation about aims and goals is difficult, if not impossible. In the most general terms the purpose of higher education may be defined as three major areas of activity: (a) the teaching of undergraduates and postgraduates; (b) carrying out research and scholarship to advance knowledge and its application at a national and international level; and (c) providing a range of services to industry and the wider society, including advising government on policy and contributing to economic development to meet the needs of employers and the economy.

Within this threefold division of activities, there is considerable overlap and interconnectedness, and different institutions place the emphasis in their missions in different places. Some universities emphasise their role in promoting scholarship, the discovery of new knowledge and the application of research – these are the so-called 'research-led' universities. Closely linked to the research function, universities are also the primary location for entry into the professions – law, medicine (and other health and care professions), dentistry, veterinary sciences, education, engineering and the sciences. Some universities emphasise their role as teaching institutions, and are often concerned with bringing into higher education individuals from groups previously underrepresented in the sector. Most in the latter category are the 'new universities' that were until 1992 the 'polytechnics', which had been under local government control until 1988. Whereas many universities are relatively large institutions, with over 10,000 students and a wide variety of subjects being taught across the sciences, arts and humanities, as well as vocational subjects, there are also many much smaller colleges with a much more specialist, usually vocational, orientation. These include colleges of art and design, agricultural colleges, specialist research and clinically orientated institutes.

The sector is also characterised by its relative autonomy from government control, although in the view of many, this autonomy has been eroded over the past decade. This reflects not only the legal status of universities defined by either Royal Charter or Parliamentary Statute, but also the methods of funding, in which there is a significant element of devolved responsibility. Many universities also have considerable funds derived from non-governmental sources, which also contributes to their relative autonomy. It should not be forgotten that approximately 11 per cent of higher education, mostly sub-degree awards such as Higher National Diplomas, are delivered in further education colleges (HESA 2000). These are very different from the research universities with international reputations – they are less autonomous, have almost no research function and are without the power to award their own degrees.

Table 14.1 summarises the current data on higher education institutions (HEIs) in the UK by country.

Table 14.1   Numbers of HEIs in the UK

	Universities	HE colleges
England	88[a]	46
Northern Ireland	2	2
Scotland	13	7
Wales	9[b]	4
Total	111	60

Notes:
[a]Includes 16 schools of the University of London.
[b]University of Glamorgan plus eight constituent colleges and universities of the University of Wales.
Source: Higher Education in the United Kingdom. Guide 99/02
(www.hefce.ac.uk/Pubs/HEFCE/1999/99_02.html).

Key structures and organisational features

Formally, higher education is defined as education provided by means of a course of any description leading to an award higher than General Certificate of Education Advanced level (GCE A level) or National Diploma or Certificate (from Edexcel).

The distinctiveness of higher education is reflected within the national qualifications frameworks. Higher education has its own government agency that oversees standards and quality, entitled the Quality Assurance Agency for Higher Education, known as the QAA (see below). In the Higher Education Qualification Framework published by the QAA, the higher levels of outcomes expected of students qualifying in the HE sector have been defined in terms of 'qualification descriptors'. These make clear that students exiting with a higher level award are expected not only to acquire more complex and specialist knowledge and understanding, but also to display increasing levels of autonomy, critical thinking, reflection and application of knowledge.

Also critical in defining standards in higher education are the professional bodies, which may be royal societies, chartered institutes or associations. Examples are the Royal Society of Chemistry, the Royal Institute of British Architects, the British Psychological Society, the British Medical Association and the Law Society. Some even have a legal right granted by Royal Charter to accredit courses and determine the requirements for successful entry into the relevant profession. In recent times the QAA has attempted to specify the expected outcomes in major subject areas by a process of 'benchmarking statements', in which panels of academics in defined subject areas (and, where appropriate, in association with the professional bodies) have described the knowledge and skills that students within the subject are expected to achieve at honours level. Twenty-two benchmark statements have been published and a further twenty-one are to be undertaken.

The levels and outcomes at degree level have also been defined by the Qualifications and Curriculum Authority, which covers oversight of school, further education and vocational qualifications. In the framework for National Vocational Qualifications (NVQs) higher education is defined as Levels 4 and 5.

Types of institution

Most higher education is provided by universities. These are self-governing institutions created by Royal Charter, or in the case of the 'new' universities, by Parliamentary Statute. Most of the 'new' universities, previously known as 'polytechnics', became higher education corporations following the Education Reform Act 1988, and under the Further and Higher Education Act 1992 were allowed to include the word 'university' in their title if they met certain conditions. Other colleges of higher education have since been allowed to be called university colleges, while others are still trying to persuade the Privy Council that they meet the criteria.

The most ancient universities in the United Kingdom trace their origins back to medieval or Tudor times. Oxford was founded between 1167 and 1185, Cambridge in 1209, St Andrews in 1411, Glasgow in 1451, Aberdeen in 1495, Edinburgh in 1582.

It was not until 1828 that a non-conformist university was created in Gower Street to challenge the power of the established universities. University College London was quickly followed by Kings College (1829) – the two becoming the first constituent colleges of London University in 1836 – and Durham was founded in 1832. Later, in the nineteenth century and at the beginning of the twentieth, Royal Charters were granted to colleges serving the fast-growing cities, such as Bristol (1876), Manchester (1880), Liverpool (1881), Birmingham (1900), Leeds (1904) and Sheffield (1905). These are sometimes collectively although loosely known as the 'red brick' universities.

London University became the largest UK federation of higher education institutions by incorporating colleges such as Imperial in 1907 and Birkbeck in 1920 (formerly the London Mechanics Institute). In the twentieth century a number of university colleges have become universities in their own right having previously offered University of London degrees, such as Southampton (1953), Hull (1954) and Keele (1962), and Oxford degrees in the case of Reading (1926) (Curtis 1968).

The Robbins Report (1963) recommended expansion of higher education from the existing level of 216,000 full-time students, to 558,000 by 1980–1. Sussex had already received its charter in 1961 and this was followed by the creation, *ab initio*, of new campus-based universities at Bath, East Anglia, Essex, Kent, Lancaster, Stirling, Surrey, Warwick and York. In addition, the colleges of advanced technology became universities, such as Aston (Birmingham), Salford (Manchester) and City (London). Also in the 1960s, the creation of the Open University as a provider of awards by distance learning was a radical and innovative step.

In 1965 the then Secretary of State for Education, Anthony Crosland, announced the government's plans for a binary policy based on two separate and distinct sectors: universities on the one hand and the technical and vocational colleges on the other. Twenty-eight (later 30) polytechnics were created between 1969 and 1973 from amalgamations of smaller specialist institutions, many tracing their history back to the nineteenth century. They remained under local authority control until 1988, and had their degrees awarded by the Council for National Academic Awards (CNAA). The reorganisation of teacher education in the 1980s had led to the creation of colleges of higher education. By 1992 four of these attained polytechnic status, so that 34 institutions became 'new' universities, which in total had enrolled over 450,000 students and included some of the largest higher education institutions in the country, such as Manchester with over 25,000 HE students (Pratt 1997).

The post-1992 universities vary in size and composition, but they have tended to have higher proportions of mature students than old universities, some have substantial numbers of part-time students and few have comparable numbers of postgraduate or research students to the old universities. Their resources, estate (inherited from the local authority control) and funding have also been more limited (see below). Nevertheless, the new universities account for over 50 per cent of students in the sector and offer a wide range of courses, not necessarily technical or vocational, have pioneered new forms of entry to HE such as access courses, accreditation of prior experiential learning, credit accumulation and transfer (CATS), have developed new modular forms of curricula and have led the way on student-centred learning (Jary 2001).

Administration and legislation

The administration and legal status of higher education in the UK is complex and different by country – particularly post-devolution. The Secretary of State for

Education has been located in a government department which has gone under different names: DES (Department of Education and Science), DfEE (Department for Education and Employment) and most recently DfES (Department for Education and Skills). The Secretary of State for Education and Skills has overall responsibility for the department and its policies and strategy, in particular responsibility for finance and public expenditure matters, including local authority finance, economic issues and major appointments. Each country in the United Kingdom has a minister with responsibility for higher education, including research, the relevant funding council (see below), student support and student loans and/or grants.

The current legal framework was established by the Further and Higher Education Act 1992. All universities and other higher education institutions are autonomous and responsible for their own internal organisations, although there are two large federal universities in London and Wales, in which some functions and responsibilities are held by the constituent colleges and some by the central university authority. It has also become increasingly common for universities to have legal agreements with other institutions to deliver higher education courses. These may be partnership agreements in which courses are delivered collaboratively, or provision may be franchised to other institutions, which may be in the UK or overseas. In these cases the ultimate responsibility for the standards of the degrees or diplomas and quality assurance matters lies with the awarding university.

By and large similar organisational patterns have emerged across British higher education. The overall head of universities is called a vice chancellor or principal. The honorary and non-executive titular head of universities is known as the chancellor, who is normally appointed but in some universities is elected. Colleges of higher education are normally headed by a principal or director. The senior administrative body in the old universities is known as the court, which determines general policy and includes representatives from the local community as well as academic representation, while day-to-day running of the university is governed by a senate. In the new (post-1992) universities ultimate responsibility for the governance of the university is held by the board of governors, while the vice chancellor is the chief executive and the senior committee for internal affairs is normally an academic board.

Typically the organisation of higher education distinguishes between central administrative functions and academic responsibility for teaching and research. The registrar is normally head of administrative functions – including admissions, university regulations and assessment processes (although the precise distribution of these functions can vary). Other significant central services include educational development, estates, finance, library and information technology (sometimes brought together in a single information and communications department), personnel or human resources and student services (including health, counselling, careers, learning support, disability services).

There are several models of academic organisation. Most common is the division of teaching and research into cognate subject areas within departments, which are in turn grouped into faculties. An alternative model groups subjects into a single organisational level known as a school. A significant variation is the college model, based on the

Oxford and Cambridge models, in which students and staff are members of a college as well as an academic department. There may also be separate research institutes, such as for agriculture, within universities with specialist interests, and some universities include semi-autonomous medical schools based in a teaching hospital.

Funding

The HE system is mostly managed by a number of government sponsored agencies and organisations. Although publicly funded, they retain general autonomy in their operations and procedures. On behalf of the government, they are required to ensure that the higher education sector remains efficient, focused and accountable to the public at large. The national funding councils, responsible for the funding and general management of higher education, are the Higher Education Funding Council for England (HEFCE), the Scottish Higher Education Funding Council (SHEFC) and the Higher Education Funding Council for Wales (HEFCW). In Northern Ireland funding is provided directly to higher education from the Department of Higher and Further Education, Training and Employment (DHFETE).

The direct involvement of government departments is small. For example, in England the DfES and Office of Science and Technology (OST) have a limited role through specific policy initiatives. In addition the Departments of Health and Defence fund a certain amount of research. Government agencies are also active at a more local level. Local education authorities (LEAs) contribute to course fees and maintenance costs for eligible UK students taking undergraduate or initial teacher training courses; for example, the Disabled Students Allowance. There are also a number of regional agencies that have an indirect influence on the operation of higher education in their areas.

The sector had a total income of £12.1 billion derived from Funding Councils' grants, tuition fees, research grants and contracts, and other income such as endowments and interest. Figure 14.1 shows the distribution of income across the UK from these sources.

However, this overall picture hides enormous variation in the source of income between institutions, both in the total amount of funding available to universities and in its distribution between different sources. A comparison of three institutions, one an 'ancient' research-oriented university, one a 'red brick' university and the third a 'new' university – all with similar numbers of students (about 16,000) – illustrates the variation (see Figure 14.2).

Research funding

An important influence over universities is the method of allocating research funding known as the Research Assessment Exercise (RAE). Panels of subject experts rate submissions from subject groups in each university. Each group's submission is then rated on a scale from 1 to 5* and special research funding is awarded to the institution on the basis of these scores for all departments. This RAE income to the university is a major

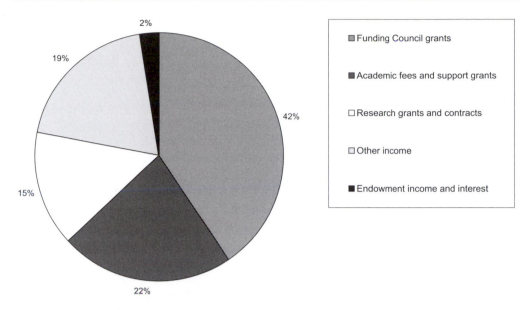

Figure 14.1   United Kingdom higher education income, by category (source: HESA 2000)

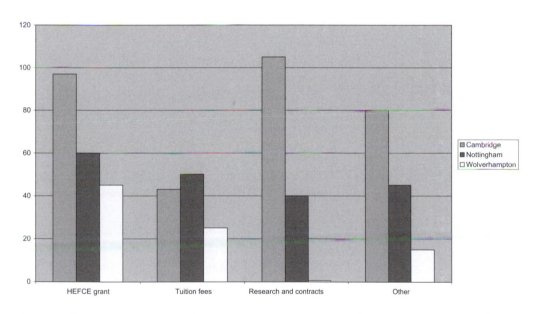

Figure 14.2   Income for three higher education institutions (£ millions) (source: HESA 2000)

source of funding if the institution has a significant number of active research staff. It is the only additional source of income that is linked to staff performance. Special funding to support teaching is described in the Initiatives section below.

Another important source of funding for research activity derives from the Research Councils. The combined budget in 1998–9 of the Councils and the Humanities Research Board was £1.3 billion. There are six major Councils: Biotechnology and

Biological Sciences Research Council; Engineering and Physical Sciences Research Council; Economic and Social Research Council; Medical Research Council; Natural Environment Research Council; Particle Physics and Astronomy Research Council. Grants are allocated to researchers, projects, programmes or designated research fellowships and postgraduate studentships.

Student tuition fees

Student tuition fees constitute another significant element of university funding. In England and Wales the government introduced an annual tuition fee of £1,075 for domiciled undergraduates, representing about a quarter of the average cost of a course. Tuition continues to be free for students from lower-income families. Other full-time students pay partial fees depending on parental income. Loans are available for maintenance costs; these are also related to parental income. Other grants, access bursaries and hardship funds are available on an income contingent loan basis to students in financial difficulty (DfEE 2001; www.hefce.ac.uk). In Scotland students do not pay tuition fees while studying. Instead, there is a Graduate Endowment which in effect pays student fees and makes student loans available. However, following graduation, once the ex-student's income reaches a specified level, it is taxed to cover the costs of funding current students in higher education. Fees for postgraduate and overseas students are set by each institution.

Courses, qualifications and credit

First degree courses generally take three years in England, Wales and Northern Ireland. Sandwich courses, which include periods of practical work, languages courses including a year abroad and certain specialist courses usually last four years, whereas medicine, dentistry and veterinary studies last five years. In Scotland the minimum age for undergraduates to start is 17 (as opposed to 18 in England) and a general degree can be attained in three years and an honours degree in four.

The main undergraduate qualification awarded in higher education is the first degree; for example, BA, BSc or BEd. Other qualifications include the Higher National Diploma (HND), normally two years of study, and the Higher National Certificate (HNC), normally one year of study. Increasingly universities and colleges are awarding credit for each 'module' of learning, based on the notional learning hours required, which can be accumulated and potentially transferred to other institutions. Credits are awarded at each level and students are awarded a degree after accumulating the appropriate level of credits.

Postgraduate courses are very varied. They can be taught courses, research-based programmes or a combination of both. They may be either full-time or part-time. Masters programmes are normally one year full-time or two years part-time. Qualifications include certificates, diplomas, masters degrees and doctorates.

Student and staff profile

Another way to capture the character of the higher education sector in the UK is to look at the student profile through some selected statistics. Figures for 1998–9 show that in this academic year there was a total of 2,081,664 enrolments on courses leading to HE qualifications and credits, 235,907 of which were at further education (FE) institutions. There were just over a million full-time students studying first degrees in HE and FE institutions and a total of 446,942 students obtained HE qualifications. Of these, 95,480 (5 per cent) were from non-European Union (EU) countries and approximately 85,000 were from the EU. Sixty-three per cent were full-time students and 37 per cent part-time. Among UK students, women (52 per cent) slightly outnumbered men. Among first year UK domiciled undergraduates 26,720 were known to have a disability and 13 per cent were from ethnic minorities. A total of 239,760 first degrees were awarded and 35,010 higher degrees, of which 2,450 were doctorates (HESA 2000).

Students studying on professional courses included 43,100 studying medicine and dentistry, 193,810 subjects allied to medicine (including nursing 121,570), 123,910 engineering and technology, 91,540 computer science, 57,850 law, 138,480 business and management studies, 99,780 creative arts and design studies and 56,510 teacher training. Other students included 222,830 on combined or general or modular courses, 23,930 studying economics, 32,680 English, 26,800 history, 5,910 philosophy, 22,660 biology, 8,330 biochemistry, 13,150 physics and 16,690 mathematics (HESA 2000).

In the whole of the UK there was a total of 112,374 full-time academic staff, of whom 35,727 were female and 76,647 were male. Just over 90,000 of these academics were in England while Scotland had 14,210 and Wales 5,419 (HESA 2000).

Teaching, learning and assessment methods

Recent government decisions to increase levels of participation in higher education throughout the UK have had a direct impact on most universities. This in turn has influenced how staff engage students in learning. One indication of this change was a special project funded in 1992 by the then Polytechnics and Colleges Funding Council (PCFC) on 'teaching more students' (Gibbs 1992). It offered workshops and materials, free of charge, to all universities in the UK on how to cope with the change in student numbers within the context of diminishing resources. In fact, there has been a widespread change in the focus of the educational experience from teaching to learning, more specifically to a student-centred approach to learning, including directly linking assessment to the student's learning experience. This has meant that learning, teaching and assessment methods have been expanded to include not only the traditional lecture and seminar methods but a wider range of learning experiences, such as case studies, computer-facilitated learning, distributed learning, on-line learning, problem-based learning, work-based learning and workshops, to name a few. Similarly, summative assessments have expanded from the traditional end-of-course unseen exam to course work, including projects, portfolios and oral presentations.

Formative assessments, those which do not count towards the final mark, are also used as a form of learning experience, and include self and peer assessments, as well as tutor assessments.

To support these changes most universities have established educational development or learning and teaching centres (Gosling 1996, 2001). The more successful centres work within the academic culture and take a holistic approach to supporting change within the institution, and also employ a combined bottom-up and top-down strategy to creating change (D'Andrea and Gosling 2001). As is noted below in the section on Initiatives, learning and teaching have been slowly receiving increased support from the funding agencies for innovation and research in pedagogic practice.

Quality assurance

Assurance of the quality and standards of the educational provision in higher education in the UK historically was determined by an extensive system of external examiners that originated as the higher education system expanded in its earliest days. From the fifteenth century examiners from Oxford and Cambridge would go to the newly established universities and read student exams to ensure the standard was similar across the UK. The external examiner system remains in place today and has been augmented by a more complex system linked to the government funding agencies in each of the four countries. Before the end of the binary divide the former polytechnics were monitored by the CNAA (as noted above). A more complex twofold system of auditing institutions and assessing subjects was put into place once the unified system was established. Institutions were audited by the Higher Education Quality Council (HEQC), while subjects were assessed by subject-specific peer review teams originally coordinated by the Higher Education Funding Councils for each country. Currently both processes are coordinated by the Quality Assurance Agency for Higher Education for all the countries. This system was criticised for being too time consuming and overly intrusive. When the results indicated that less than 1 per cent of the provision was unsatisfactory the cost-effectiveness of this system was questioned. Combined with recommendations for a UK-wide quality assurance system in the Dearing Report (NICHE 1997), there was enough impetus to review this quality assurance process once again. From January 2003 a new integrated 'lighter touch' method of review is expected to be in place across the UK. This system is more like an institutional audit of universities and colleges. The new quality assurance system is currently under review (www.qaa.ac.uk).

In addition to the QAA quality review, universities with departments of education that provide initial teacher training (ITT) are inspected by the Office for Standards in Education (Ofsted). Low scores in these inspections can cause the closure of ITT programmes offered by the university under scrutiny. This system remains in effect at the present time.

Initiatives

Following the Dearing (NICHE 1997) and Garrick (1997) Reports a number of initiatives have been put into place across the HE sector in the UK. A Teaching Quality Enhancement Fund (TQEF) has recently been established. It has three major strands of activity, some of which are UK-wide and others of which apply to England and Northern Ireland only. The three strands cover institutional, subject and individual support for the development of teaching and learning. The institutional strand applies to England and Northern Ireland only and provides funding to institutions for their teaching and learning strategies on a per capita student basis to improve the quality of the educational experience. At the subject level a Learning and Teaching Support Network (LTSN) has been established across the UK. It includes 24 separate subject centres whose remit is to support developments in teaching and learning at the subject level. A Generic Learning and Teaching Centre (GLTC) has been established to coordinate teaching and learning developments across all subjects. At the individual level a National Teaching Fellowship Scheme has been established to identify and reward excellence in teaching. Two cohorts of 20 fellows each have been selected thus far. Another notable innovation was the creation of the Institute for Learning and Teaching in 1999. It was established to enhance the quality of the professional development of university teaching staff via a professional accreditation scheme and encouragement of innovation in learning and teaching.

One outcome of national government devolution is the impact it has had on initiatives supported by the funding of HE in each country. In some cases these are distinct and in some they are overlapping. In England and Northern Ireland, for example, there is the Higher Education Reach Out to Business and Community (HEROBAC) fund. It is intended to initiate a third stream of funding, complementing the HEFCE's existing grant for teaching and research, to reward and encourage HE institutions to enhance their interaction with business. The fund provides core funding to help HE institutions to contribute to economic growth and competitiveness. The HEROBAC fund was established in partnership with the Department of Trade and Industry (DTI), the Department of Higher and Further Education, Training and Employment in Northern Ireland and the former Department for Education and Employment (www.hefce.ac.uk).

Special funding for widening participation initiatives is broadly supported in all countries. This funding is intended to encourage institutions to enrol underrepresented groups and to ensure that all students have the best possible chance of succeeding in their studies. The funding provided to institutions is in proportion to their success in recruiting students from neighbourhoods with low rates of participation in higher education (www.hefce.ac.uk and www.shefc.ac.uk).

In England, a major new initiative focuses on rewarding and developing staff. As part of the year 2000 spending review, the government announced additional resources to help HE institutions to recruit, retain and develop staff, and to help to modernise management processes in the sector. Each HE institution will receive funding on receipt of a human resource strategy that identifies objectives, describes how the money will be spent and sets specific targets for these activities.

In recent years, the SHEFC has reduced the number of special initiatives based on 'top-sliced' funding (particularly competitive project-based schemes), in response to sector demands to increase the unit of resource. Instead SHEFC has allocated 2 per cent of its available resources to support strategic change in the HE sector to enable institutions to address future strategic priorities and implement strategic change programmes. Also included in this funding is money for human resources improvements, as noted in the special initiatives in England and Northern Ireland (www.shefc.ac.uk/content/shefc/strategy/planning/strategychanegrantl.html).

Additionally, in 2002–3, the SHEFC will require institutions to develop strategies for enhancing the quality of learning and teaching, as a condition of their teaching and learning grant (www.shefc.ac.uk/content/library/circs/01/he1101.html). Although this is not a special initiative, it will have similar outcomes.

Prospects

The government has set a target of an additional 500,000 students in higher education by 2005. The pressure will continue to widen participation to include those previously underrepresented in the sector, particularly students from the lower socio-economic groups. Much of the additional provision will be made in the FE sector in order to achieve a participation rate approaching 50 per cent, compared to its present level of approximately 30 per cent. The new two-year foundation degrees, intended to focus on vocational learning and delivered in collaboration with FE and employers, are currently being piloted, and if adopted as government policy will challenge traditional assumptions about the delivery of HE. Increasingly HE is being seen in government policy terms as part of the wider notion of lifelong learning.

A trend towards increased flexibility of delivery can be expected to continue, with more on-line or e-learning, and more distance and part-time provision using computer-based technologies. The Internet will be a vehicle to deliver HE, leading to increasingly global competition between major suppliers. In the UK the government's push for a national e-university is just one example of the expected changes in this direction.

Internationalisation of HE, already apparent with large numbers of students moving primarily from poorer to richer countries for their HE, is set to be a continuing trend. Closely linked to this development is the increasing marketisation of HE – that is, competition between institutions to increase fee income and research funding as traditional sources of government funding diminish even further. There are likely to be more institutions merging or entering into strategic alliances in order to improve their market share, while universities and colleges that cannot maintain student numbers will come under increasing pressure to close or merge.

The recent trend towards highlighting teaching is likely to continue as governments emphasise accountability of universities to the wider public, employers and students. The creation of the Institute for Learning and Teaching is an important step towards the professionalisation of HE staff as teachers. Educational development or learning and teaching centres will continue to grow as important sources of quality improvement, and some of the more intrusive forms of external quality assurance will be significantly reduced in scope – partly in response to the sector's concern for a more useful exercise and partly to reduce costs.

Conclusion

British universities have a high reputation internationally for the quality of the education provided to undergraduate and postgraduate students and for the contribution they make to research, scholarship and innovation in all fields of academic endeavour. The sector is well placed to continue to compete successfully at the global level. Yet it is also facing a period of rapid change and uncertainty, as knowledge production ceases to be the exclusive preserve of universities and is increasingly in the hands of multinational corporations.

Furthermore, many universities are facing a challenge to their traditional exclusivity as the government maintains the political pressure to widen participation to groups hitherto underrepresented in HE. As increasing numbers of students enter HE with more demanding and different expectations, reflecting their varied cultural and educational histories, the sector will be required to maintain its diversity to meet their needs. But, as one commentator has written, 'The higher education system as at present financed is inequitable, inadequate and inefficient. It is also unsustainable' (Barnett 2000: 42).

Universities have to negotiate the transition from an elite to a mass system of HE, while also facing increasingly tough competition from overseas and corporate-funded research. This critical situation must be tackled in the context of continuing underfunding from government. Nevertheless, the long history of UK universities suggests that they will find ways of meeting this challenge to maintain their place as centres of teaching and research respected across the globe. In any case these are very interesting times to be learning or teaching in UK universities.

POINTS FOR DISCUSSION

1 What are the critical issues raised by the shift in university education from an elite system to a mass system?
2 Why are universities important to the future of the constituent countries of the UK?

INTERNET SITES

Department for Education and Skills: www.dfes.gov.uk/index.shtml
Department of Higher and Further Education, Training and Employment: www.nics.gov.uk
Higher Education Funding Council for England: www.hefce.ac.uk
Higher Education Funding Council for Wales: www.wfc.ac.uk/hefcw/index.html
Higher Education Statistics Agency: www.hesa.ac.uk
Joint Information Systems Committee: www.jisc.ac.uk/about.html
Office for Standards in Education: www.ofsted.gov.uk

Quality Assurance Agency for Higher Education: www.qaa.ac.uk
Scottish Higher Education Funding Council: www.shefc.ac.uk
Universities Scotland: www.Universities-Scotland.ac.uk
Universities UK: www.universitiesuk.ac.uk

REFERENCES AND FURTHER READING

Barnett, R. (2000) 'Realizing a compact for higher education', in K. Gokulsing *et al.* (eds) *A Compact for Higher Education.* Aldershot: Ashgate.

Committee on Higher Education (1963) *Report of the Committee appointed by the Prime Minister under the chairmanship of Lord Robbins, 1961–63* (Robbins Report), Cmnd 2154. London: HMSO.

Curtis, S. J. (1968) *History of Education in Great Britain.* London: University Tutorial Press.

D'Andrea, V. and Gosling, D. (2001) 'Joining the dots: reconceptualising educational development', *Active Learning*, 2(1), 64–80.

DfEE (2001) *Financial Support for Higher Education Students in 2001/2002: a Guide.* London: DfEE.

Garrick Report (1997) *Higher Education in the Learning Society.* Report of the Scottish Committee, National Committee of Enquiry into Higher Education. London: HMSO.

Gibbs, G. (1992) *Developing Teaching: Teaching More Students, Volumes 1–5.* Oxford: Oxonian Rewley Press.

Goren, C., Cohen, A. and Gregory, J. (2000) *Education Year Book 2000/2001.* Harlow: Pearson Education.

Gosling, D. (1996) 'What do UK educational development units do?', *International Journal for Academic Development*, 1(1), 75–83.

Gosling, D. (2001) 'What educational development units do – five years on', *International Journal of Academic Development*, 6, 74–92.

Higher Education Statistics Agency (HESA) (2000) *Higher Education Statistics for the United Kingdom 1998/99.* Cheltenham: Higher Education Statistics Agency.

Holt, G., Boyd, S., Dickerson, B., Loose, J. and O'Donnell, S. (1999) *Education in England, Wales and Northern Ireland: a Guide to the System.* Slough: National Foundation for Educational Research.

Jary, D. (2001) 'Access and UK higher education', *Higher Education Digest*, Supplement (Summer), 1–12.

NICHE (National Commission of Inquiry into Higher Education) (1997) *Higher Education for a Learning Society.* London: HMSO.

Pratt, J. (1997) The Polytechnic Experiment 1965–1992. Buckingham: SRHE and Open University Press.

CHAPTER 15

Developing Models for Initial Teacher Training: Challenges, Changes and Future Directions

Ian Morrison and John Gray

CHAPTER SUMMARY

This chapter provides:

- A historical overview of the issues surrounding teaching as a profession.
- An assessment of key issues affecting the recruitment and training of teachers.
- A review of procedures for the inspection of initial teacher training.

Introduction

Schools need a regular flow of new teachers who are well qualified, well trained and committed to their new profession. The agenda for teacher education flows from these requirements. Over the past three decades, however, virtually every aspect of the process of preparing intending teachers for their classroom duties has been contested and reformed. In the process new routes into teacher training have been constructed and new requirements have been imposed on all training institutions.

At the centre of the debates have been divergent views about what training is required to be a teacher and what institutions might be best placed to provide it. This chapter seeks to describe the current situation, to explore some of the factors that have been shaping it, to comment on recent trends and to speculate about future directions.

Many of the changes in initial teacher training (ITT) have been driven by central government, which has argued that teacher education has needed major reforms. Not surprisingly, those responsible for its provision have countered this view. As a direct consequence, and over a period of years, relationships between the higher education institutions (HEIs) and government agencies have moved towards a system of precise expectations about what intending teachers will be taught. At the same time, HEIs' relationships with schools have changed as the latter have been given a larger position, reflected in payments to schools, in training the profession. Overall, then, there has been a general transition from autonomy and freedom to control, prescription and accountability. The relationship between the HEIs and the government agencies has moved from partnership and professional dialogue to prescription and fears for future funding depending on the outcome of inspections. The relationship between the HEIs and the schools involved in training students has changed from one based on goodwill to a system of contracts with money transferred from the HEIs.

Such developments parallel and mirror some of the losses of autonomy schools and individual teachers have experienced during this period. For well over a decade now, the National Curriculum has described both what should be taught and, in some respects, how – by the late 1990s, for example, views about some of the ways in which particular subjects (notably literacy and numeracy) should be handled had become incorporated into national strategies. Thus changes to the school curriculum and its assessment, combined with changing views of teaching, especially in primary schools, have contributed further to the pressures to bring ITT more closely into line with contemporary classroom developments.

Key structures

For most of the period under discussion there have been two major routes into the teaching profession. One of these has involved a three- or four-year period of initial training leading to a bachelor's degree (either a BA or a BEd), followed by a year as a probationary teacher. Such courses have performed a dual function, providing students simultaneously with a higher education in a particular subject(s) and a preparation for a teaching career. This has been a particularly popular route for those intending to pursue a career in primary education. The other has been taken by students *after* they have completed a bachelor's degree and completed a one-year training course, specifically directed at turning them into a teacher and leading to a teaching qualification known as the PGCE (Postgraduate Certification of Education). Between them these two routes have provided the vast majority (over 95 per cent) of the 30,000 or so entrants to the teaching profession required each year. Recently, there has been a trend away from the 'undergraduate' towards the 'degree plus PGCE' approach, in which the training for teaching component is more intensive, confined to the last year and almost entirely focused on preparation for the classroom.

Historically, alongside these two dominant approaches, there have always been a variety of alternative ways of entering the teaching profession. In one form or another their construction has mostly been driven by teacher shortages, especially in some regions of the country. Essentially, they have involved different approaches to providing 'on-the-job' training. In their current manifestations these 'third ways' include school-centred initial teacher training schemes (SCITTs), where consortia of schools commit themselves over a number of years to recruiting students directly and providing them with a series of training experiences alongside their time in the classroom, and graduate teacher programmes (GTPs), where training is provided by individual schools to 'top up' the knowledge and skills of the graduates they have recruited to teaching posts.

Both these schemes have been seen by those supporting them as pragmatic strategies, designed to increase the 'diversity' and 'flexibility' of routes into the profession. There has been a further difficulty, however, which has formed part of the backdrop for these initiatives. HEIs have traditionally offered the undergraduate and PGCE routes, while consortia of schools, local education authorities and other bodies (such as religious groups and not-for-profit organisations) have been involved in SCITTs and the like. While there has frequently been a role for higher education in validating or contributing to these routes, it has usually been a much reduced one. Not surprisingly, therefore, they have often been seen by HEIs as a form of 'competition', a perception which has been fuelled by some of those who have been ideologically opposed over the years to higher education's dominant position in teacher training.

Pressure to change: the era of CATE

The so-called 'Great Debate' about education, which dominated the mid-1970s, was not primarily about the contribution of teacher education and training to educational standards – however, it was shortly to implicate them. A consultative paper from the Department for Education and Science (DES) maintained that 'Teachers lacked adequate professional skills, and did not know how to discipline children or to instil in them concern for hard work or good manners' (DES 1977: para. 1.2). Schools, it went on, needed to demonstrate their accountability to society. This would require a coherent and soundly based system of assessment, a theme which had been canvassed more widely by central government and others. The attacks, no matter their origin, focused on teaching methods as part of the malaise. From the late 1970s onwards concerns about what was taught, and how, were expressed increasingly often. Indeed, by 1987 a potential National Curriculum had been published (DES 1987). Among a range of significant proposals, it described the curriculum in terms of academic *subjects* rather than the 'topic work', 'areas of experience' and 'themes' to which primary practitioners had mostly been committed. It was clear from these interventions that efforts to reform teacher education would follow in their wake.

Prior to 1984, there had been little government control of ITT. Entrants were simply required to have passed GCE O level in English language and mathematics and institutions were expected to adhere to general specifications for student numbers for the different age ranges. Inspections, when they occurred, were relatively low key and reports were not made public. Courses, whether primary or secondary, undergraduate or postgraduate, provided a mixture of training in the HEIs and in schools, in the education disciplines and, on undergraduate courses, in one or two specialist subjects. In the vast majority of institutions the bulk of the preparation for a career in teaching took place in the HEIs rather than in the schools, a distinction which was sometimes couched (and justified) in terms of 'theory' and 'practice'.

A central government circular (DES 1984) was to provide the first indications of a possible change of direction. The circular established the Council for the Accreditation of Teacher Education (CATE) to oversee and approve teacher education on behalf of the government. It covered four areas: course structure; approval at central and local level; partnership with local schools; and the need for 'relevant experience' for those involved in teaching students aspects of 'pedagogy'. Courses began to be developed in partnership with local schools, and local committees were set up as part of the process.

The requirements stipulated: a minimum length for PGCE courses (36 weeks); the number of weeks in school on a four-year undergraduate course (20 weeks); and the minimum number of hours devoted to the study of teaching language and mathematics in primary curriculum courses (100 hours). Furthermore, staff involved in pedagogy needed 'recent and relevant' experience in the classroom, and experienced teachers were to be involved in assessment and training. This circular caused HEIs to audit their courses and remedy gaps before inspections took place. Primary undergraduate courses often needed to place students in school for extra days, to give more emphasis to the teaching of reading and to strengthen the place of the specialist subject, often at the expense of the education disciplines.

As a direct result all institutions were inspected by HM Inspectors (HMI); in many cases an inspection of this depth was a novel experience. When HMI had reported and the institutional response had been written, documentation was sent to CATE. A team from each institution then attended a meeting of the CATE scrutiny committee. The questioning ranged from the response to the HMI report, through the involvement of schools in the selection of trainees, to details of course content.

The impact of Circular No. 3/84 was very considerable. HEIs were undoubtedly losing some of their autonomy in planning courses and there were significant tensions. Looking back, however, it is clear that the circular also contained issues that were to grow in prominence relating to the nature of 'professionalism', for example, and 'partnerships with schools'. Some examples of partnership-based approaches already existed (at Oxford, Leicester and Sussex Universities, for example) but notions of 'school-based' training were not yet widespread.

The next circular (DES 1989) was a good deal more specific and prescriptive. Science was added as a 'core subject' to primary courses. Education and professional studies were to emphasise child development, special educational needs and the variety of children in a class. There was an increased emphasis on subject studies and on 'main subject *application*' for primary undergraduate courses, the latter intended to provide 'subject leadership' in a student's specialist subject. This emphasis promoted the idea of the specialist teacher or curriculum leader, as opposed to the generalist class teacher, in primary schools. This requirement still poses difficulties for some HEIs involved in primary teacher training.

Further inspections followed and gave some courses 'quality' awards. CATE committees asked questions about how education and professional studies enhanced students' understanding of their school experiences and how 'serial' and 'block' school placements were integrated into the elements of the courses provided by HEIs.

The numbers of graduates opting to take up careers in teaching still lagged behind the numbers of vacancies. In the late 1980s the search for viable new routes to Qualified Teacher Status (QTS) was revived. The Articled Teachers Scheme for graduates, for example, ran for five years and provided school-based training for those not attracted by the conventional courses. Other new routes were also introduced, such as a two-year part-time PGCE course in secondary 'shortage' subjects. Nevertheless, overall, this was a period of relatively quiet evolution – at least compared with what was to come.

Pressure to change: changing the training partnership with schools

Pressures on HEIs were to continue throughout the next decade. In 1992 the Secretary of State, Kenneth Clarke, signalled a further raft of reforms, stressing that 'the changes in initial teacher training which I am about to propose will attract into teaching some of those who might have been put off by some of the orthodoxies of the past and by fear of lacking the practical experience to cope in the classroom' (Clarke 1992). To those who are attuned to these matters it was significant that he referred to initial teacher *training* (and not *education*), attacked the theoretical framework included in courses and highlighted the need to strengthen the practical experience of students.

An HMI report on 'school-based' training (DES 1991) had underlined the need for clearly understood roles for HEI tutors, students and the teachers helping to train them. Clarke claimed that schools were still unclear about their responsibilities, that teachers were given little opportunity to assess students and that schools lacked the resources (and teachers the time) to carry out their training tasks. He argued for a more equal partnership between schools and HEIs, with newly qualified teachers (NQTs) having had the experience that could only come from school-based work supervised by serving teachers. In short, he spelled out a model of secondary partnership involving the whole school – the head, school mentors, the head of department and the teachers who would work with the student. For primary training, however, he wished to delay the introduction of school-based training until he had received the report of the 'three wise men' – Alexander, Rose and Woodhead (Alexander *et al.* 1992) – on how the National Curriculum could best be delivered in primary schools. Furthermore, in future, accreditation would be decided by the *outcomes* of training rather than the process and content of courses, suggesting that many of the criteria relating to the courses should be recast in terms of what employers expected of newly qualified teachers.

These proposals heralded the introduction of a competence-based model for teacher preparation in which new arrangements would be made with 'partner schools'. Furthermore, Clarke argued, 'as more of the responsibility for teacher training moves from the colleges to the schools most of the costs of that training will have to move with it'. After a brief transitional phase, the introduction of the reforms would be supported and reinforced by a further round of inspections.

The speech was to set the agenda for the next decade and was to prove a watershed for teacher training institutions, for their relationship with schools, for the structure and content of courses and for their relationships with central government. Later CATE advised the DfE that there should be three main principles for the new criteria and for procedures of accreditation. These were that:

- schools should play a much larger part in ITT as full partners of higher education institutions;
- the accreditation criteria for ITT courses should require HEIs, schools and students to focus on the competencies of teaching;
- institutions, rather than individual courses, should be accredited for ITT.

Two circulars were to follow laying out the 'competencies' expected of NQTs. The one for secondary teachers (DfE 1992) described these under the following areas: subject knowledge, subject application, class management, assessment and recording of pupils' progress and further professional development. The requirements for primary schools (DfE 1993) were fairly similar, although there was rather more detail: whole curriculum, subject knowledge and application, assessment and recording of pupils' progress, pupils' learning, teaching strategies and techniques, and further professional development. Teaching strategies was divided into two sub-headings and then into 15 competence statements. Courses were required to include a minimum of 150 hours on each of the core subjects of mathematics, English and science. In addition, training in the teaching of arithmetic and reading was to last at least 50 hours, while the number of weeks in school was raised from 20 to 32 weeks in four-year courses. In marked contrast to earlier proposals, HEIs were asked to consider six-subject, three-year BEd courses to prepare primary teachers to work across the curriculum. Furthermore, the new criteria no longer required courses to cover all subjects of the primary curriculum.

HEIs established partnership committees to oversee their relationships with schools, including the planning, teaching and assessment of students. The chairs were headteachers, to symbolise the new relationships, and the number of headteachers and school coordinators balanced HEI tutors. Secondary heads, in particular, perceived an expansion of their roles and were demanding in the transfer of funds from HEIs to schools in return for their contribution to training. Primary schools, for their part, were unsure whether they wished to take on the extra responsibility and needed some persuasion. As Furlong *et al.* (2000) comment, 'in both primary and secondary circulars, "training" was explicitly presented as involving only two elements: subject knowledge, which was largely, though not exclusively the province of the higher education institutions, and practical teaching skills, which students were to learn in schools'.

Further innovations were to follow. In 1993, the DfE introduced the 'school-centred' teacher training initiative. This encouraged schools to train postgraduates, and was intended to demonstrate the profession 'gaining control of training'. Schools formed consortia, only sometimes buying in HEI expertise to deliver or assess the courses. Funding went to the SCITT, not the HEI. The scheme greatly concerned HEIs because it often developed in schools with which they had previously been in partnership and which they had actually trained. SCITTs were undoubtedly in competition with HEIs, diverted resources, had favoured status and reduced the number of training places in schools available for conventional training. SCITTs were also given an enhanced level of resource, even though their performance in inspections has not matched expectations, and they contribute only a tiny fraction of entrants to the profession.

The pressure of inspections

Government could lay out its requirements for ITT, but in the first half of the 1990s it was clear that it lacked mechanisms for ensuring implementation. From the mid-1990s onwards the power to inspect became the vehicle for enforcement and compliance. Inspections occur every three years for each of the secondary subjects that an institution provides and every other year for primary courses. Much of the political controversy surrounded the inspections of institutions involved in primary training. The so-called Primary Sweep inspection finished in 1996 and was followed by the PFUS (Primary Follow-up Survey) and two cycles of PITTI (Primary ITT Inspection), which finished in 2002. These focused on the training of students in literacy and numeracy, then on English and mathematics, then on English or mathematics plus a specialist subject. The 2000–2 cycle should have inspected English or mathematics, science and another specialist subject. This was reduced to English or mathematics, with ICT assessed in the chosen subject as it is in secondary inspections. The decision emphasised a view in primary education and ITT that English and mathematics are *core* subjects and ICT and science *subsidiary* core subjects, but still ones that need strict control by statutory orders.

The inspection programme has shifted attention away from institutional provision towards student outcomes. Training was inspected in the HEIs but the outcomes of such training were inspected in schools where students were observed and questioned, according to the *Framework for the Assessment of Quality and Standards in Initial Teacher Training* (Ofsted 1998). The outcomes were graded; HEIs doing less well lost student numbers, with little possibility of a successful appeal. There was little or no professional dialogue during or after an inspection. The pressure was not just on HEIs. Inspectors themselves found they were required to apply the criteria to the letter, as otherwise HEIs might lodge objections during the inspection process. Relationships were made more difficult because the inspection cycles started around the same time that the circulars were being implemented and new partnership relationships were being developed. No 'allowance', however, was made for such 'excuses'.

HEIs, for their part, were initially irritated and then became angry, voicing their concerns about the process, especially at meetings of the Universities Council for the Education of Teachers (UCET). A number threatened to pull out of ITT, and not always because of poor inspection grades. A tightening funding regime meant that some lost out and resources were not always available to develop the new courses and partnerships. Indeed, for a mixture of reasons, a small group of institutions did close down operations.

In the second half of the 1990s the ITT sector began to articulate its concerns more forcefully. In a comprehensive survey of providers, Graham and Nabb (1999) suggested that the majority perceived Ofsted's inspection of ITT as:

- inconsistent;
- lacking validity and reliability;
- failing to acknowledge the realities of partnership courses;
- unacceptably dominated by the funder's grading procedures;
- imposing excessive burdens;
- insufficiently promoting quality enhancement;
- representing poor value for money to the system.

The problems were to continue beyond the millennium. By 2001 inspection policies were beginning to bite quite hard. A small number of universities said they were actively considering whether they wished to sustain their commitment to teacher training and claimed to be on the point of withdrawing. Meanwhile, several SCITTs, whose overall record in inspections fell well below that of more traditional providers, had already dropped away.

The control of ITT in the years after 1997

Further changes were to follow the election of the new Labour government in 1997. The government wanted schools to focus on English, mathematics, science and information technology and to give particular attention to literacy and numeracy. From 1998, schools were not required to deliver the foundation subjects in full, while literacy and numeracy strategies were introduced to enable more 11-year-olds to achieve higher standards by 2002. So-called 'desirable outcomes' were also introduced for nursery-age children (DfEE 1998a). Training institutions were expected to be completely up to date with these changes.

By this stage CATE had given way to a new government body known as the Teaching Training Agency (TTA), at arm's length from but reporting to the DfEE. In a further signal of what was to come it was given responsibility for the funding of ITT, which was separated from the rest of higher education. Universities had to bid for student numbers and the resources to manage them. A key feature of the new agency's strategy was the decision to link funding to 'quality': institutions that performed well in inspections were given greater opportunities to expand; those that did particularly badly had numbers taken away from them. In its *Annual Report* for 2000 the TTA states that its purpose is to raise standards in schools by attracting able and committed people to teaching and by improving the quality of teacher training. This is developed into four strategic aims, agreed with ministers, three of which are relevant to ITT (TTA 2001a). They are to:

• increase the number and quality of recruits to teaching;
• raise the standard and quality of initial teacher training;
• increase the proportion of trainees in high quality ITT provision.

As part of its strategy, the TTA aims to have 10 per cent of NQTs trained on 'new' routes. These include the introduction of a greater degree of 'flexibility' into the postgraduate routes, designed to take account of prior achievement and to meet the needs of those changing careers who may have major financial commitments. The advantages of the Graduate Teacher Programme (GTP) and other employment-based routes were also canvassed. Whatever the route, however, the general principle is that all entrants should be assessed against the same standards of performance. Interestingly, perhaps given the considerable criticism to which they had previously been exposed, there was no specific reference to SCITTs. The same report also provided evidence on the changing levels of 'quality' among providers. Out of 195 secondary subjects inspected, 87 had improved and only 15 had lower quality categories. However, of the 57 primary providers inspected, 15 had lower quality categories than before, while only seven had improved.

The general reasons for these disparities between the primary and secondary sectors are not clear, although annual reports from Ofsted in 2000 and 2001 provide some insights. Primary trainees' subject knowledge in English, the assessment of trainees against the standards, and monitoring, assessment, recording, reporting and accountability are all mentioned.

The reforms initiated in the mid-1980s had resulted by the end of the 1990s in a 'national curriculum for initial teacher training' to parallel that provided for pupils. Circular 4/98, in particular, demanded in its 'Standards for the Award of Qualified Teacher Status' that '*All* courses must involve the assessment of *all* trainees to ensure that they meet all *the standards specified*' (DfEE 1998b). This sentence has proved controversial, especially during Ofsted inspections. Universities, for their part, have complained that these 'standards' are too numerous to verify and continue to encourage a 'ticklist' mentality. Policy-makers, by contrast, have tried to argue that a more holistic view of training teachers is also implied, suggesting in the same document (page 8) that:

> It is necessary to consider the standards as a whole to appreciate the creativity, commitment, energy and enthusiasm which teaching demands, and the intellectual and managerial skills required of the effective professional . . . the award of QTS . . . should not require a mechanistic, tick-list approach or entail each standard being supported by its own evidence base.

In late 1999 a review of Circular 4/98 was announced. The TTA wrote to providers, chief education officers, the General Teaching Council and other organisations announcing a programme to monitor the requirements in Circular 4/98. It would collect evidence and views to feed into a review. A new circular would be ready for September 2002. Stakeholders were asked to provide evidence, and the TTA would take into account evidence from Ofsted and other sources. At the end of the exercise (TTA 1999) the TTA wished to be able to provide sound advice to ministers on where:

- changes to the circular would help to improve further the quality of ITT;
- the circular might need to be adjusted to reflect national policy developments, such as the introduction of the revised National Curriculum for pupils and the National Literacy and Numeracy Strategies.

The monitoring and review were more conciliatory in tone than previous consultations and the whole process was to last more than two years.

The present system

By the end of the 1990s, then, the structures for educating and training intending teachers had been thoroughly reformed. Nevertheless, pressures for change continued. The first Green Paper from the newly elected Labour government (DfEE 1998c) maintained that the present system still did not guarantee that every new teacher had a thorough grounding, and announced the introduction of skills tests (in numeracy, literacy and ICT) for all trainees. Another proposal, running in parallel with the modularisation of PGCE courses, was to include appropriate modules in undergraduate courses; this can be seen as part of the continuing shift from undergraduate ITT to PGCE courses. The Green Paper also proposed a 'Training Schools' initiative, in which certain schools would be given a higher profile in providing training, as well as a 'fast-track' system to attract and support 'high-flying' graduates to run in parallel with some existing PGCE courses.

At the same time there were some signs that the TTA wished to come to an accommodation with its main providers. New and less draconian arrangements for allocating places were proposed, along with a less punitive approach to the handling of institutions whose provision had fallen below acceptable levels (TTA 2001b), revised and possibly 'lighter' arrangements for inspection and the provision of support and guidance to continue to improve provision (TTA 2001c).

Looking to the future

After so much turmoil what were the results? The Green Paper (DfEE 2001) concluded, rather optimistically, that since the Labour victory in 1997 primary teacher training had 'greatly improved', so that, 'for the first time, we can have confidence that all trainee teachers are being taught the best practice in English and Mathematics'. Ofsted grades had been used by the TTA to reduce and, in extreme cases, close down low-quality provision, and more trainees were being trained in institutions that had received the highest inspection grades (65 per cent in 1999, compared with 56 per cent in 1997). The Green Paper's conclusion was that the reforms of previous years had improved both the quality of ITT and the standard of teaching by NQTs (which, Ofsted reported, nearly matched the profile of the whole profession). Teacher educators would doubtless agree that training provision had been transformed over the previous decade. Many would be more reluctant, however, to see this as a 'success' in the same terms as those propounded by the government of the day. The 2001 Green Paper, nevertheless, implies that the government will continue to set standards, will want to influence the curriculum of ITT and will still be prepared to tell teachers (and hence trainees) how to teach.

Meanwhile, a bigger threat to the stability of ITT reforms has begun to emerge. During its first year in office the Labour government changed the arrangements for the funding of students in higher education. Students were expected to make some contribution to the costs themselves, and began to accumulate debts on graduation. Teaching, which has never been a particularly popular profession among university graduates, began to come under strains that were compounded by a relatively buoyant economy. As a partial response to the problems the TTA introduced a 'training salary' for those undergoing the one-year PGCE course after their degree course. To the dismay of students following the BA/BEd routes into a teaching career, this 'salary' was not initially extended to those in the last year of their undergraduate training, even though their position was comparable. As a result the pressures for more courses to move towards a three years plus one year pattern of preparation have increased along with the development of employment-based routes (which also pay a salary from the beginning). After an extended period in which the major concern has been with what intending teachers are taught, training providers find themselves having to come to terms again with a longstanding problem. How can promising young graduates be persuaded of the opportunities and satisfactions a career in teaching can offer? It is a question that successive governments have had difficulty in answering and one that the next circular in 2002 will be expected to address.

POINTS FOR DISCUSSION

1 What are the attractions of teaching as a profession today?
2 What are the major obstacles to recruitment and retention in teaching?

INTERNET SITE

The Teacher Training Agency: www.tta.org.uk

REFERENCES AND FURTHER READING

Alexander, R., Rose, J. and Woodhead, C. (1992) *Curriculum Organisation and Classroom Practice in Primary Schools: a Discussion Paper.* London: DES.

Clarke, K. (1992) 'Speech for the North of England Education Conference, 4 January'. London: DFE.

DES (1977) *Education in Schools: a Consultative Document*, Green Paper, Cmnd 6869. London: HMSO.

DES (1984) *ITT: Approval of Courses*, Circular 3/84. London: DES.

DES (1987) *The National Curriculum 5–16: a Consultation Document.* London: DES.

DES (1989) *ITT: Approval of Courses.* Circular No. 24/89. London: DES.

DES (1991) *School-based Initial Teacher Training in England and Wales: a Report by HM Inspectorate.* London: HMSO.

DfE (1992) *Initial Teacher Training (Secondary Phase).* Circular No. 9/92. London: DFE.

DfE (1993) *The Initial Training of Primary School Teachers: New Criteria for Courses.* Circular No. 14/93. London: DFE.

DfEE (1998a) *Nursery Education: Desirable Outcomes for Children's Learning on Entering Compulsory Education.* Sudbury: DfEE Publications.

DfEE (1998b) *Teaching: High Status, High Standards.* Circular No. 4/98. London: DfEE.

DfEE (1998c) *Teachers Meeting the Challenge of Change.* London: The Stationery Office.

DfEE (2001) *Schools: Building on Success.* Norwich: The Stationery Office.

Furlong, J., Barton, L., Miles, S., Whiting, C. and Whitty, G. (2000) *Teacher Education in Transition: Re-forming Professionalism?* Buckingham: Open University Press.

Graham, J. and Nabb, J. (1999) *Stakeholder Satisfaction Survey of Ofsted Inspection of ITT 1994–1999.* London: UCET.

Ofsted (1998) *Framework for the Assessment of Quality and Standards in Initial Teacher Training.* London: Ofsted and TTA.

Ofsted (2000) *Working Together in Initial Teacher Education and Training: Making Inspection Work.* London: Ofsted.

TTA (1999) *Monitoring and Review of DfEE Circular 4/98* (Letter and Annex dated 14 December). London: TTA.

TTA (2001a) *Teacher Training Agency Annual Report 2000*. London: TTA.

TTA (2001b) *Consultation on the Use of Information about Quality in Allocations Decisions for 2002/2003* (Letter and consultation document dated 9 February). London: TTA.

TTA (2001c) *Monitoring and Review of DfEE Circular 4/98* (Letter and Annex dated 19 February). London: TTA.

CHAPTER 16

Induction for New Teachers

Linda Gillard and Pat Mahony

CHAPTER SUMMARY

- This chapter places the current induction arrangements into an historical context.
- The induction process is summarised and the stated aims are discussed.
- The use of standards in professional development and performance management is considered.
- It is suggested that induction is an important phase in the development of teachers and should be perceived as an opportunity for teachers to take control of their professional development.

Introduction

This chapter discusses current induction policy and how the arrangements could contribute to the professional development of teachers. It outlines provision for newly qualified teachers (NQTs) prior to the introduction in 1999 of the current induction arrangements, and suggests that the treatment of NQTs has been an issue for many years. It has generally been agreed that new teachers need support during the early years of teaching, and in the present managerial culture it is not surprising that this is now combined with assessment of each NQT against National Professional Standards. New teachers now have a statutory period of induction, which follows on from a training period, a large proportion of which is school-based. The induction period is intended to provide a supportive environment as they make the transition from training to an employment context. Continued assessment against the standards for the award of Qualified Teacher Status (QTS) (already met in training) and against a further set of induction standards is carried out. The degree to which teachers take control of the way the standards framework is used will have a significant impact on the future development of the profession.

Before 1992

Teachers qualifying prior to 1992 would have been subject to the regulations of Administrative Memorandum 4/59, *Probation of Qualified Teachers* (DES 1959), in which the initial period of service in school as a qualified teacher was the 'probationary year', during which an assessment of the new teacher's ability to teach was made. It was predicated on the need to ensure that new teachers, who had a mainly theoretical training, could teach in a classroom setting. Collins's (1969) study, based on comments from probationers, headteachers, chief education officers and research carried out in the 1960s, concluded:

> It is not, as yet, at all clear what probationers can reasonably be expected to do when they begin teaching and what kinds of skills can be left to be developed during the probationary year. A consensus of opinion on this question is urgently required and would make for more realistic expectations on the part of everybody concerned. It would help to clarify the part to be played by colleges and departments of education, LEAs and schools to set more limited goals for the young teacher at each stage of his career. (Collins 1969: 89)

The James Report (DES 1972) proposed reforms to teacher education and training. It located probation within a second cycle of training, in which support in the early years of teaching is linked to pre-service training. In response to James, the University of London Institute of Education (1972) acknowledged that the probationary year was ineffective and questioned whether this second cycle would be better. James was not implemented but was followed by a period of DES-sponsored research into 'induction' for new teachers in schools (Bolam 1973, 1975). This research proposed a support programme of 'induction' to run concurrent with probation and not to replace it. Induction continued to be developed on an *ad hoc* basis depending on the interest and enthusiasm in individual schools and local authorities, but examples of good practice did not become widespread.

The development of induction was supported not by statute but by 'recommendation' in an Administrative Memorandum (DES 1983). Reports by HMI on the new teacher in school published in 1982 and 1988 were critical of the provision for NQTs in schools (DES 1982, 1988). The 1988 report expressed similar concerns to those raised by Collins nearly 20 years earlier, and suggested that more definition was needed in the following areas:

- the responsibilities of each party (LEA, trainer, school);
- the competence levels at the end of training;
- the aspects of training that could not be developed until the teacher is in post.

It also suggested that information from initial teacher training (ITT) about the trainees' strengths and weaknesses needed to be passed to schools.

In January 1992 at the North of England Education Conference in Southport the government commitment to a shift of ITT from higher education institutions (HEIs) to schools was announced by Kenneth Clarke (DES 1992a). This marked a change in the focus of education policy away from schools and curriculum (evident in the Education Reform Act 1988), and towards teachers and their training. Clarke announced the abolition of probation from September 1992. The regulations were replaced by non-mandatory guidance in the *Induction of Newly Qualified Teachers* (DES 1992b) amidst considerable controversy (Sidgwick *et al.* 1993; Sidgwick 1996). This guidance shifted responsibility for induction from local authorities to schools, and responses from local authorities, a teacher union, trainers and teachers in schools are recorded in a special issue of the *British Journal of In-Service Education* (1993). At this time competences, which have since developed into standards, were controversially introduced into teacher training (DfE 1992, 1993; Mahony 1996). The development of a Career Entry Profile from 1995 provides for communication between ITT and schools and the introduction of induction standards has indicated areas for in-post training. Thus concerns about new teachers have resulted in the production of a legislated framework within which beginning teachers work. The next two sections consider what the current induction arrangements involve, and some of the issues that will need to be addressed.

Key structures and organisational features

The main documents relating to the induction of teachers are:

* DfEE Guidance 90/2000 (DfEE 2000);
* TTA support materials (TTA 1999, 2001a);
* TTA Career Entry Profile (TTA 2001b);
* DfEE Circular 4/98 relating to the standards for the award of QTS (DfEE 1998a).

The expectation is that on completion of training, QTS is awarded and new teachers register with the General Teaching Council (GTC). Successful induction confirms this registration. Initiatives included in *Learning and Teaching: a Strategy for Professional Development* (DfEE 2001) place induction at the start of professional development and confirm its place within the performance management framework.

The Career Entry Profile (CEP), which provides information to the employer about strengths and professional development needs, is completed at the end of training and is intended to support the development of an individualised induction programme. The DfEE guidance, in conjunction with the TTA support materials, details the arrangements that schools, teachers and local authorities need to make in order to provide NQTs with such a programme. Under the *School Teachers' Pay and Conditions* document (DfEE 1999) NQTs should have a teaching load not exceeding 90 per cent of the average. It is recommended that the extra time released is spread over the induction period and is protected so that induction and professional development are planned and coherent.

The induction programme normally lasts for one year (or pro rata equivalent for part-time teachers), during which the NQT should be monitored, supported and assessed. The most important restriction is that induction can only be completed once. Induction involves:

* the identification of a named induction tutor to support the NQT;
* observation, with follow-up discussion, of the NQT's teaching each half term;

- half-termly meetings to review progress;
- the NQT observing experienced teachers;
- participation in professional development activities based on individual needs;
- target setting with respect to the QTS and induction standards;
- formal assessment meetings.

The assessment of progress should be based on a range of evidence. This must include written reports on the NQT's teaching and on the progress review meetings. Further evidence could include lesson plans, evaluations, the professional profile and information about liaison with colleagues.

Within the new arrangements two important questions are whether new teachers are being inducted into the profession or the particular school and whether the professional standards can really guarantee the required level of proficiency. In the introduction, the guidance describes the induction arrangements in terms of providing:

- a bridge between ITT and continuing professional development;
- support for NQTs so that they can contribute to school improvement and raising standards in the classroom;
- a basis for professional and career development.

The bridge metaphor suggests that new teachers need help in order to move from teacher training to effective practice. It also suggests that instead of this being an easily negotiable pathway there are specific difficulties that the new teacher needs help to overcome. This raises questions about what these difficulties are and whether the new induction arrangements best meet these needs. For example, workload and administration are major factors cited by new and experienced teachers as barriers to their effective practice. The reduced teaching load during induction may not be a workload reduction because the released time is used for induction activities, which may add to rather than reduce administration. Furthermore, ATL data (2001) indicate that nearly 20 per cent of new teachers are not being supported in this way, and Bubb (2000) found that there were problems with the provision of cover for this release. At a time of teacher shortage more schools may find this difficult. Another issue is the variable use of the CEP completed by the ITT institution and the NQT, which forms part of the architecture of the bridge. Research by Bubb (2000) found that the CEP was a useful starting point for the induction process, although 20 per cent of the NQTs did not discuss it with their school. The ATL surveys in 2000 and 2001 also showed that between 13 and 21 per cent of respondents had not used their CEP for setting objectives for professional development (ATL 2001). This may be because the 'needs' identified at the end of the period of initial training change in the context of the development plan of the particular school, or because ITT is geared towards training to teach (anywhere), while the induction period is inevitably oriented to the local school context.

Furthermore, some induction tutors will be better skilled than others. Turner (1994) showed that successful induction depended on an appropriate placement, successful relationships with tutors and the new teacher's attitude. These are likely to be variable. The NQT needs to be confident that discussing his or her development as a teacher will lead to support and not a negative assessment. The induction tutor may experience conflict between the roles of providing support on one hand and assessment on the other.

The intention in the induction arrangements is that the NQTs will receive targeted support and so become effective teachers able to contribute to school improvement. In this way the induction policy is securely located within the government's overall aim of school improvement and raising standards in the classroom. This raises the point that, whatever else the benefits of such support are, the link between the support given to NQTs and their ability to contribute to school improvement is not straightforward. The performance of NQTs during school Ofsted inspections is measured on the same performance scale as other teachers, and it should be possible to look at these data and make comparisons between NQTs and other teachers. HMI surveys of the new teacher in school in the 1980s and early 1990s (DES 1982, 1988, 1992c) found that new teachers were rated as being as good as more experienced teachers. Data from 1997 to 2000 show that almost half of new teachers' lessons observed by inspectors are judged to be good or very good (Howson 2001). This suggests that new teachers are effective in the classroom and have been successful without the benefit of the current arrangements. This leads us to ask (though not to answer): what is the (real) problem that induction is designed to address? (Mahony and Hextall 2000).

In the guidance the induction year is also described as providing a basis for continuing professional and career development. As such, induction is further located within the policy to restructure teaching found within the Green Paper *Teachers: Meeting the Challenge of Change* (DfEE 1998b). This performance management framework links professional development to a series of national standards. They include standards for the award of QTS for entry into teaching, the induction standards, threshold standards that link performance to pay, standards for appointment of Advanced Skills Teachers and finally standards for the award of a National Professional Qualification for Headship. At present the standards are not designed to discriminate between the good teacher and the average, but only require a judgement of whether the standards have been met. Induction and career development are also linked by the requirement for NQTs to take responsibility for their own professional development. Under proposals in *Learning and Teaching* (DfEE 2001) all teachers will have a contractual responsibility to take charge of their own professional development. This is intended to support the introduction of performance management, and depending on how schools translate it, will become either an administrative burden or a professionally empowering activity.

Administration and legislation: local, national and devolved governance

The induction arrangements are statutory and described in the DfEE Guidance 90/2000 (DfEE 2000). The statutory requirements are given in the Teaching and Higher Education Act 1998, the Education (Induction Arrangements for School

Teachers) (England) Regulations 1999 and amendments. They are also supported by the School Teachers' Pay and Conditions documents. Within the induction arrangements are administrative procedures that require documentary evidence to be kept by those involved.

NQTs should:

- be actively involved in their induction programme and be familiar with the standards that they are required to meet;
- complete their CEP (this may develop into a professional profile and could be used by NQTs to provide evidence of their progress);
- receive a job description and school policy documents relating to their employment and induction;
- receive dated copies of reports on teaching observed, feedback given, progress review meetings and targets set;
- receive dated copies of the summative assessment meeting report.

The induction tutor should:

- prepare the reports on teaching observed, feedback given and the review meetings;
- if acting on behalf of the headteacher, keep a record of the evidence used to inform the judgements made about the standards.

The headteacher is *responsible* for the induction training and assessment and should:

- provide a job description, policy documents and induction programme as set out in the guidance;
- keep a record of the evidence used to inform judgements made about the standards if the summative assessment is not delegated;
- return summative assessment forms to the LEA, ensuring that they have been signed by the headteacher, the induction tutor and the NQT;
- make all induction records available to the LEA;
- for any NQT completing induction in more than one school, the records must be kept for five years or until requested by another school;
- where there is concern that progress is unsatisfactory, observe the NQT to confirm the judgement, check that a support programme is in place, inform the NQT of the concerns and inform the LEA;
- where final summative assessment is unsatisfactory, records should be kept until after the appeal process and a decision on registration has been made by the GTC.

The school governing body should:

- ensure that a good induction programme is available for any NQTs that they appoint;
- be aware of the implications, in terms of staff time and costs, of the induction arrangements.

The LEA (as the appropriate body) should:[1]

- provide summative assessment forms to the schools as per Annex B to the guidance;
- when informed that there is concern about progress, check the assessment and ensure that a support programme is in place.

Induction policy is an example of centralised control of policy leading to increased regulation and inspection, with roles for bodies such as the Teacher Training Agency. The statutory standards for QTS and for induction are backed by a plethora of non-statutory support documents provided by the TTA, which interpret and develop the framework. The focus on standards and assessment within the documentation illustrates how responsibility for implementing policy has been devolved and a management/inspection framework used to ensure that the centrally defined model is followed. Quality assurance procedures at the local level are the responsibility of the appropriate body and at the national level the process is to be monitored and reviewed as part of the Ofsted inspection of both schools and LEAs. This is in line with the general trend of policy change over the past ten years, in which there has been centralised control by the production of regulations and guidance on how policy will be implemented, combined with inspection and local accountability.

The finance to support induction is provided within a larger budget (the Standards Fund). The significance of the devolution of responsibility for the implementation of this national policy to individual schools is that any inadequacies in funding are masked. Research findings suggest that the real cost of induction is greater than the funding made available (Williams and Prestage 2000). The School Teachers' Pay and Conditions document makes participation in initial training and induction part of the employment conditions for teachers, and induction tutors are assigned this role as part of their 'other duties'. The time used by experienced teachers is a major cost of induction and is subsumed into the staff salary budget. The NUT recommended that the allocation in the Standards Fund be increased to enable induction tutors to have time allocated for their role (NUT 2000). Schools and LEAs can use part of the money allocated to the induction process to monitor and evaluate the process. It will be interesting to see whether the findings from such evaluations result in local changes or can be used to inform national policy. LEAs have been given an important role in the success of induction and need to allocate sufficient funds to administration and staffing. The NUT report on induction recommended that the cost of LEA induction coordinators should be funded centrally, particularly where many NQTs were employed or local circumstances made the work of new teachers difficult (NUT 2000).

Teaching and learning: inspection frameworks

The development of induction represents one of the changes to teacher training within the government's wider policy of radically restructuring teaching and teacher training. Details of this policy were laid out in the Green Paper *Teachers: Meeting the Challenge of Change* (DfEE 1998b). During the 1990s there has been a move to increased school-based training, which has changed the relationship between schools and HEIs, with different models of partnership emerging (Furlong *et al.* 1996, 2000).

As we have noted, the current induction arrangements use two sets of standards. The new teacher is required to meet the QTS standards independently and within an employment rather than training situation, and also to meet the induction standards set out in the DfEE guidance. This presupposes that a standards framework supports professional development and that it can be interpreted fairly and consistently. Any NQT who does not successfully complete the induction period will not be eligible to work in state schools, so the consequences of unfair judgements are potentially severe. Each teacher, school and lesson provides a unique experience and so inevitably each NQT will have a unique experience of induction and be assessed against interpretations of the standards across many different schools and local authorities. This inevitably makes it difficult to ensure fairness and a standardised interpretation. Furthermore, Mahony and Hextall's (2000) research found that the use of standards does not resolve issues of consistency and fairness when used for assessment purposes. Not only do they rely heavily on interpretation for translation into practice, but they are framed in a way that provides no measurable yardsticks: as one headteacher put it, 'the "standard" of the Standards is not clear . . . the devil is in the interpretation' (Mahony and Hextall 2000: 54–5). Mahony and Hextall also found that headteachers were worried that energy can be diverted away from teaching and into providing the documentary evidence that the standards have been met (or not). The induction arrangements suggest that more evidence will be needed where a teacher is failing to reach the standards required, yet these are the very teachers who need to be more supported in order to develop their teaching skills rather than burdened with the increased bureaucracy of evidence gathering. It is yet to be seen how many teachers fail to meet the induction standards and how many of these are successful with their appeals. Initial data compiled by the NUT suggest that 90 per cent of NQTs successfully completed induction in 1999/2000, 0.4 per cent failed, about 1 per cent were given an extension and the remainder had not completed their induction, had resigned or had moved. Their main conclusion is that '0.5% failure rate does not mean a 99.5% success rate' (NUT 2000: 10). This is because of the number of new teachers (8.5 per cent) not completing induction and so not appearing in the figures as 'failures'. The reasons for non-completion need to be further investigated.

Attempts to make more open and explicit the expectations of what is required of teachers are generally supported by those involved with the training of teachers. These explicit statements (which are more properly described as descriptors of the job than as 'standards') can be used within a developmental approach that provides structured opportunities for teachers to learn professionally and improve their teaching throughout their careers. Standards can also be used within a regulatory approach as a managerial tool for 'measuring' the efficiency and effectiveness of systems, institutions and individuals, as at the present time. It is the latter that has resulted in an inspection regime experienced by many as negative in its impact and discouraging innovation and development.

Current education policy links economic success with improving pupils' academic standards. To achieve this, the government's goal is effective teaching and effective training of teachers within a performance management framework. The current policy of using 'teaching standards' or competence-based models in teacher training and continued professional development to define and assess good teaching is not confined to England and Wales. There have been similar trends in Australia, New Zealand, the USA and Sweden (see Smyth *et al.* 1997; Ingvarson 1998; Whitty *et al.* 1998; Mahony and Hextall 2000).

The proposed model for induction implies that professional learning takes place in a particular way and that the provision of centrally determined standards will support this process. The process of learning to teach is not simple and does not take place in isolation: it requires the intervention of significant others, such as other teachers, mentors, advisers and experts. Research by Elliott and Calderhead (1995) concluded that professional growth takes place over a long period and is idiosyncratic, personal and affected by previous knowledge. Berliner (1995) proposes a theory of skill learning in which the novice moves through advanced beginner, competent and proficient stages before becoming an expert. Schon (1983) has argued that effective learning of professional competences occurs through 'reflection-in-action' and not just 'reflection-on-action', which takes place after the event. What is clear from research is that effective teaching is not the result of technical expertise in a variety of competences or standards. Effective teaching results from the way the separate parts are brought together to meet the unique needs of different groups of pupils at different times. This requires an understanding of learners as well as pedagogy, and time to consider practice against an appropriate theoretical background. It is to be hoped that the reduced timetable for NQTs will enable this to happen and that more urgent but less important issues will not take up the time.

Inspection is a central feature of the drive to improve standards. This includes schools and teacher training, which are subject to demanding and frequent inspections that affect the allocation of trainees to each institution. Induction will be subject to inspection at both school and LEA levels and new teachers will continue to be graded during school inspections according to the same scale as more experienced teachers. It remains to be seen whether information generated by the inspection processes will be used to develop induction policy.

Conclusion: initiatives and prospects

Within the current performance management framework new teachers need to make judgements and take control of their own professional development. New teachers need to be supported in a positive way by more experienced teachers and governors so that they continue to develop their expertise. A notion of professionalism that encourages an imaginative use of the standards framework would enable individual talents, creativity and skills to blossom and this might go some way to encouraging new entrants into teaching and retaining those already in post. This will not happen unless the balance between professional development and the hard regulatory use of standards is weighted in favour of professional development.

The aim of the government, according to the DfES web pages, is 'to give everyone the chance, through education, training and work, to realise their full potential, and thus build an inclusive and fair society and a competitive economy'. This means that there is a need to ensure that all pupils receive a quality education from high-quality teachers. Professional standards can be used to focus help and support, to challenge and to provide a framework for critical self-reflection. For the vast majority of teachers there is a need to recognise and support their ability to direct their own career by selecting continuing professional development courses that consolidate, challenge and motivate. Governors and school development plans need to support the professional development of all staff at whatever stage of their career. Induction is an important phase in the development of a new teacher. There is widespread support for an induction process that enables new teachers to survive and flourish during their first year of teaching and in the years to follow. Time will tell whether the new arrangements are adequate or appropriate for the task in hand.

POINTS FOR DISCUSSION

1 What should new teachers be inducted into and why: the local authority, the school or the profession?
2 How should professional standards be used: as a checklist (the driving test model) or as a focus for development? Can the problems of fairness and consistency be overcome?
3 Should a new teacher who fails be prevented from teaching in the future? Should he or she be able to opt for further training or try again in a different school?
4 What do you predict will be the longer-term effect of current induction? Will it improve: teachers' practice; pupil achievement; recruitment and retention; teacher professionalism?

INTERNET SITES

Association of Teachers and Lecturers: www.askatl.org.uk
Department for Education and Skills: www.dfes.gov.uk
DfES Guidance: www.dfes.gov.uk/circulars/5_99/index.htm
General Teaching Council: www.gtce.org.uk
National Association of Schoolteachers Union of Women Teachers:
    www.teachersunion.org.uk/members/nqts
National Union of Teachers: www.data.teachers.org.uk/nut
Teacher Training Agency: www.canteach.gov.uk/info/induction

NOTE

1 For Independent Schools the appropriate body is the Independent Schools Council Teacher Induction Panel (ISCTIP). Where progress is unsatisfactory there are procedures and an appeal process outlined in the DfEE guidance.

FURTHER READING

Bleach, K. (1999) *The Induction and Mentoring of Newly Qualified Teachers*. London: David Fulton Publishers.

Bleach, K. (2000) *The Newly Qualified Secondary Teachers Handbook*. London: David Fulton Publishers.

Bubb, S. (2000) *The Effective Induction of Newly Qualified Primary Teachers*. London: David Fulton Publishers.

Bubb, S. (2001) *A Newly Qualified Teacher's Manual*. London: David Fulton Publishers.

Mahony, P. and Hextall, I. (2000) *Reconstructing Teaching: Standards, Performance and Accountability*. London: Routledge Falmer.

REFERENCES

Association of Teachers and Lecturers (2001) *Induction: So How Has It Been for You?* London: ATL.

Berliner, D. (1995) 'Teacher expertise', in B. Moon and A. Shelton Mayes (eds) *Teaching and Learning in the Secondary School*. London: Routledge.

Bolam, R. (1973) *Induction Programmes for Probationary Teachers: a Report of an Action Research Project Funded by DES and Carried out at Bristol University 1968–72*. Bristol: Bristol University School of Education.

Bolam, R. (1975) *The Teacher Induction Pilot Schemes (TIPS) Project: a National Evaluation Report*. Bristol: Bristol University School of Education.

Bubb, S. (2000) *The First Year of Statutory Induction: Research Findings from One LEA*. London: London Institute of Education.

Collins, M. (1969) *Students into Teachers*. London: Routledge and Kegan Paul.

DES (1959) *Probation of Qualified Teachers*. Administrative Memorandum 4/59. London: DES.

DES (1972) *The James Report*. London: HMSO.

DES (1982) *The New Teacher in School. A Survey by HM Inspectors in England and Wales 1981*. London: HMSO.

DES (1983) *The Treatment and Assessment of Probationary Teachers*. Administrative Memorandum 1/83. London: DES.

DES (1988) *The New Teacher in School. A Survey by HM Inspectors in England and Wales 1987*. London: HMSO.

DES (1992a) 'Speech of the Secretary of State for Education and Science to the North of England Conference', Southport, 4 January.

DES (1992b) *Induction of Newly Qualified Teachers*. Administrative Memorandum 2/92. London: DES.

DES (1992c) *The Induction and Probation of New Teachers 1988–1991*. London: DES.

DfE (1992) *Initial Teacher Training, Secondary Phase*. Circular 9/92. London: DfEE.

DfE (1993) *Initial Teacher Training, Primary Phase*. Circular 14/93. London: DfEE.

DfEE (1998a) *Teaching: High Status, High Standards*. Circular 4/98. London: DfEE.

DfEE (1998b) *Teachers: Meeting the Challenge of Change*. London: DfEE.

DfEE (1999) *School Teachers' Pay and Conditions of Employment.* Circular 12/99. London: DfEE.

DfEE (2000) *The Induction Period for Newly Qualified Teachers.* Guidance 90/2000. London: DfEE.

DfEE (2001) *Learning and Teaching: a Strategy for Professional Development.* London: DfEE.

Elliott, R. and Calderhead, J. (1995) 'Mentoring for teacher development', in T. Kerry and A. Shelton Mayes (eds) *Issues in Mentoring.* London: Routledge.

Furlong, J., Whitty, G., Whiting, C., Miles, S., Barton, L. and Barrett, E. (1996) 'Re-defining partnership: revolution of reform in initial teachers' education?', *Journal of Education for Teaching,* 22(1), 39–55.

Furlong, J., Barton, L., Miles, S., Whiting, C. and Whitty, G. (2000) *Teacher Education in Transition: Re-forming Professionalism?* Buckingham: Open University Press.

Howson, J. (2001) 'Young guns are going for it', *Times Educational Supplement,* 2 March.

Ingvarson, L. (1998) 'Professional development as the pursuit of professional standards: the standards-based professional development system', *Teaching and Teacher Education,* 14(1), 127–40.

Mahony, P. (1996) 'Competences and the first year of teaching', in D. Hustler and D. McIntyre (eds) *Developing Competent Teachers.* London: David Fulton Publishers.

Mahony, P. and Hextall, I. (2000) *Reconstructing Teaching: Standards, Performance and Accountability.* London: Routledge Falmer.

National Union of Teachers (2000) *Crossing the Winning Line or Falling at the First Hurdle?* London: NUT.

Schon, D. A. (1983) *The Reflective Practitioner: How Professionals Think in Action.* New York: Basic Books.

Sidgwick, S. (1996) 'Government policy and the induction of new teachers', in R. McBride (ed.) *Teacher Education Policy.* London: Falmer Press.

Sidgwick, S., Mahony, P. and Hextall, I. (1993) 'Policy and practice in the professional development of teachers', *International Studies in the Sociology of Education,* 13(1), 91–108.

Smyth, J., Shacklock, G. and Hattam, R. (1997) 'Teacher development in difficult times: lessons from a policy initiative in Australia', *Teacher Development,* 1(1), 11–19.

TTA (1999) *Supporting Induction for Newly Qualified Teachers.* London: TTA.

TTA (2001a) *Into Induction.* London: TTA.

TTA (2001b) *Career Entry Profile 2001.* London: TTA.

Turner, M. (1994) 'The management of the induction of newly qualified teachers in primary schools', *Journal of Education for Teaching,* 20(3), 325–41.

University of London Institute of Education (1972) *The James Report: Some Questions.* London: University of London.

Whitty, G., Power, S. and Halpin, D. (1998) *Devolution and Choice in Education.* Buckingham: Open University Press.

Williams, A. and Prestage, S. (2000) *Still in at the Deep End?* London: ATL.

PART V:

Continuing Professional Development and Educational Research

CHAPTER 17

Continuing Professional Development

Karen Evans

CHAPTER SUMMARY

This chapter:

- Considers approaches to continuing professional development (CPD) that have been adopted in a variety of professions.
- Proposes some new ways of thinking about CPD.
- Discusses some implications for teaching professionals.

Introduction

The crucial importance of professional development has been underlined by public interest in a series of 'new crises' in the professions. High profile cases have identified unacceptable practices, arrogance and closed communities in parts of the medical community. Recruitment and retention crises in public service professions such as teaching, social work, nursing and general medical practice have reflected the feelings of many professionals that they are being overburdened with increasing demands for high-quality service and improvements in performance, without commensurate input of resource. In both public and private professions, such as law and financial services, the culture of consumerism has generated additional pressures: 'clients tend to be more precise about what they expect and less forgiving about failures to deliver the outcome desired' (Swinson 2001). Professional bodies are caught in the tensions of serving and representing members' interests, while ensuring the public interest is served.

Professions are under pressure to find ways to manage expectation and risk so as to achieve an appropriate balance and ensure both safety nets and continued commitment to improving practice through innovation and development. But there is also a responsibility on government and on the wider society to play their part. A culture in which citizenship sits alongside consumerism (and is not replaced by it) recognises that those who provide services can become caught in contradictions in trying to meet multiple, sometimes incompatible, demands for higher levels of performance against proliferating 'indicators', while receiving reduced support and input of resource.

This is the environment that has given professional bodies a new impetus to develop policies, frameworks and programmes for continuing professional development (CPD). It has created expanding markets for higher education institutions offering post-experience courses to professional criteria and standards. These developments reflect the need, as a minimum, for professionals to stay current and up-to-date in their fields. The chartered professions of 100 years ago were underpinned by articles and qualifications that applied for life. They were often 'gentlemen's clubs', exclusive and monopolistic. At the start of the new millennium almost one-third of the British population regards itself as professional, the status being closely linked with qualification through higher education. According to Burley (2001), 'the professions are now locked into higher education, lifelong learning and into the research community'. The majority of entrants to the professions are now female. The professional cadre to which CPD potentially applies is thus very different from the exclusive gentlemen's club of 100 years ago. The expectations, demands and access to information of their clients are also transformed, and as service providers professions have to demonstrate that they are worthy of public trust and confidence.

At a professional level, competence means attaining standards for admission to the profession and subsequent improvement of both individual and collective standards; CPD thus has individual and collective dimensions. This chapter argues that, while early approaches to 'continuing professional education' emphasised entry to the profession and maintenance of standards, approaches suitable for a 'learning society' now require greater emphasis on the continuing collective development of the profession and professional standards.

There are several strands of development that come together in current perspectives on CPD. Vaughan (1991: 5) typified the *individual maintenance* model in a definition of CPD as: 'Ongoing learning that professionals need to undertake throughout their career in order to maintain their professional competence.' An *individual developmental* approach, emphasising a lifelong process of learning, is reflected in definitions that emphasise 'the systematic maintenance, improvement and broadening of knowledge and skills, and the development of personal qualities necessary for execution of professional and technical duties throughout the individual's working life'. The dominance of the individual in the previous two definitions is balanced by attention to the wider social context and employment relationship in *mutual benefit developmental* definitions. These emphasise systematic and planned approaches to the maintenance, enhancement and development of knowledge, skills and expertise that continue throughout a professional's career, to the mutual benefit of the individual, the employer, the professional body and society as a whole.

Lines of development

Early concepts of continuing professional education centred on ideas of individual updating, *education permanente* and recurrent education. The idea that professional knowledge had a 'half life' under conditions of accelerating change became fashionable in the 1970s. Continuing professional education in its original forms emphasised the need to counter the deterioration of knowledge and skills gained through initial professional education and training. It focused on the provision of a variety of courses on the latest developments in the field, sometimes termed 'refresher courses'. Gardner's work in the 1970s led to adoption of the term 'continuing professional development' to represent a larger concept in which 'the purely educational element becomes one alongside others, a full professional life, good practice, career advancement, increased capacity and well-earned profit or its equivalent'.

'Updating' and 'refresher courses' remained the dominant form of provision in 1987 at the time of the first major review of provision. As part of its policy to promote professional, industrial and commercial updating (PICKUP), the Department of Education and Science commissioned a review of continuing professional education and development. Welsh and Woodward's (1989) study provided a detailed picture of the state of the field at that time. Its findings can be compared with the results of a comprehensive survey undertaken by Friedman *et al.* (2001). In this way it is possible to gauge the shifts in the field over a 15-year period. In 1987 approximately half of the professional bodies surveyed by Welsh and Woodward had a CPD policy. By the mid-nineties, Friedman *et al.* showed that CPD had become 'firmly established' within a high proportion of professions. Friedman *et al.*'s national survey of CPD and the vocational lifelong learning reports (Field and Moseley 2000) have confirmed the continuing increase and the trend away from hours on courses towards the 'continuous development' models, and have provided evidence of the extent of the shift from 'CPE and updating' towards 'CPD'. This has been accompanied by the movement towards competence development, and accreditation of evidence of performance and outcomes.

The long-term continuous development view of CPD has been fuelled further by the government's promotion of individualised versions of lifelong learning, and the promotion of the stakeholder view of the responsibility to 'invest' in learning.

> Individuals have a responsibility to invest in learning for their own career development. This will make it easier for them to change job or become more secure by improving their skills in their current workplace. It will give them the chance to earn more. Learning accounts are aimed at encouraging more people to invest in their own future. They will give people the chance to gain the portable skills they need. (DfEE 1998)

Key players: professional associations, higher education institutions, examining bodies

Roles and functions of professional associations

Core functions of professional associations include preservation and enhancement of the status of the professions, support for their members and maintenance of public confidence in the professions. To perform their roles and fulfil their functions, professional associations are finding it increasingly necessary to emphasise the role of CPD.

This is part of the dynamics of 'self-regulation', but professional associations differ greatly in the extent to which they exercise control in this domain.

In those professional associations for which membership is required as part of the licence to practise (e.g. nursing, UKCC), CPD can be prescribed as a condition of continued membership, and the professional's continued ability to practise is dependent upon meeting the requirements. Other professional associations 'offer' voluntaristic CPD frameworks as part of the benefits of membership, emphasising professional enhancement, broader career development options and job satisfaction. Friedman *et al.*, in their 1999 review of professional associations, found that, across the board, there is evidence of converging policies and practices among the professional associations, involving the provision of structured frameworks, and emphasis on individual learning plans and competence outcomes over 'input'-driven programmes based on course attendance. Encouragement rather than sanction is emphasised in the drive to promote participation. These developments were found to apply across the boundaries of 'obligatory' and 'voluntary' schemes. This may be a consequence of benchmarking practices, as associations seek to review their own practices and performance against those of peers and competitors in the field.

The central tension for professional associations, according to Friedman *et al.* (1999: 202), is 'to seek a balance between fashionable educational theory, the best interests of individual professionals, the reputation of the profession and the requirements of the contexts, social and economic, in which they operate'. The tension referred to is the tension between individualised ownership of learning plans and the need to reassure government and the public that professional standards are being properly safeguarded, monitored and implemented. This is well illustrated by Blair and Ramones's analysis of the impact of adult education theories of 'andragogy' on the effectiveness of CPD provision in the nursing profession, which argues that these have had a negative impact: 'Making the assumptions that professional nurses respond to the elements of andragogy is erroneous and dangerous to consumers. These assumptions may be at the very heart of the problem of the lack of effectiveness or utilization of continuing professional education in nursing' (Blair and Ramones 1998).

The role of higher education

Higher education (HE) institutions are major providers of CPD. Many universities collaborate with professional associations in the development of CPD programmes. These programmes are largely funded by the associations and members themselves, with underpinning from government funds where university awards are involved or where new programmes are able to attract initial pump-priming funds for development costs through special targeted measures.

This HE–professional body collaboration can take the form of a university-led award recognised by the professional association, a professional body-led award validated by a university or a jointly developed award. By validating learning in a public way, academic institutions can 'legitimise the professions' claims to expert knowledge' (Bryans *et al.* 1998: 120). This requires collaborative arrangements that can ensure the independence of the university while promoting developments in the CPD domain, which are underpinned by critical engagement with important ideas, issues and practices. Intellectual challenge to the received wisdom of professions can move them from enclaves to developing communities of social practice. This is the potential strength of university involvement. Field and Moseley (2000) provided guidelines for HE institutions seeking to expand their share of the CPD market, as part of a government funded review. One outcome was a set of pointers (reproduced in Box 17.1) for HE institutions seeking to engage in CPD. This emphasised complementarity, financial incentives and positive working relationships between the HE institution and the professional associations concerned. The dangers are omitted, in that partnerships may become too cosy, with HE providers losing their critical edge as they are increasingly dependent on the resources from the partnership arrangement.

Box 17.1

Key recommendations for promotion to professional bodies

- Identify those professional bodies that relate to areas of Vocational Lifelong Learning in which the institution has significant VLL activity.
- Develop a working relationship based on complementarity.
- Keep abreast of professional bodies' approaches and attitudes towards CPD.

Good practice

- Where the professional body has an accreditation system, identify opportunities and procedures to meet its requirements to ensure that VLL courses can be accredited, and if necessary registered with the professional body.
- Offer course fee discounts to members of professional bodies.
- Use professional bodies as a vehicle for marketing; for example, by offering discounts to regional members in return for access to mailing lists, placing inserts in regional mailings, providing editorial for newsletters or involving the professional body in market research.
- Use professional bodies to identify clusters of local SMEs.
- Identify the requirements of the professional body for CPD, and build this into the course design.

Barriers

- Professional bodies may draw back from partnerships with HEIs if they do not wish to be seen as favouring one institution over another.
- Professional bodies may see themselves as being in competition with HEIs.

Box 17.1 (*cont.*)

Reflection

* Is it possible to identify professional bodies and employers' associations that are complementary to the niche markets for which the institution offers VLL activities? Have contacts been made at local, regional and national level?
* Are there opportunities to expand and diversify markets by exploring links with professional bodies in Europe and elsewhere?
* Are there opportunities for joint HEI/professional body events that are to the advantage of both parties?

Source: Field and Moseley (2000).

Examining bodies

The ability of examining bodies such as Edexcel or City and Guilds to accredit programmes up to National Vocational Qualification Level 4 and above has brought them into the CPD field as key players. Many of these will also be aiming to develop working partnerships with the other stakeholders in the field to realise their potential markets, and their ability to accredit units of professional development, including experiential and workplace learning, positions them strongly for this.

Accreditation as recognition and control

Accreditation is potentially an instrument of self-regulation and of external control. Accreditation of policies, of courses, of portfolios of evidence and of individual activities is high on the agenda of many professional associations, and Friedman *et al.* (2001) showed that 81 per cent of professional associations had some form of accreditation associated with their CPD policies and programmes.

Over half of the associations surveyed incorporated accreditation in their policy and approximately one-half accredited CPD courses. Only 13 per cent were involved in accreditation of policies involving benchmarking between equivalent bodies or using external agencies, and these were concentrated in the engineering sector (under the umbrella of the Engineering Council) and in the financial sector, where cross-accreditation takes place between related associations. Whether the associations had voluntary, obligatory, compulsory or mixed policies towards CPD did not appear to be linked to the pattern of accreditation.

Course accreditation by professional associations can place a heavy administration burden on them. The process usually involves issuing guidelines on requirements that have to be met, with the constitution of specific accreditation panels comprised of selected association members and peers. These evaluate course specifications, processes, outcomes, quality assurance and staff development procedures and other features against the guidelines and criteria, and usually involve site visits (CIPFA, UKCC and ILT all provide examples of accreditation panels and processes; see Box 17.2).

The 'accreditation' of individual members' CPD involves verification of evidence of CPD activity and is often linked to membership upgrades. Specified CPD requirements for those wishing to upgrade their membership are laid down. These can provide incentives for members.

Box 17.2 Three Examples of Accreditation of CPD

1 Chartered Institute of Public Finance and Accountancy (CIPFA)

CIPFA has established a three-year cycle of CPD for members. After the first and second years, successful completion is recognised by inclusion in the List of Members. On completion of the full three-year cycle, members are awarded the Cert CPD as an additional qualification (and additional letters after their names).

2 United Kingdom Central Council for Nursing, Midwifery and Health Visiting (UKCC)

UKCC's post-registration education and practice (PREP) requirements involve nurses undertaking the equivalent of 35 hours of continuing professional development in five recommended study areas: reducing risk; care enhancement; patient, client and colleague support; practice development; and education development. The Royal College of Nursing, as the professional association, promotes the use of the personal professional portfolio, to record study days, 'unstructured' learning, work experience and current projects, as well as reflections on experience and action planning. The RCN states that 'Nurses face a perpetual cycle of learning and achievement – which makes the concept of lifelong learning so important to their profession' (RCN 2001).

3 Institute of Learning and Teaching (ILT)

The ILT is the newly established professional association for university teachers. Many institutions are now building in requirements for membership into probationary periods and conditions of appointment. ILT has an initial entry route for experienced teachers, for the first period of its operation up to 2002. Once they have joined ILT, members are 'expected to remain in good standing', and a newly constituted CPD Working Group is exploring and monitoring the most appropriate ways of 'tracking and monitoring' CPD, through a consultation exercise.

Communities of practice

Some of the examples given above illustrate how professional associations act as 'communities of practice' in ensuring and developing standards of practice of their members.

Situated learning is an approach to thinking about and theorising learning that has generated much recent interest. It is important for professional development because it tries to understand more about the learning processes that take place *informally* in naturally occurring work environments outside the structures of formal institutions.

The concept of 'socially situated learning' emerged strongly in the 1980s. It was, in part, a reaction against the dominant views of learning derived from psychological traditions that emphasised learning as:

- *individual*, in the sense that the locus of intelligence is taken to be the single person;
- *rational*, in that deliberative, conceptual thought is viewed as the primary example of cognition;
- *abstract*, in the sense that implementation and the nature of the physical environment are treated as of secondary importance (if relevant at all);
- *detached*, in the sense that thinking is treated separately from perception and action;
- *general*, in the sense that cognitive science is taken to be a search for universal principles, true of all individuals and applicable in all circumstances.

Situated approaches question all these assumptions, arguing instead that cognition (indeed, all human activity) is:

- *social*, in the sense of being located in humanly constructed settings among human communities;
- *embodied*, in the sense that physical constraints of realisation and circumstance are viewed as of the utmost importance;
- *located*, implying that context dependence is a central and enabling feature of all human endeavour;
- *specific*, dependent on particular circumstances;
- *engaging*, in that ongoing interaction with the surrounding environment is recognised as of primary importance.

Learning, as it normally occurs, is a function of the activity, context and culture in which it occurs. In that sense it is situated. It sits at the heart of the model of learning-in-context and learning-in-action (see Figure 17.1). I propose that this model has particular value in enabling us to examine, at a deeper level, the potential and the tensions within CPD. In this model, conceptual knowledge is built up and understood through use and activity in social settings. This contrasts with those learning activities which involve knowledge that is abstract and learned 'out of context'.

Social interaction is a critical component of situated learning. Extending that idea, learners become involved in a 'community of practice' that embodies certain beliefs

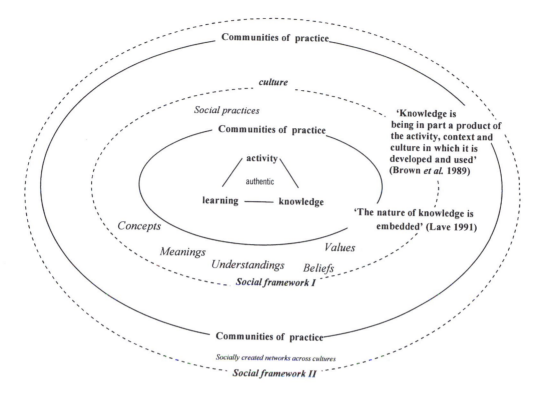

Figure 17.1 Situated learning

and behaviours to be acquired. Situated professional learning is defined by approaches, methods and processes that are consistent with the ideas of community.

As the beginners or newcomers move from the periphery of the community into the centre, they become more active and engaged within the culture and eventually assume the role of expert or old-timer. As they do so they become able to influence that community in different ways. This feature is not linear or simple, in that expert status also has to be continuously renewed and newcomers can challenge existing practices with fresh ways of thinking.

Communities of practice form themselves or are set up within *social frameworks* – explained broadly as the environment that all communities of practice share.

- *Outer social frameworks* are created by the outer world and are hard to influence (but not impossible, e.g. legislation, geographical and cultural conditions).
- *Inner social frameworks* are generated through the communities of practice themselves (and can generate microcultures with altered values and beliefs).

Ideas of community of practice hinge on balances of power, which may be disturbed when structured learning environments and structuring of experiences are introduced. These may reflect the goals and interests of dominant groups, such as governmental agencies, in ways that run counter to the ways in which communities of practice operate.

The tensions in the accountability of professionals and the debate between self-regulation and external regulation can be analysed with reference to their inner and outer social frameworks. The inner framework can be shaped by the professional body, the external framework is moving to impose greater control. CPD involves learning situated in the professional work context and within the community of social practice. It involves ongoing continuous development that has both individual and mutual learning components. A working definition of situated professional learning is:

- a specific approach to learning, viewing learning as a social process of interaction situated in a community of social practice;
- a set of methods situating learning in authentic contexts;
- a process aiming for full participation.

Situated approaches strengthen learning processes and the prospects of enhancing learning success through 'engagement'. The following principles apply:

1 *Engagement* is essential for learning to take place.
2 Learning may be *situated* in three ways: (a) practically; (b) in the culture of the profession; (c) in the social world of the participants.
3 Learning that is *well situated* in each of these three ways will promote strong professional development.
4 Learning that is *poorly situated* in any of these three respects will impede CPD.

In arguing that learning may be well situated or poorly situated, I have the following scenarios in mind.

The situation of learning in *practical tasks* has been a method used in educational programmes ranging from woodwork classes in school to the experiment in the science laboratory or the workshop activity in the CPD programme. In professional development, learning that is well situated in practical terms is based on reflection on practical experience, on reflection on action and in action, to use Schon's (1996) terms. Learning that is *well situated* in a practical sense occurs when the task has meaning and the status of being somehow 'necessary'.

Similarly, experimentation which arises in response to a problem identified 'naturally' by the learner is more likely to lead to professional development. Mentors can aid this process. *In the workplace*, activities that are performed as part of the daily work process are linked into the *culture of the workplace and the profession*. Here, the power of authentic work settings can be harnessed as a resource for learning. The culture of the workplace embodies the social practices that are crucial to engagement and learning. Learning that is poorly situated in relation to the culture of the profession is unlikely to enhance learning. This is not to say that learning programmes should not engage in critical dialogue with the cultural norms and expectations of professional groups. Here, the engagement of the professional bodies with higher education providers has particular potential for improvement through critical analysis and challenge, thus countering the tendencies towards cultural enclaves.

In modern workplaces, how can conflicts between authenticity and the time/resources needed for deep learning be resolved? Paper-based CPD involving a lot of form filling ('paper exercises') is sometimes seen as contributing to the intensification of work, impeding rather than contributing to deep professional learning.

Learning has also, I argue, to be well situated in *the social world of the participants*, in the sense of taking the social and biographical position of the learner fully into account. This applies to adjustments that must be made within the shared communities and working groups of workplaces. It also recognises that people have their own occupational and career trajectories, which may involve changes of direction in the future, and CPD increasingly recognises the possibility of mobility. The management of situated learning processes within CPD involves developing the support structures and creating the learning environments and activities needed. It has to recognise the strengths of individuals and teams, building positively on previous experience and overcoming blocks or impediments to learning.

Most CPD provision appears now to recognise that new knowledge, competencies, skills, work-related skills and attitudes can be best acquired and developed in the context of 'situated activity'. This emphasises 'the relational character of knowledge and learning, and . . . the concerned (engaged, dilemma-driven) nature of learning activity for the people involved' (Lave and Wenger 1991: 33).

It furthermore includes learning in communities of practice, which combines individual and social learning. For the individual as a learner, social learning is learning in the context of a 'community of practice' that enables and supports personal/social learning (see Evans and Hoffmann 2000). *'Good' practice* means that the programmes aim at reaching out for the individual participant, acknowledging his or her specific needs, interests and situations, with mentoring and support becoming the crucial 'glue' for the process.

Inner social frameworks, communities of practice and good CPD practice

The professional community of practice itself shapes the inner social framework. Within this social framework professional development takes place through collaboration, reflection, coaching, mentoring, multiple experiences of practice and articulation of learning skills. Here 'situated learning' can be seen as a framework for the enhancement of professional development environments. It has been argued in a previous analysis (Evans and Hoffmann 2000) that learning will be fostered and knowledge created in learning environments that feature the following characteristics:

- an authentic context that reflects the way knowledge will be used in real life;
- insight into multiple perspectives and changing roles for the members of the community;
- support for collaborative construction of knowledge;
- help and mentoring;
- the promotion of reflection to enable abstractions;

- the promotion of articulation to enable tacit competencies to be built up;
- a clarification for one's own position.

The 'situated learning' perspective also draws upon the learner's previous experiences, links concepts and practices, and encourages reflection and the transfer of knowledge from one situation to another. These features can be elaborated with reference to professional learning as follows.

Authentic activity

The learner is involved in the continual search for solutions to problems. The problems occur from the situation of the learner itself, they are real-world problems. The professional interacts with the 'community of practice' in order to find solutions and explore possibilities, and CPD occurs through this process.

Multiple perspectives and changing roles

A situated learning environment provides the professional with the opportunity to investigate multiple roles and perspectives. The wide range of the 'community of practice' will provide a variety of perspectives for professionals, allowing them to explore several possibilities and to choose and live multiple roles within the 'community of practice'. This is part of being fully engaged in the community and the process of learning.

Collaboration

A situated learning environment supports the collaborative construction of knowledge. In the case of professional communities it involves the development of practice standards and quality assurance. Collaboration demands interaction and the exchange of ideas, and engages thinking and reflection, which in the end creates the conditions for self-review and the improvement of practice understanding.

Reflection

A situated learning environment promotes reflection to enable abstraction and self-determination. Reflection is a very important attribute of the environment, as it represents an opportunity to articulate, negotiate and defend certain issues, positions and knowledge.

Support and encouragement

Situated learning environments can provide a safety net for novice participants of the 'community of practice' and challenges for expert practitioners. For novices, the learners' situation needs to be acknowledged, perhaps assessed or identified at the beginning of the programme in order to offer suitable, effective and specific support. The support that is going to be offered depends on each individual's personal needs and must allow a wide range of assistance. Support and encouragement are offered in several ways and will lead the learner in the right direction, but also point out strategies and suggestions. For expert practitioners, coaching and mentoring to challenge and extend can provide a crucial aid to stretching and enlarging their repertoire, while the experts will themselves also be expected to mentor newer colleagues.

Role models

Coaches and mentors should themselves exemplify the principles of continuing professional development, through their own ongoing and visible engagement with learning and development activities and a reflective approach to their own practice.

The inner social framework

A situated learning environment is not restricted to the world, work or life environment, but extends to 'situations', beliefs and values. The 'community of practice', when operating ideally, embraces the context and sets free a learning environment. At the same time, 'space' is being created and this provides an opportunity for active engagement of the participants within the 'community of practice'. Within the inner social framework self-regulation takes place in ways that may be outwardly recognised through accreditation and audit, but that should contribute fundamentally to safeguarding standards. External assessments and checks can achieve a degree of control, but will not provide safeguards in the absence of professional commitment, ethics, self-responsibility and motivation.

The outer social framework

This involves regulation from the outside on the communities of professional practice. Strong outer social frameworks will maintain and improve standards, and challenge any tendencies to closed enclaves that seek to protect their members over the public or client interests. The features of professional commitment need to be secured by a regulatory framework in which the external world can have confidence. The key issue for CPD is the extent to which self-regulation can provide the controls necessary to ensure maintenance of standards, and can provide the evidence that testifies to the competence and professionalism of its members. The balance between sanctions and benefits also needs to be established.

Friedman *et al.*'s (2001) research observed that:

> Again and again throughout the research . . . such tensions were in evidence. For example, a set of guidelines will intersperse its promotion of CPD as a dynamic and empowering process with looming 'extracts', which function essentially as faceless warnings, about the need to take control of one's career given the insecurities and precariousness of the modern workplace. These positive and

negative aspects sit uneasily together, the veiled threat and the happy vision of an empowered, enlightened future. . . . Sanctions and accreditation, the two sides of the motivational coin, are used selectively, and at times in an apparently *ad hoc* way. For all the vaunted dynamism of the CPD process, it also contains a great potential for instability and internal conflict.

Most professional bodies wish to maximise self-regulation and minimise the need for external intervention to shore up public confidence in standards. To achieve this, their policies should set out, as a minimum:

- rationale and purpose;
- clear aims and objectives;
- underpinning assumptions;
- ethical framework;
- benchmark standards;
- sanctions and benefits;
- evaluation and quality assurance procedures;
- external review arrangements;
- publication of results.

Implications for teaching professionals and future directions

The review presented in this chapter has discussed continuing professonal education and development in ways that extend beyond the current preoccupations of the teaching profession. The intention has been to introduce some ideas and perspectives that can enrich the debate on the challenges that now face teaching professionals, not only in schools, but also in further and higher education. The government published a new strategy for teachers' continuing professional development in March 2001. The strategy aims to provide more funds for individual teachers and 'the control to decide how they wish to spend it', and to provide more opportunities for teachers to learn from good professional development practice in other schools.

'The government recognises that high quality professional development is crucially important if teachers are to keep their skills and knowledge up-to-date' (DfES 2001). The commitment includes more professional bursaries, 'best practice' research scholarships and the extension of an international professional development programme. The planned programme thus reflects strongly several features of CPD discussed above. While emphasising the rather restricted concept of 'updating', it also recognises the importance of situated learning, space for reflection and the need for the sharing of practices linked to benchmarking. The programme is also linked to a 'standards framework' that sets out the standards of practice that teachers should expect to demonstrate at different points in their career, and makes suggestions for supporting development activity: 'The Framework will support career planning, performance management and enable development activity to be targeted in recognition of the individual teacher's needs and aspirations' (DfES 2001).

In further education too, the Standards Fund is promoting CPD for teachers as a high priority alongside mandatory initial teacher training. For both school and further education, the policies are strongly linked to the objective of 'driving up standards' and increasing levels of attainment of learners.

The various stakeholders are now positioning themselves in relation to these developments. Subject associations and teachers' unions are seeking appropriate ways to engage with these developments, as part of the 'inner social framework' described above. Examining bodies, which can now accredit professional development to NVQ Level 4 and above, perceive a strengthening market, as do higher education institutions. The accreditation of CPD will be a central issue as these developments unfold, and the linkage to standards, as publicly defined, is part of the outer social framework. The ways in which the teachers' communities of practice engage with the regulatory framework, and the ways in which the tensions between professional development and performance management are resolved, will determine the direction and the ultimate success of the new programmes.

POINTS FOR DISCUSSION

- How can the tensions between professional development and performance management be resolved?
- How far can self-regulation by associations provide the controls necessary to ensure maintenance of standards, while supplying evidence that testifies to the competence and professionalism of their members?
- In modern workplaces how can conflicts between intensification of work and the time/resources needed for deep learning be resolved?
- What is the proper role of higher education in continuing professional development?

INTERNET SITES

Chartered Institute of Public Finance and Accountancy: www.cipfa.org.uk
Department for Education and Skills: www.dfes.gov.uk
Royal College of Nursing: www.rcn.org.uk
United Kingdom Council for Psychotherapy: www.psychotherapy.org.uk

REFERENCES AND FURTHER READING

Allaker, J. and Shapland, J. (1994) *Organising UK Professions: Continuity and Change.* Research Study No. 16, Research and Policy Planning Unit. London: The Law Society.
Blair, D. T. and Ramones, V. A. (1998) 'A question of nursing competence', *Perspectives*, January–March.
Brown, A., Evans, K., Blackman, S. and Germon, S. (1994) *Key Workers, Technical and Training Mastery in the Workplace.* Bournemouth: Hyde Publications.
Brown, J. S., Collins, A. and Duguid, P. (1989) 'Situated cognition and the culture of learning', *American Educator*, 18(1), 32.

Bryans, P., Gormley, N., Stalker, B. and Williamson, B. (1998) 'From collusion to dialogue: universities and continuing professional development', *Continuing Professional Development Journal*, 1, 120–8.

Burley, P. (2001) 'Response to "Professions under fire"', *Royal Society of Arts Journal*, 1 April, 26.

DfEE (1998) *Individual Learning Accounts Summary Document*. London: DfEE.

DfES (2001) *Continuing Professional Development*. London: DfES.

Evans, K. and Hoffmann, B. (2000) *Engaging to Learn* in Walraven, G., Parsons, C., van Veen, D. and Day, C. (eds) *Combating Social Exclusion through Education*. Apeldoorn: Garant.

Field, J. and Moseley, R. (2000) *Promoting Vocational Lifelong Learning: a Guide to Good Practice in the HE Sector*. London: Higher Education Funding Council for England.

Friedman, A. L., Durkin, C. M. and Hurran, N. K. (1999) 'Good Practice in CPD among UK professional associations', *Continuing Professional Development*, 2, 99 (www.open-house.org.uk/virtual-university-press/cpd).

Friedman, A., Davis, K. and Phillips, M. (2001) *Continuing Professional Development in the UK*. London: Professional Association Research Network.

Gardner, R. (1978) *Policy on Continuing Education: a Report with Recommendations for Action*. York: University of York.

Lave, J. (1991) 'Situated learning in communities of practice', in L. Resnick, J. Levine and S. Behrend (eds) *Perspectives on Socially Shared Cognition*. Washington DC, American Psychological Association.

Lave, J. and Wenger, E. (1991) *Situated Learning: Legitimate Peripheral Participation*. New York: Cambridge University Press.

RCN (2001) Continuing Professional Development and PREP (www.rcn.org.uk/services/promote/cpd).

Schon, D. (1996) *The Reflective Practitioner*. Aldershot: Arena.

Swinson, C. (2001) 'Professions under fire', *Royal Society of Arts Journal*, 1 April, 20.

Vaughan, P. (1991) *Maintaining Professional Competence: a Survey of the Role of Professional Bodies in the Development of Credit-bearing CPD Courses*. Hull: University of Hull.

Welsh, L. and Woodward, P. (1989) *Continuing Professional Development: Towards a National Strategy*. Glasgow: Planning Exchange.

CHAPTER 18

Education and Research

Lucy Palfreyman and Sally Power

CHAPTER SUMMARY

- This chapter begins by outlining some of the recent debates over education research, and particularly the criticism that the education research community is less engaged with the practitioner community than it should be. The authors argue that education research *is* relevant to practitioners, but that it comprises a large, complex and contested range of activities that are unlikely to provide quick and easy answers to the challenges of the classroom.
- The chapter then outlines the structure of education research in the UK, the different ways in which it is funded, the main 'producers' and some of the tensions between the needs of 'producers' and 'users'.
- It concludes by identifying some of the main challenges facing education research in the future.

Introduction

Education research is currently enjoying a high profile. Policy-makers frequently talk of the need for 'evidence-based' policy and practice. Significant and increasing amounts of money are being spent on education research activities, leading to the employment of hundreds of researchers and the publication of thousands of articles and books each year. More teachers than ever before are now engaging in research as part of taking a higher degree or, more recently, as part of the government's new schemes designed to bolster teacher expertise. However, for many of those closely involved in the day-to-day workings of schools, education research can seem at best distant and at worst an irrelevance.

This chapter begins by outlining some of the recent debates over education research and its relevance to those working in schools and colleges. It argues that although more could be done to make research accessible education research is complex and contested and unlikely to provide clearcut and simple 'answers' to the issues that confront teachers and policy makers.

Education research is undertaken by different organisations and funded in different ways. The chapter outlines the structure of education research in the UK and identifies the main funders and producers. It discusses tensions between research producers and users and concludes by identifying some of the main challenges facing education research in the future.

Perspectives on education research

Recent critiques

While much importance is placed on the value of education research in *principle*, a number of concerns have been voiced about what it currently offers in *practice*. Criticisms have been levelled about the conduct, content and impact of education research from inside and outside the academy.

In a speech to the Teacher Training Agency (TTA) in 1996, David Hargreaves criticised the education research community on the grounds of a low level of stakeholder involvement in setting the research agenda, a low level of application of findings, poor coordination between researchers and funders and the non-cumulative nature of educational research, which, Hargreaves argues, has failed to add up to a coherent corpus of knowledge.

These criticisms were reflected in varying degrees by two reports – one commissioned by the Office of Standards in Education (commonly known as the Tooley Report) and one commissioned by the Department for Education and Employment (commonly referred to as the Hillage Report).

The Tooley Report (Tooley and Darby 1998) was based on an analysis of a selection of papers in four education journals. On the basis of these papers, it argued that while much education research was relevant, it suffered from: partisanship in the conduct and presentation of research; lack of rigour in the conduct of research; inadequate reporting of research procedures; and the adulation of 'great thinkers'.

The Hillage Report (Hillage *et al.* 1998), based on a review of the literature and interviews with key 'stakeholders' and focus groups, was less critical of the content and conduct of research, but did find that 'the actions and decisions of policy-makers and practitioners are insufficiently informed by research'. Key factors in this lack of impact were identified as the small-scale nature of education research, the lack of a basis in existing knowledge and inaccessibility to non-academic audiences.

Both of these reports have themselves been subjected to extensive criticism. In terms of inaccessibility of findings, for instance, it has been claimed that the Hillage Report does not recognise the extent to which different outputs are intended for different audiences (Lomax 1998) and that it was too narrow in its definition of education research (Edwards 1998). There have also been concerns that the Hillage Report would tie research in too closely with politics (BERA 1998). The Tooley Report in particular was criticised for its own political partisanship (e.g. Atkinson 1998) and research method (Hodkinson 1998).

However, while the methods and conclusions of these reports can be seen as questionable, they do indicate something of a mismatch between current education research practice and the expectations of those working in schools and colleges. They also suggest that the research community is perhaps not as close to the practitioner community as it needs to be.

In order to address this lack of engagement and its underlying causes, the Hillage Report recommended, among other things, that a National Educational Research Forum be set up to enable researchers, policy-makers and practitioners to work together more closely. The Forum was established in 2000 with a remit of providing strategic direction for education research and raising its quality, profile and impact. More specifically, it aims to:

- stimulate high-quality research;
- provide advice and guidance on priorities for research;
- advise on the capacity, organisation and funding needed to address these priorities;
- identify gaps in knowledge;
- advise on ways of involving teachers and others in the research process;
- advise on horizon scanning and foresight requirements;
- promote the importance of, and identify ways of, investigating the impact of research.

The Forum's National Strategy Consultation Paper *Research and Development in Education* was sent out to key stakeholders for comment in 2000. Although the research community broadly welcomed the establishment of a body designed to promote research, many respondents raised concerns that its proposals might be based on too narrow a definition of education research. In particular, there were worries that it over-estimated the direct utility of research findings and might eventually compromise the independence of research in the UK (Bassey 2001; Hodkinson 2001; Stronach 2001; Utley 2001). If research is to be made more accessible and provide a basis for guiding policy and practice, it is important that there is a more widespread appreciation of the complex and often contested nature of research and of the difficulty of straightforwardly applying 'findings' to 'practice'.

What is education research?

What counts as 'research' is in itself contested and precise definitions are hard to come by. It is even more difficult to find tidy definitions for education research. It comprises more than just knowledge about education. As William Taylor (1973: 192) has argued,

> everyone has knowledge about education, even if it only amounts to knowing the name and reputation of the local primary school . . . or having opinions about comprehensive reorganisation. . . . The more involved in education activities people become, as parents, teachers, politicians or administrators, the greater the number of facts and opinions about these activities they come to possess.

While such knowledge is important, indeed essential, for everyday practice, it is what Schutz (1964) refers to as 'recipe knowledge' – assemblages of context-specific guidance and values. Education research is different inasmuch as it is 'sustained systematic enquiry' (Peters and White 1973). In addition to being systematic, research is generally distinct from other knowledge activities (even those such as consultancy) because of the expectation that the outputs (and process) of the investigation will be made available to others and have some application beyond the immediate cases under study.

A key distinction is often made between 'pure' (fundamental) and 'applied' (policy- or practice-oriented) research. However, in education, this distinction can be quite problematic. As Glennerster and Hoyle (1973) argue, it is impossible to draw a line between the two in practice. Fundamental research can often reveal important areas and strategies for intervention and practice- or policy-oriented research needs to be based on a solid understanding of theory. A further related distinction (adapted from Moore 1996: 159; Ball 1997: 269) can be made between studies *of* education and studies *for* education. The former take a more distant, critical and outsider perspective of education, while the latter operate within the concerns of those working within the service. Again, though, in practice, there is likely to be significant overlap in most education research.

A further complication in the definition of education research is its multidisciplinary nature. Glennerster and Hoyle (1973) argue that 'probably of all the fields of social policy, education has the richest background of international and policy-oriented research'. It draws on many different disciplines: sociology, psychology, history and economics to name but a few. In addition, it has significant overlaps with research in other social policy fields. There would often appear to be no clear-cut or useful boundary to be drawn between education and other research – for instance, research in health, social welfare and social policy.

Education research is also extraordinarily diverse in the range of perspectives and methods employed. Although early education research tended to use quantitative methodologies, during the 1970s and 1980s qualitative approaches achieved widespread credibility – to the extent that there are now concerns that the capacity of the research community to undertake quantitative analysis has been dangerously diminished. It is to be hoped that we have now moved beyond some of the more sterile debates about the intrinsic superiority of particular methods and approaches. This does not, of course, mean there is no such thing as 'bad research', but each piece of research needs to be judged in terms of the appropriateness of its methods and analysis for the question under consideration. For some research questions, the answer lies in the analysis of large and complex data sets. For other issues, a small action research project undertaken by a teacher may offer the most illuminating insights. As we discuss below, unless the complexity of research is understood, those who attempt to use its outputs may well be disappointed.

The organisation of education research

The increasing importance placed on education research is evident in increasing expenditure. Burt (1960) estimated that in 1959, £50,000 was spent on education research – about 0.008 per cent of the total expenditure on education. Forty years later, the Hillage Report estimated that £66 million was spent on education research annually – comprising 0.2 per cent of total expenditure. However, while these figures show that the proportion of money spent on research is increasing relative to the total education expenditure, it remains relatively low. According to the Office of National Statistics, 1.9 per cent of the gross domestic product is spent on research and development nationally (BERA 1998). In the next sections, we examine how this research expenditure is funded, distributed and 'used'.

Funders and producers

The main organisations undertaking research are universities, government departments and agencies, specialist research organisations, commercial organisations and, increasingly, individual practitioners.

Government departments and agencies

Government departments and agencies, at both national and local levels, often undertake their own research – as do professional organisations, such as the National Union of Teachers and the Secondary Heads Associations. The newly reorganised Department for Education and Skills (DfES, formerly DfEE), for example, undertakes a significant amount of research in education. Between 1997 and 2001/2, DfES annual research expenditure rose from £5.4 million to £10.4 million. Much of the research is conducted 'in-house' by the DfES Analytical Services section, and comprises analyses of a wide range of statistics covering education, training and lifelong learning. These are disseminated as *First Releases*, *Bulletins*, *Volumes* and *Performance Tables* and can be found on a website (www.dfes.gov.uk/statistics).

The DfES also commissions research from external contractors – notably universities and specialist research organisations. Details of future research programmes can be found in the research prospectus (also available on-line at www.dfes.gov.uk/research). The findings from DfES-funded projects are disseminated through *Research Reports* and *Research Briefs* (summaries of key findings from the longer reports) and can also be found on the website.

Universities

Universities are the main producers of education research. Funding for research in universities can be divided into two broad categories – externally funded research and research funded by the annual quality-related grant from the funding councils.[1]

Quality-related funding
Quality-related research funding is designed to support those institutions with the highest quality research within their subject area. The funding council identifies the budget available for quality-related research in universities across all subject areas on an annual basis. This is then distributed among subject areas by a formula. Each subject is allocated a cost weight (in descending weight order: clinical/laboratory subjects, intermediate cost subjects and other; education is 'other'), which is multiplied by the

Table 18.1   Research Assessment Exercise grades

Grade	Description
5*	International excellence in more than half of the research activity submitted and national excellence in the remainder
5	International excellence in up to half of the research activity submitted and national excellence in virtually all of the remainder
4	National excellence in virtually all of the research activity submitted, showing some evidence of international excellence
3a	National excellence in over two-thirds of the research activity submitted, possibly showing evidence of international excellence
3b	National excellence in more than half of the research activity submitted
2	National excellence in up to half of the research activity submitted
1	National excellence in none, or virtually none, of the research activity submitted

volume of research in each subject to arrive at the total funding for that subject. Volume is measured by criteria such as the number of research-active academic staff and the number of research assistants. This income is then distributed between institutions by a further formula so that universities and colleges with the highest quality research (as assessed by the regular Research Assessment Exercises) receive a larger share of the money for that subject area.

The Research Assessment Exercise (RAE) takes place every four to five years and aims to assess the quality of research within a subject area by undertaking a peer review exercise of academics' publications. The grade allocated at the end of this exercise is a crucial part of the funding allocation formula and will therefore affect each institution's income for the next four to five years. The grades currently used are shown in Table 18.1. The current ranking of universities can be found on the RAE website.

The formulae used for allocating funding and the RAE itself have both been subject to extensive criticism and debate. Some of this concerns the way in which those who are already successful continue to be rewarded – leading to a growing gap between universities that specialise in research and those that have largely teaching responsibilities. Related to this are concerns about the extent to which the newer universities can compete with the older universities that have much longer established research traditions. There are also criticisms that the nature of the peer-review process has not provided sufficient incentives for researchers to disseminate their findings to broader audiences. However, a review undertaken before the 2001 RAE (HEFCE 1997) reinforced the broad approach as appropriate, and it is likely to continue for some time.

Externally funded research

A diverse range of research activities in universities is supported by external funders. Total educational external research income in UK universities was £28 million in 1998/9 – see Figure 18.1 (HESA 2000). This is only 1.5 per cent of total UK university income from research in that year, but as Table 18.2 shows, education was fifteenth

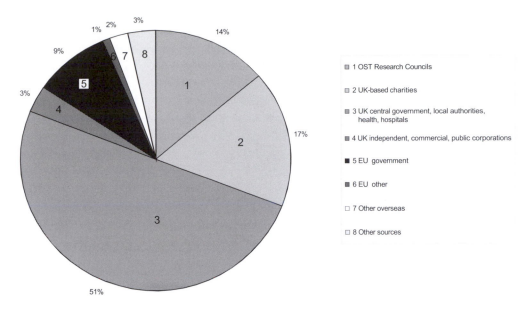

Figure 18.1 Education research grants and contracts income by source, 1998/9

in the league table of subject areas by research income. Given that the medical, engineering and scientific disciplines are expensive areas in which to undertake research, due to the infrastructure costs, education has performed well in attracting research income.

Approximately half this funding came from central and local government, health and hospitals. Central government funders include the DfES, the Department of Health, the Home Office and the Department of Social Security. As we commented above, educational research crosses many boundaries and this is so in funding terms as well. Almost all government departments have an educational aspect to their work and are, at some time, interested in supporting relevant research.

Almost all the research funded by the DfES is offered out on a tender basis (through advertisement in the *Times Higher Education Supplement* (*THES*), the *Guardian* or registered contacts) to research questions set centrally. Although universities and other organisations are offered the opportunity to respond to draft DfES research strategies, the formulation of research questions and the management of this strategy are undertaken by central research and policy departments.

Specific interests of other departments include the Department of Health's focus on health education research and the Department for International Development's interest in comparative education research. Research opportunities are advertised in the *THES* and *Guardian* as well as through websites such as www.doh.gov.uk/research/index.htm and www.dfid.gov.uk.

While government research may offer the opportunity to feed directly into the policy-making process, it also creates its own tensions as the government departments seek to respond to the political agenda and university researchers bring their own academic perspectives. This manifests itself most often in the issue of time scale – in university terms the 'lead-in' time between advertisement of a research opportunity and

Table 18.2 External research income by subject area, 1998/9 (£ thousands)

	OST research councils	UK-based charities	UK central government, local authority, health, hospitals	UK independent commercial, public corps	EU government	EU other	Other overseas	Other sources	Total
1 Clinical Medicine	76,809	227,451	99,461	52,558	15,455	7,829	32,835	11,360	523,758
2 Biosciences	95,992	88,052	23,660	19,961	19,966	4,117	11,511	1,811	265,070
3 Physics	87,683	4,025	8,039	5,338	6,786	778	2,361	546	115,556
4 Chemistry	45,584	7,812	6,952	17,110	8,954	1,173	5,105	1,158	93,848
5 Electrical, Electronic and Computer Engineering	38,504	811	8,438	12,479	12,032	1,680	3,768	1,376	79,088
6 Social Studies	18,801	8,766	26,971	3,551	8,620	781	4,297	1,645	73,432
7 Mechanical, Aero and Production Engineering	23,230	1,172	10,738	20,919	11,297	1,691	3,458	456	72,961
8 Earth, Marine and Environmental Sciences	19,172	1,677	6,953	8,061	7,842	639	4,007	633	48,984
9 General Engineering	15,937	1,139	8,099	13,003	5,808	383	1,550	871	46,790
10 Anatomy and Physiology	9,082	22,954	1,232	1,399	1,888	381	2,994	181	40,111
11 Agriculture and Forestry	4,058	859	18,536	5,871	5,853	1,076	1,270	1,649	39,172
12 Mineral, Metallurgy and Materials Engineering	17,926	883	3,281	7,819	2,931	483	2,951	584	36,858
13 Business and Management Studies	7,391	2,114	8,003	9,096	4,450	2,502	833	2,009	36,398
14 Psychology and Behavioural Sciences	12,374	7,902	5,426	2,624	1,539	333	784	538	31,520
15 Education	3,862	4,783	14,135	914	2,581	197	667	903	28,042
16 Computer Software Engineering	10,596	457	1,904	5,081	6,785	159	330	272	25,584
17 Veterinary Science	4,295	9,525	6,477	3,197	1,262	298	454	66	25,574
18 Civil Engineering	10,077	353	5,093	4,486	4,242	184	326	626	25,387
19 Mathematics	11,518	1,150	2,630	2,342	3,964	67	1,025	237	22,933

Subject									Total
20 Chemical Engineering	12,429	312	962	3,195	2,289	354	1,230	95	20,866
21 Pharmacology	2,922	10,209	1,193	2,792	573	516	1,851	466	20,522
22 Pharmacy	3,007	6,122	2,134	5,875	671	316	1,317	926	20,368
23 Architecture, Built Environment and Planning	3,744	1,192	6,367	2,772	2,806	101	518	1,031	18,531
24 Geography	4,865	1,656	5,027	2,017	3,725	84	662	391	18,427
25 Health and Community Studies	1,401	2,274	10,393	651	544	121	122	403	15,909
26 Information Technology and Systems Sciences	6,697	248	1,428	827	3,484	559	826	267	14,336
27 Humanities	3,289	4,774	2,782	692	570	162	1,160	371	13,800
28 Nursing and Paramedical Studies	372	1,678	7,428	767	1,033	313	88	369	12,048
29 Clinical Dentistry	1,036	3,344	3,355	1,763	731	239	845	405	11,718
30 Design and Creative Arts	788	1,048	645	565	1,190	265	1,033	396	5,930
31 Archaeology	657	1,140	1,387	1,680	224	15	263	384	5,750
32 Language Based Studies	2,308	1,129	425	34	385	69	352	219	4,921
33 Sports Science and Leisure Studies	31	508	507	375	26	11	96	538	2,092
34 Librarianship, Communication and Media Studies	428	220	478	280	370	32	9	208	2,025
35 Continuing Education	99	224	611	188	320	42	3	50	1,537
36 French, Spanish and German Modern Languages	384	207	265	3	50	12	40	8	969
37 General Sciences	31	26	296	200	267	9	43	89	961
38 Other Modern Languages	242	73	97	-25	231	5	19	80	722
39 Catering and Hospitality Management	25	8	263	111	65	91	11	83	657
40 Other Technologies	51	5	0	95	2	0	0	0	153
Total	557,697	428,282	312,071	220,666	151,811	28,067	91,014	33,700	1,823,308

Source: HESA (2000).

proposed start date is short and the time given for completing a project is often 'tight' given the restraints of recruitment procedures and other commitments academics are involved in. For the government departments, the need to meet targets to feed into the political process and the constraints of the public sector funding processes (which limit expenditure to specific financial years) mean that quick turnarounds are required from their academic partners.

Local authorities, health authorities and hospitals also contribute to the £14 million worth of educational research in this category. They share a common focus in seeking independent researchers to investigate specific research issues of direct relevance to their field of operation. Evaluations of pilot projects and assessments of 'what works' are common themes of this type of funded research. As with central government, opportunities may be advertised in national publications, but informal contact or partnership working are also just as likely to lead to a research opportunity.

The second largest funders of university-based educational research are UK-based charities. While university administrators may not welcome the funding policies of many charities, which pay little or no overheads and often do not contribute to the teaching replacement or direct salary costs of permanent university teaching staff, many charities do offer the researcher more flexibility in developing a proposal, and open applications are sometimes welcomed (as opposed to the submission of tenders to specific advertisements). The Leverhulme Trust has a wide remit to 'support excellence' novelty and significance . . . across a wide range of fields' (Leverhulme Trust 2001), but excludes school education as a field of enquiry. Similarly, the Nuffield Foundation 'keeps an "open door" to projects that are in some way concerned with the advancement of social well being' (Nuffield Foundation 2001) but includes educational research and innovation as an area of special interest. The Joseph Rowntree Foundation works slightly differently, by establishing umbrella research programmes under which applications for funding are welcomed, but recipients are regarded as partners in a common enterprise with the Foundation. Other charitable funders include the Wellcome Trust, which includes within its medical remit funding for wider health and social education issues, and smaller specialist trusts – many of which can be identified through specialist publications such as the Charity Aid Foundation's *Directory of Grant Making Trusts* and the Directory of Social Change publication *A Guide to the Major Trusts*.

Research councils are a further substantial stream of education research funding in universities (14 per cent of income in 1998/9). The councils are organised around specific activity themes, e.g. the Engineering and Physical Sciences Research Council, or the Medical Research Council. While the broad base of education research means that proposals developed to meet the different boards' criteria but with an educational remit may well be funded, the majority of educational research is funded through the Economic and Social Research Council. The annual budget of £46 million (the smallest of the research councils) funds work across the social science field. While specific themes are identified each year, funding is also allocated reactively to proposals submitted by researchers. The ESRC recently managed the Teaching and Learning Programme, a £23 million programme to 'support research projects and related activities which will lead to significant improvements in the achievement of learners at all ages and stages in all sectors and contexts of education and training, including formal settings and beyond, throughout the United Kingdom'. As well as substantial project grants, the ESRC also offers a small grants programme, which is a 'fast track' procedure designed particularly to appeal to new researchers. Research fellowships are available to support individual researchers in the development of their careers.

While research councils, central government and charities together accounted for over 80 per cent of external research funding in education in 1998/9, the European Union (EU) is an expanding funder. The organisation of the EU can appear confusing to the researcher new to the field and many universities employ specialists to assist in the provision of information and development of proposals. Umbrella organisations in Brussels, such as the UK Research Office (UKRO), also offer expertise and contacts. European research offers its own opportunities and challenges. Proposals are often developed on a partnership basis with universities in other EU countries. While this can offer valuable experience in comparative work, it offers specific challenges in terms of administration and coordination.

As universities look to expand their funding base, business and commercial organisations are often proposed as a 'third funding stream'. For example, the Higher Education Funding Council for England (HEFCE) has as one of its strategic aims: 'to promote and support productive interaction between HE and industry and commerce in order to encourage the transfer of knowledge and expertise and enhance the relevance of programmes of teaching and research to the needs of employers and the economy'. The Higher Education Innovation Fund is a new strand of funding designed to support this aim. However, educational research has a poor track record in terms of achieving funding from these sources (3 per cent of income in 1998/9). This is, perhaps, not surprising given the lack of commercial opportunities in the traditional UK education field. However, the expanded involvement of private sector organisations in the running of education (as in Islington) and the Labour government's policy intention to expand public–private initiatives might, in the long term, lead to increased opportunities for collaborative research work with commercial organisations.

As well as analysing the sources of university research funding, it is interesting to consider the spread of work between institutions. In 1998/9, 48 per cent of research income in educational research was spread between just seven universities. Specialisation appears to be a trend that the funding bodies support – not least by the selective funding mechanisms described above.

Specialist and commercial research organisations

In addition to universities, there are a number of research organisations that specialise in education research. The largest of these is the National Foundation for Education Research (NFER), based in Slough. The NFER has over 200 staff and an income of over £9 million. Most of this is derived from sponsored research, particularly for government agencies such as the Qualifications and Curriculum Authority, the DfES and the Curriculum and Assessment Authority for Wales. The NFER offers a specialised research and consultancy service to local education authorities.

There are also smaller independent foundations that produce education-related research. The Tavistock Institute, for instance, specialises in evaluations that examine organisation and policy dynamics through action-research and organisational analysis. Although not specialising in education research, commercial research organisations such as MORI (Market and Opinion Research International) have increasingly been looking at areas such as education as it becomes more politically high-profile.

Individual practitioners

Individuals also undertake research, usually in association with a university as part of a higher degree. Many students taking taught masters degrees undertake small pieces of empirical research for their dissertations. MPhil degrees are more research-based and often lead on to the more advanced study required for a doctoral degree. The PhD used to be the only form of doctoral degree that those specialising in education and related social science research could undertake. However, in the UK an increasing number of 'professional doctorates' are available. The doctor of education (EdD) degree is now available in over 40 UK universities, and although its components vary, it usually comprises a series of taught and assessed elements focusing on specialist content (e.g. education policy and management) and research methodologies, followed by a dissertation. Even more recently, universities have been developing doctoral degrees for educational psychologists (DEdPsy) who wish to extend their professional expertise and training and to carry out research relevant to their professional practice.

In addition, however, a number of schemes have been developed which are designed to encourage individual teachers to engage in their own research without necessarily undertaking a higher degree. Of particular relevance to teachers will be the TTA's *Teacher Research Grant Scheme* and the DfES's *Best Practice Research Scholarship Programme*. The Teacher Research Grant Scheme was launched in 1997 with the intention of contributing to 'the development of a cumulative stock of high-quality, small-scale, classroom-based research carried out by teachers, to raise other teachers' interest in research and evidence, and to extend the debate about the role of teachers in classroom research in order to raise standards and improve classroom practice'. Teachers are encouraged to undertake classroom-based research, usually with the support of a higher education institution or local education authority (LEA). The grants are usually made available for one year and consist of awards of £2,500 to individual teachers or £3,500 for collaborative projects. Guidelines on how to submit and how to prepare reports of findings are available from the TTA. At the time of writing, the future of the scheme is uncertain. It is in the final year of its three-year trial period. However, it is likely to be extended rather than abolished. The TTA claims that 'given the success of the scheme to date the TTA is currently discussing the possibility of other organisations supporting teachers who wish to pursue deeper systematic classroom enquiries'.

The DfES Best Practice Research Scholarship Programme is also available to teachers. At the time of writing it was in its pilot year – when £3 million was made available. It too is aimed at developing small-scale classroom-based research by practitioners, who will be supported by mentors.

Alongside the Best Practice Research Scholarships are two other related schemes. The new *Teachers' International Professional Development Programme* invites teachers to visit schools elsewhere in order to identify new and different kinds of practices that might be incorporated in their own teaching. Also announced were the 'professional bursaries' launched in nine pilot LEAs. These comprise grants of £500 or £700 over two academic years.

Using education research

Recent years have seen many pronouncements about the importance of 'evidence-based policy and practice'. As we discussed above, many of the criticisms of education research focus on lack of user-engagement, and this has been seen as one of the main stumbling blocks to wider awareness and application of research findings among practitioners and policy-makers. In this section, we examine the issues of 'using' research, current initiatives to broaden research awareness and challenges that need to be overcome.

The research community

Education researchers themselves are the main users of education research – which is why so many research outputs are aimed at other researchers. Within-community dialogue is important in order to sustain the intellectual health of research. Higher education depends not just on research income, but on attracting students, and the high profile of education research in the UK is an important aspect in universities' ability to attract students and funding from home and overseas. So, while dialogue with other users needs to be strengthened, it is important that this does not weaken collaboration *within* the research community.

Policy-makers

In February 2000, David Blunkett, then Secretary of State for Education and Employment, set out a number of issues concerning closer collaboration between the research community and policy-makers (Blunkett 2000). As indicated by the title of his speech 'Influence or irrelevance: can social science improve government?', Blunkett argued that research is currently too 'detached from and irrelevant to the real debates which affect people's life chances'. In addition to insularity within the research community, he identified a number of problems within the policy-making community. He referred, for instance, to 'a seam of anti-intellectualism running through government both at the political level and amongst officials' and 'a culture in which ideas are unwelcome'.

Certainly, as researchers we often feel that it is hard to identify the evidence on which policies have been based. There is also a common perception that when findings are disseminated that may suggest that policies are perhaps less successful than their architects hoped, the research is either ignored or dismissed.

To some extent, these tensions are probably an inevitable part of the relationship between the research community and government. Apart from the complexity and contested nature of many research findings, political imperatives can make it understandably difficult for policy-makers to accept research findings that illuminate the ineffectiveness or negative consequences of their policies. Moreover, the time scale in which political decision-making takes place is frequently shorter than that needed for rigorous research.

Nevertheless, it is good to see proposals being put in place to bring researchers and government into a closer partnership – provided, of course, these do not compromise the independence of research. Current developments include the establishment of dedicated policy-oriented research centres such as the Centre for Research on the Wider Benefits of Learning (a joint initiative by the Institute of Education and Birkbeck College) and the Centre for Evidence Informed Policy and Practice (based at the Institute of Education), as well as new policy units within government, such as the Performance and Innovation Unit in the Cabinet Office. A key function of these centres and units is to draw together and organise existing evidence in a systematic way.

Practitioners

Education practitioners also feel they are somewhat detached from the research community. A number of factors contribute to this. One we have already discussed is the lack of accessibility of many research publications. To varying degrees, universities are attempting to address this themselves. At the Institute of Education, for instance, we regularly publish monographs and bulletins aimed at practitioners. *Issues in Practice* is aimed at primary and secondary school teachers and reports on the practical implications of research. *Viewpoints* are short overviews of research and debate on contemporary topics. The International School Effectiveness and Improvement Centre produces *Research Matters* for 1,100 schools and colleges and 65 LEAs throughout the UK. Other research organisations also have practitioner-oriented dissemination strategies. The NFER, for example, publishes *TOPIC* twice a year, which contains articles on current research issues for teachers, students and educational administrators, and provides practical advice.

There are commercially produced practitioner papers and journals that often disseminate research findings. Some are directed at subject specialists (e.g. *Language Learning Journal, Mathematics in School*), some at school managers (e.g. *Leading Edge*) and others have more general audiences – notably the *Times Educational Supplement* and the *Educational Journal*. National papers also often have weekly supplements that include items of research.

It is often claimed (e.g. NERF 2000) that new information and communication technology (ICT) will facilitate teacher engagement with research. However, it also creates a number of challenges. The Internet, for instance, has the capacity to provide unparalleled access to research findings. However, these will need to be arranged and presented in a digestible form without oversimplifying the research method or results. It needs to be remembered that access to searchable websites and databases is most likely to be individually motivated and dependent on appropriate ICT. In addition, teachers do not have equal access to the new technologies or, in many cases, the time to use them.

While increasing dissemination will help to make research findings more *accessible*, other barriers could prevent them from being particularly *useful*. One very real problem is that research findings can rarely be straightforwardly 'applied' by teachers and managers. Many findings are highly context-specific – and many are also hotly contested. For researchers, disputes are healthy as they lead to further debate and refinement of methodologies. For practitioners, however, disagreement and the lack of any clear-cut 'answers' can be frustrating.

Professional imperatives and conditions of work can also make teachers unwilling and/or unable to be involved in research. Certainly, at the current time, the culture and workload of many schools is not yet one in which research is considered possible or valuable.

Future opportunities and challenges

It is apparent that much is being done to address some of the problems identified at the beginning of this chapter. However, it is also clear that improving access to research is only one aspect of engaging policy-makers and practitioners. We believe that it is perhaps more important to engage users in more meaningful ways than just giving access to findings. In particular, it might be useful to reconceptualise the relationship between practitioners and research.

In the current 'evidence-based' climate, practitioners are cast very much as people who will look to research for answers – without necessarily engaging more fully or having more awareness of the complexities of the research process. This approach not only might lead to disillusionment with research, as it becomes clear that research does not provide straightforward answers to problems, it also to some extent presents the teacher as a technician rather than a professional.

Hargreaves (1996) claims that 'there is no virtue in expert teachers and newly qualified heads studying substantial bodies of educational theory and research that is mostly remote from practical engagement'. However, as Ball (1997) argues, this conception of teachers does not present them as 'intellectuals'.

The most beneficial uses of research are those that extend professional awareness and encourage reflective and intellectually engaged practices – in other words, teachers developing their 'professional imagination' (Power 2000). In order to do this, they need to be able to think critically about their practices in a systematic way and to understand the relevance, the limits and the strengths of research findings for their practice. Seeing research and its underlying theoretical orientations as part of an ongoing process rather than a set of answers held on a knowledge base should also help to 'mainstream' research throughout the system as a whole by generating lively debate and a questioning approach.

POINTS FOR DISCUSSION

1 Is educational research an identifiable discipline in its own right?
2 Does educational research have relevance for the concerns of those involved with the practicalities of education?

3 Should educational research be more concerned with the development of links with other subject disciplines? Is educational research too restricted to a social science paradigm?

4 What difference can and should educational research make to issues of global justice?

INTERNET SITES

Economic and Social Research Council: www.esrc.ac.uk
Teacher Training Agency: www.canteach.gov.uk
Research Assessment Exercise: www.rae.ac.uk
National Foundation for Educational Research: www.nfer.ac.uk
British Educational Research Association: www.bera.ac.uk
Arts and Humanities Research Board: www.ahrb.ac.uk
National Educational Research Forum: www.nerf-uk.org
Joseph Rowntree Foundation: www.jrf.org.uk
Leverhulme Trust: www.leverhulme.org.uk
Nuffield Foundation: www.nuffieldfoundation.org
Wellcome Trust: www.wellcome.ac.uk
Tavistock Institute: www.tavinstitute.org
MORI: www.mori.com

NOTE

1 England, Wales, Scotland and Northern Ireland each have their own higher education funding councils – HEFCE (Higher Education Funding Council for England), HEFCW (Higher Education Funding Council for Wales), SHEFC (Scottish Higher Education Funding Council) and DHFETE (Department for Higher and Further Education Training and Employment for Northern Ireland). However, in relation to research, the quality-related funding formulae and Research Assessment Exercise are jointly conducted.

REFERENCES AND FURTHER READING

Atkinson, E. (1998) 'Partisan research and the pursuit of truth', *Research Intelligence*, 66 (October), 18–19.
Ball, S. J. (1997) 'Policy sociology and critical social research: a personal review of recent education policy and policy research', *British Educational Research Journal*, 23(3), 257–74.
Bassey, M. (2001) 'NERF need not be naff', *Research Intelligence*, 74 (January), 1.
BERA (1998) 'BERA's response to the DfEE enquiry', *Research Intelligence*, 64 (May), 9–13.
Blunkett, D. (2000) 'Influence or irrelevance: can social science improve government?', speech to the Economic and Social Research Council, 2 February. Reprinted in *Research Intelligence*, 72 (March), 12–21.

Burt, C. (1960) 'The Crowther and Albemarle Reports', *British Journal of Educational Psychology*, 30 (November), 277–82.

DfEE (1997) *Higher Education for the 21st Century* (commonly known as the Dearing Report). London: Stationery Office.

Edwards, A. (1998) 'A careful review but some lost opportunities', *Research Intelligence*, 66 (August), 15–16.

Glennerster, H. and Hoyle, E. (1973) 'Educational research and educational policy', in W. Taylor (ed.) *Research Perspectives in Education*. London: Routledge and Kegan Paul.

Hargreaves, D. H. (1996) 'Teaching as a research-based profession: possibilities and prospects', Teacher Training Agency Annual Lecture.

HEFCE (1997) *Research Assessment: Consultation Document* RAE 2/97. Bristol: HEFCE.

HESA (2000) *HE Finance Plus 1998/99*. London: Higher Education Statistics Agency (CD-ROM).

Hillage, J., Pearson, R., Anderson, A. and Tamkin, P. (1998) *Excellence in Research on Schools*. London: Department for Education and Employment.

Hodkinson, P. (1998) 'Naivete and bias in educational research: the Tooley Report', *Research Intelligence*, 65 (August), 16–17.

Hodkinson, P. (2001) 'NERF strategy proposals: a major threat to academic freedom', *Research Intelligence*, 74 (January), 20–2.

Leverhulme Trust (2001) *Policies and Procedures. A Guide for Applicants*. London: Leverhulme Trust.

Lomax, P. (1998) 'Researching the researchers', *Times Educational Supplement*, 4 September.

Moore, R. (1996) 'Back to the future: the problems of change and possibilities of advance in the sociology of education', *British Journal of Sociology of Education*, 17, 145–62.

NERF (2000) *Research and Development in Education: National Strategy Consultation Paper*. London: National Educational Research Forum.

Nuffield Foundation (2001) *Guide for Applicants*. London: Nuffield Foundation.

Peters, R. S. and White, J. (1973) 'The philosopher's contribution to educational research', in W. Taylor (ed.) *Research Perspectives in Education*. London: Routledge and Kegan Paul.

Power, S. (2000) 'Fostering the professional imagination: why teachers should study for higher degrees', *Education Review*, 14(1), 69–72.

Schutz, A. (1964) 'The stranger: an essay in social psychology', in A. Schutz (ed.) *Collected Papers*, Vol. II. The Hague: Martinus Nijhoff.

Stronach, I. (2001) 'NERF strategy proposals: not national, not educational, not research-based, not a forum – otherwise a good idea', *Research Intelligence*, 74 (January), 22–8.

Taylor, W. (1973) 'Knowledge and research', in W. Taylor (ed.) *Research Perspectives in Education*. London: Routledge and Kegan Paul.

Tooley, J. and Darby, D. (1998) *Educational Research: a Critique*. London: Ofsted.

Utley, A. (2001) 'Fear of censorship in education research strategy', *Times Higher Education Supplement*, 12 January.

Index